MANCHESTER
UNIVERSITY PRESS

CONTEMPORARY WORLD WRITERS

SERIES EDITOR   JOHN THIEME

ALREADY PUBLISHED IN THE SERIES

Peter Carey   BRUCE WOODCOCK
Timothy Mo   ELAINE YEE LIN HO
Toni Morrison   JILL MATUS
Alice Munro   CORAL ANN HOWELLS
Ngugi Wa Thiong'o   PATRICK WILLIAMS
Salman Rushdie   CATHERINE CUNDY
Derek Walcott   JOHN THIEME

FORTHCOMING

Anita Desai   SHIRLEY CHEW
Hanif Kureishi   BART MOORE-GILBERT
Les Murray   STEVEN MATTHEWS
R. K. Narayan   JOHN THIEME
Caryl Phillips   BENEDICTE LEDENT
Wole Soyinka   ABDULRAZAK GURNAH

Kazuo Ishiguro

BARRY LEWIS

Manchester University Press

Manchester and New York

distributed exclusively in the USA by St. Martin's Press

The right of Barry Lewis to be identified as the author of this work has been
asserted by him in accordance with the Copyright, Designs and Patents Act 1988.

Published by Manchester University Press
Oxford Road, Manchester M13 9NR, UK
and Room 400, 175 Fifth Avenue, New York, NY 10010, USA
http://www.manchesteruniversitypress.co.uk

Distributed exclusively in the USA by
St. Martin's Press, Inc., 175 Fifth Avenue, New York, NY 10010, USA

Distributed exclusively in Canada by
UBC Press, University of British Columbia, 2029 West Mall,
Vancouver, BC, Canada V6T 1Z2

British Library Cataloguing-in-Publication Data
A catalogue record for this book is available from the British Library

Library of Congress Cataloging-in-Publication Data applied for

ISBN 0 7190 5513 x *hardback*
     0 7190 5514 8 *paperback*

First published 2000
07 06 05 04 03 02 01 00   10 9 8 7 6 5 4 3 2 1

Typeset in Aldus
by Koinonia, Manchester
Printed in Great Britain
by Bell and Bain Ltd, Glasgow

To the memory of my father,
Henry Lewis (1925–1996)

Contents

Series editor's foreword

Contemporary World Writers is an innovative series of authorita-tive introductions to a range of culturally diverse contemporary writers from outside Britain and the United States, or from 'minor-ity' backgrounds within Britain or the United States. In addition to providing comprehensive general introductions, books in the series also argue stimulating original theses, often but not always related to contemporary debates in post-colonial studies.

The series locates individual writers within their specific cul-tural contexts, while recognising that such contexts are themselves invariably a complex mixture of hybridised influences. It aims to counter tendencies to appropriate the writers discussed into the canon of English or American literature or to regard them as 'other'.

Each volume includes a chronology of the writer's life, an intro-ductory section on formative contexts and intertexts, discussion of all the writer's major works, a bibliography of primary and second-ary works and an index. Issues of racial, national and cultural identity are explored, as are gender and sexuality. Books in the se-ries also examine writers' use of genre, particularly ways in which Western genres are adapted or subverted and 'traditional' local forms are reworked in a contemporary context.

Contemporary World Writers aims to bring together the theoretical impulse which currently dominates post-colonial studies and closely argued readings of particular authors' works, and by so doing to avoid the danger of appropriating the specifics of particular texts into the hegemony of totalising theories.

Acknowledgements

My first thanks go to Ish himself for his kind assistance during the preparation of this study. I'd like to express my appreciation to the University of Sunderland, for sabbatical leave and financial support. Also, my gratitude to the Daiwa Anglo-Japanese Foundation and the Japan Foundation Endowment Committee, whose funding made possible a research visit to Japan. I am especially indebted to John Thieme and Matthew Frost for their careful editing, and to Peter Dempsey, Sarah Gamble and Shuhei Takada for perusing the drafts. Many thanks to those who gave me useful materials: Peter Bolger, Janet Graham-Russell, Norio Irie, Brian McHale, Tomoko Nagaoka, Ann Skinner of Skreba Films, Kern Trembath, Karine Zbinden and the staff at the Chester Road Library in Sunderland. I am much obliged to Brian Hulme, Cynthia Wong, Brian Shaffer and those at Manchester University Press and Faber & Faber for their help. Finally, thanks to the following for their support: Niran Abbas, Amalia Bourou, Kristin Nervik Forseth, Carey and Pat Nutman, Danielle Ramsay, Peter and Eliane Wilson and Colin and Alison Younger. Special nods to my mother, Elizabeth, sisters Lesley and Maureen – and Vita, for her vitality.

List of abbreviations

AFW	*An Artist of the Floating World*
PVH	*A Pale View of Hills*
RD	*The Remains of the Day*
U	*The Unconsoled*
WWWO	*When We Were Orphans*

Chronology

1954   Kazuo Ishiguro born (8 November) in Nagasaki, Japan. Son of Shigeo (an oceanographer) and Shizuko (maiden name, Michida).

1960   Family (including two sisters, Fumiko and Yoko) moves to Guildford, Surrey; father works on development of oil fields in the North Sea.

1960–66 Attends Stoughton Primary School.

1966–73 Attends Woking County Grammar School for Boys, Surrey.

1973   Grouse beater for Queen Mother at Balmoral Castle, Aberdeen, Scotland. Other sundry jobs.

1974   During 'gap year', travels in America and Canada, where he writes journal, and unsuccessfully hawks demo tapes around music companies.

1974–78 Attends University of Kent, Canterbury, where he graduates with a BA (Honours) in English and Philosophy.

1975   Suspends his studies for a year and writes fiction.

1976   Community worker at Renfrew Social Works Department, Renfrew, Scotland.

1979–80 Resettlement worker at West London Cyrenians, helping the homeless. Meets future wife, Lorna Anne MacDougal.

1979   Writes four short stories during the summer at a farmhouse in Cornwall.

1979–80 Attends University of East Anglia, where he completes an MA in Creative Writing. Tutors include Malcolm Bradbury and Angela Carter.

1980   Moves to a bed-sit in Cardiff, Wales. Bill Buford, editor of *Granta*, contacts him after submission of short story. 'A Strange and Sometimes Sadness' published in small journal *Bananas*.

1981   'A Strange and Sometimes Sadness', 'Getting Poisoned' and 'Waiting for J' published in *Introduction 7: Stories by New Writers*. Robert McCrum, editor at Faber & Faber, commissions him to write a novel. Settles in Sydenham, London, with Lorna.

1982   *A Pale View of Hills* published in UK and the US; becomes British citizen; included in 'Best of Young British Novelists' campaign.

1983   Awarded Winifred Holtby Prize from the Royal Society of Literature for *A Pale View of Hills*; 'A Family Supper' published in *Firebird 2*, edited by T. J. Binding. Included as one of twenty 'Best Young British Novelists' in Book Marketing Council campaign.

1984   *A Profile of Arthur J. Mason* broadcast on Channel 4 television; wins Golden Plaque for Best Short Film at Chicago Film Festival. Receives writer's bursary from the Arts Council of Great Britain.

1986   Publishes *An Artist of the Floating World* in UK and the US; wins Whitbread Book of the Year Award, and is shortlisted for Booker Prize. Marries Lorna Anne MacDougal (9 May). *The Gourmet* broadcast on Channel 4 television. Visits Singapore and Malaysia.

1987   'A Family Supper' appears in *The Penguin Book of Modern British Short Stories*, edited by Malcolm Bradbury.

1989   Publishes *The Remains of the Day* in UK and the US; awarded Booker Prize. Harold Pinter purchases the film rights. Returns to Japan for short visit in collaboration with the Japan Foundation.

1990   Awarded honorary D.Litt. by University of Kent, Canterbury. 'A Family Supper' published in *Esquire*. Guest at the Houston International Festival.

1992   Daughter, Naomi, born in March.

1993   *The Remains of the Day* feature film released by Merchant-

Ivory Productions, starring Anthony Hopkins and Emma Thompson; film is nominated for eight Oscars. Included in second 'Best of Young British Novelists' campaign.

1994   Member of jury at Cannes Film Festival (other jurors include Catherine Deneuve and Clint Eastwood).

1995   Publishes *The Unconsoled*; wins Cheltenham Prize; is shortlisted for Booker Prize. Receives the Order of the British Empire (OBE) for services to literature; awarded Premio Scanno for literature, Italy.

1998   Attends State Banquet in May to mark visit of Emperor Akihito of Japan to England. Receives the Chevalier dans l'Ordre des Arts et Lettres in France.

2000   Publishes *When We Were Orphans* in UK and US.

Contexts and intertexts

'HOME' is a simple noun – with tentacles. Home is many different things to many different people. It is an origin, a base, a shelter, a returning point. It is a house, a town, a country, an ideology. You are 'at home' wherever you feel comfortable, and it is where you want to be when things go wrong. As a character says in a Robert Frost poem, 'Home is the place where, when you have to go there, / They have to take you in.'[1] Home is sweet, there is no place like it, it is where the heart is.

What is home to Kazuo Ishiguro? No doubt, in everyday terms, it is the house in London that he shares happily with his wife, Lorna Anne MacDougall, and his daughter, Naomi. But at a deeper level, down in the recesses of identity and belonging, where is his home? He was born in Nagasaki, Japan, in 1954, and came to England at the age of five with his oceanographer father, Shizuo; his mother, Shizuko Michida; and his two sisters. The move was only supposed to be for a short time, but Ishiguro has lived there ever since.

So Ishiguro's home is a halfway house, neither Japanese nor English, somewhere in-between departure and arrival, nostalgia and anticipation. He is, in short, a displaced person, one of the many in the twentieth century of exile and estrangement. Peter Berger would no doubt class him as one of those 'discontents [who] can be subsumed under the heading of "homelessness"' as the 'pluralistic structures of modern society have made the life of more and more individuals migratory, ever-changing, mobile.'[2] It is precisely because Ishiguro demonstrates such a 'homeless mind' that it is therefore useful to examine his fictions through the optic of displacement, and its effect upon his themes, characters and style. There are, naturally, other ways of approaching his work, but the concepts of dislocation and homelessness and all that they imply are versatile tools for exploring the richness of Ishiguro's writings.

Homelessness appears only once as a literal, rather than as a figurative, motif in Ishiguro's work. In his play for television *The Gourmet* (1986), the central protagonist Manley Kingston – a rich food aficionado in search of the perfect meal – joins a queue of homeless people outside a church offering soup and shelter. He has not come to partake of the customary gruel doled out to the hapless down-and-outs. He is there for the altogether more exotic purpose of capturing and eating a ghost due to appear in the vestry that night. Although successful in his mission, he is violently ill the next day. As he staggers through an underpass where some other homeless people have made their cardboard abode, he is accused of having had too much to drink the night before. He rebuffs this suggestion:

> *Manley looks at the homeless man with disdain.*
> *Then with dignity:*
> MANLEY: I was hungry. I ate. Now I am sick.[3]

Notice the script direction, 'with dignity'. Dignity is a keyword in Ishiguro's most famous novel, *The Remains of the Day* (1989). It is the opposite of displacement. To be dignified is to be 'at home' with oneself and one's circumstances. To have dignity is to be correctly placed *vis-à-vis* your self-demands and the expectations of others. The novel spotlights the predicament of the butler Stevens, who realises that his lifetime of stalwart service to Lord Darlington has been wasted, and has brought him little happiness. This is not the only feature of Ishiguro's other fictions to grace *The Gourmet*. The ghost motif is explored at length in *A Pale View of Hills* (1982). The connoisseurship of Manley is mirrored by the dedication of Masuji Ono and Ryder in their respective professions of painter and pianist in *An Artist of the Floating World* (1986) and *The Unconsoled* (1995). And the motif of homelessness in its wider, metaphorical aspects is sounded out through the character of Christopher Banks in *When We Were Orphans* (2000). Etsuko, Ono, Stevens, Ryder and Banks, like Manley, are no longer at home with themselves, as they strive to regain the dignity they have lost after being displaced from their natural surroundings.

This, then, will be one of the key oppositions traced in this study: the struggle between displacement and dignity. Each chapter will look at an individual novel by Ishiguro, stressing particular aspects of the work: the representation of Japan and the atomic bomb in *A Pale View of Hills*; the issue of blame in *An Artist of the Floating World,* and the book's filmic structure; the conflict between personal and national identity in *The Remains of the Day*; the surreal world of *The Unconsoled*; and the strange amalgam of reality and dream in *When We Were Orphans*. Underlying all of these books is a tug-of-war between a sense of homelessness and being 'at home'.

Ishiguro worked with the homeless for a brief spell in the 1970s, as a member of the community group the Cyrenians who provide food, accommodation and welfare advice for itinerants. His then wife-to-be, Lorna, was also active in this organisation. Perhaps there is some truth in the idea that people are attracted by occupations answering some psychological need, and that this work helped Ishiguro wrestle with his own special form of homelessness. If so, then what can be made of the fact that in the summer of 1973 Ishiguro was employed as a member of the Queen Mother's Royal grousebeating party at Balmoral Castle?[4] It is difficult to say, other than to note that this furnished him with some direct experience of life as a retainer for the English upper classes, a subject central to *The Remains of the Day*.

It may seem incongruous for a Japanese to have such familiarity with both ends of the English social ladder. Yet Ishiguro never particularly felt himself to be Japanese, or English either for that matter:

> I was very aware that I had very little knowledge of modern Japan. But I was still writing books set in Japan, or supposedly set in Japan. My very lack of authority and

lack of knowledge about Japan, I think, forced me into a position of using my imagination, and also of thinking of myself as a kind of homeless writer. I had no obvious social role, because I wasn't a very English Englishman and I wasn't a very Japanese Japanese either.

And so I had no clear role, no society or country to speak for or write about. Nobody's history seemed to be my history.[5]

So added to Ishiguro's homelessness and classlessness is his lack of a country to call his own. Nationalised as a United Kingdom citizen in 1982, he thinks of himself as British rather than English,[6] a passport distinction increasingly uncommon among the peoples of England, Scotland, Wales and Northern Ireland. Interestingly he prefers to live in big cities, with their mixtures of ethnic backgrounds. He feels quite at home in London, that most cosmopolitan of cities, where he has resided since the early 1980s. It is the perfect environment for someone who straddles different cultures. In those syncretic streets and suburbs, he can blend into the background. As Kate Kellaway puts it, 'Ishiguro is a chameleon. He's not quite at home anywhere, but can seem to be at ease everywhere. His placelessness gives him freedom and he has mastered the art of projection and protective coloration.'[7]

The twentieth century was the age of both exiles and chameleons, those displaced involuntarily and those who chose to drift and adapt. Two World Wars and hundreds of minor conflicts precipitated the mass movements of entire populations against their will. Forced relocation of large ethnic communities in Croatia, Bosnia and Kosovo blighted the end of the century during the Balkan conflicts. Yet there was also a more positive trend encouraging placelessness. Technological advancement and new forms of transport made travel easier and faster, and accelerated a globalisation of culture. Pico Iyer believes that this led to the formation of a new breed of displaced person, one who is proud not to feel affiliated to any specific country or culture. 'We pass', Iyer writes, 'through countries as through revolving doors, impermanent residents of nowhere. Nothing is strange to us, and nowhere is foreign'; or, to put it the opposite way, 'If all the world is alien to us, all the world is home'.[8]

Iyer nominates Ishiguro as 'a great spokesman for the privileged homeless',[9] because of his unusual mixed background. His departure from Japan was not his decision: small children are seldom captains of their fate. But immersion in the cultures of both East and West, and his fame as an international writer, enables Ishiguro to become rooted in his rootlessness. The phrase 'privileged homeless' is thus not necessarily an oxymoron in an era of displacement. It is a label which Salman Rushdie, another spokesman for the privileged homeless, might recognise. In an open letter to Rushdie during the crisis of *The Satanic Verses* (1988), Ishiguro referred to 'this age of migration and "multi-culturalism"'.[10] Indeed it is, as the Rushdie case proves. At stake throughout the affair of *The Satanic Verses*, a book deemed to be a blasphemous attack on Islam, was the clash of two incompatible world views. Muslim fundamentalists sought to maintain the purity and integrity of their culture, whilst Western liberals encouraged the melting of old nationalistic boundaries and the development of a pluralist internationalism. Rushdie and his supporters wished to construct 'a vision of home where diversity is not calumny.'[11] But the surge towards diversity creates in its wake, inevitably, a sense of homelessness. This, in turn, can lead to an intense desire for home and stability. As Abdul R. JanMohamed suggests, 'the notion of exile always emphasises the absence of "home", of the cultural matrix that formed the individual subject; hence, it implies an involuntary or enforced rupture between the collective subject of the original culture and the individual subject.'[12]

It is arguably precisely because of such social and cultural ruptures that each of Ishiguro's novels is 'very rooted in a particular house or a particular place.'[13] The fictions re-enact the struggles between the individual and the collective, the vision of home and the sense of homelessness, with settings that literally house these crucial themes.

In *A Pale View of Hills* the narrator is a middle-aged Japanese woman, Etsuko. She is finding her English country house too large following the deaths of her husband (Mr Sheringham) and eldest daughter (Keiko), and the departure of her youngest daughter (Niki) to London. On the last day of Niki's short visit to her mother, Etsuko reveals that she is thinking of selling the house and moving into somewhere smaller. It would be a wise decision, not least because it is now a haunted house, possessed by memories of Keiko who committed suicide after leaving her family home.

At the beginning of *An Artist of the Floating World*, Ono tells the story of how he acquired his splendid house through an 'auction of prestige' (*AFW*, 9) before the war. He was nearing the height of his career as a politically motivated artist, and basking in what he thought was his high social standing. However, after the war his work is discredited as nationalist propaganda, and he is reduced to spending his days repairing the damage sustained to the house during the Allied bombing raids. Like Etsuko, he too is now alone at home, as his wife and son died during the war, his eldest daughter (Setsuko) is married, and his youngest daughter (Noriko) is contemplating marriage. His only pleasure is to spend time with his grandson, Ichiro, who seems more interested in pretending to be Popeye or the Lone Ranger than humouring his ageing relative.

Stevens in *The Remains of the Day* has served as a butler in the stately home of Darlington Hall for over forty years, without taking a holiday. He is so unused to being outside its confines that his motoring trip to the West Country brings him into contact with a democratised 1950s England of ordinary people that he never knew existed. He fools himself into believing that the reason for his journey is to recruit his former housekeeper, Miss Kenton, to help with a staff shortage. Yet it is clear that this professional rationale veils amatory ambitions. As Joseph Coates says, Stevens has 'turned himself inside-out like a glove: he can express his needs only as the needs of the house.'[14] Ironically, whilst at the Taylors' cottage in Moscombe, a villager mistakes the butler for a member of parliament – also called Stevens – who '[h]ad some very sensible things to say about housing' (*RD*, 187).

In *The Unconsoled*, Ryder is constantly on tour as a concert pianist, and his travels induce unbearable strains upon his life. His partner, Sophie, pins all her hopes of improving the relationship with Ryder on finding a new place to live: 'Once I find a proper home for us ... then everything will go better. It's bound to' (*U*, 89). However, an attempt to organise an ideal family night in – with a special meal and board games with the son, Boris – ends in disaster. Ryder refuses to play happy families, sticks his nose behind a newspaper, grumbles about the food and leaves early.

Perhaps the most puissant probing of the meaning of 'home' is presented by the plight of Christopher Banks in *When We Were Orphans*. Banks, a distinguished detective in 1930s London, returns to the place of his birth in Shanghai to investigate the possible kidnapping of his parents eighteen years earlier. He visits again the 'big white house' (*WWWO*, 51) where he lived as a child, only to discover that it has been extensively altered by its current and previous occupants. His childhood obsession of solving the mystery of his parents' disappearance drives his adult enquiries, and brings him to the point of madness as he scrabbles through the ruins of war-ravaged tenements in search of a lost cause. His will-o'-the-wisp wish to settle back in the house with his family evaporates, but many years later in London he finally accepts his loss: 'This city ... has come to be my home, and I should not mind if I had to live out the rest of my days here' (*WWWO*, 313).

So the main characters in Ishiguro's novels live in houses that are not quite homes. As Kana Oyabu observes, their houses 'are neither their birthplaces, nor where their parents lived, nor even where they have full and happy family lives.'[15] They are simply dwellings, convenient places from which to manage their private and public affairs. Etsuko, Ono, Stevens, Ryder and Banks are exiles, displaced persons, 'lone rangers' in their memories and imaginations. Their homeless minds make them perfect representatives of the century of displacement.

To what extent are the predicaments of these characters reflections of Ishiguro's experience? The question is a beguiling one because of his peculiar biographical circumstances. He has disclosed in several interviews that leaving his home in Japan was a wrench for him as a child. He lived in a three-storey house in Nagasaki (still owned by Ishiguro's father), with a large garden. The paternal grandparents occupied the ground floor, whilst Ishiguro and sister had the run of the second floor where his parents slept. This traditional extended family provided Ishiguro with a secure and stable infancy. When he left for Britain in 1961, he was suddenly exiled from this safe haven, an exile made even more unsettling by the uncertainty about when or whether the family would return.

As it happens, the family never did return, and for many years Ishiguro delayed visiting his grandparents' Nagasaki house in case it disturbed his inward vision of home. He said in 1987: 'The house as I remember it is a rather grand and beautiful thing, and if I went back, the reality would be rather shabby and horrible; and in a way, that is how I feel about that whole area of my life. It's very powerful to me while it remains a land of speculation, imagination and memory.'[16] For a long time, then, Japan was as remote to Ishiguro as it was to the children in Guildford who would follow him around the playground at school. They had never seen a Japanese before, so it was as if he had beamed down from outer space. Such intense curiosity prompted Ishiguro to become a performer. He was conscious both of the difference perceived in him by others, but also of the sameness perceived in others by himself. It is not surprising, given these early alienating experiences, that Ishiguro became 'Janus-minded'.[17]

Despite this distinctive background, Ishiguro chooses not to write directly about himself. He finds it more productive to deal with characters who are *unlike* him. Distancing forces him to look at his subjects from the outside. It helps him to avoid the temptation to deal with material that may be personally interesting, but artistically irrelevant. This is not to say that there are no autobiographical elements in his work. The young boy Ichiro in *An Artist of the Floating World* undoubtedly reflects many aspects of Ishiguro's childhood, particularly his love of popular

American culture and its icons. Scenes involving a film poster draw upon some of Ishiguro's earliest memories of his Japanese grandfather.[18] The writing is autobiographical in a broader sense, too, in that it expresses Ishiguro's views on how the world works.

But by and large, Ishiguro is absent from his novels. Nevertheless this careful excision of himself from his fictions has not prevented many commentators from reading them almost exclusively in terms of his Japanese origins. When Ishiguro first became a public figure he suffered greatly from stereotyping by critics and reviewers, who could not resist 'compulsory analogies to Sumo wrestling, geisha girls and Toyotas' and nicknamed him the 'Shogun of Sydenham'.[19] It was as if the Japaneseness of his name and his appearance acted as a screen to hide the possibility that behind it there was a complex person. One reviewer even seemed to think that *A Pale View of Hills* was translated from Japanese. This worked to Ishiguro's advantage to some extent, as it gave him a distinct marketable image, especially in a literary climate where there was an active search for non-native English writers. But the limitations soon became apparent:

> These stereotypes are all right as part of a publicity game. Where it starts to get irritating is when people read your work in a certain sort of way: it seems my Japanese novels are so exotic and remote that I could have written bizarre Márquezian or Kafkaesque stuff and people would still have taken it as straight realism. I've always struggled with this literal-minded tendency in British audiences.[20]

He even joked that if he wrote a book like Kafka's *The Trial* (1925), reviewers would comment on the strangeness of the judicial process in Japan. It was because of these sorts of pressures that Ishiguro began talking in 1989 about wanting to write a 'messy, jagged, loud kind of book',[21] unlocateable in any specific socio-political reality. This became *The Unconsoled*, a novel in which a surreal, rambling picaresque style replaced Ishiguro's trademark concision and stylistic reticence. Márquez and Kafka are indeed two of the obvious reference points, and the novel is structured with techniques borrowed from the *non sequiturs* of dreams.

Another way in which Ishiguro is stereotyped is through comparisons with well-known Japanese writers. Yukio Mishima is perhaps the most famous twentieth-century novelist from Japan in the West, though this is probably as much to do with his colourful personal life as his writings. This bisexual extrovert, part-time film-actor and political agitator committed ritual suicide in a spectacularly public manner in 1970, as a protest against the decline of militarism and the *samurai* warrior tradition in Japan. He produced some fine books, too, including *Confessions of a Mask* (1949) and *The Temple of the Golden Pavilion* (1956) which experiment with both Western and Eastern novelistic conventions. His act of *harakiri*, however, has tended to eclipse his literary achievement, and has confirmed certain preconceptions about the alien customs of Japan. Ishiguro quickly became tired of being asked about Mishima by journalists. It is not as if they had much in common either in their life or their work. Ishiguro's every instinct 'goes against demonstrativeness';[22] the reverse was true with Mishima, whose excesses of self-publicity rivalled those of the nineteenth-century American poet, Walt Whitman.

Whitman wrote favourable reviews of his own work under assumed names, and posed defiantly for the frontispiece of *Leaves of Grass* (1855) in an open-necked shirt. Ishiguro has suggested that if his own books had been published pseudonymously, and someone else hired to stand in for jacket photos, nobody would think of comparing him with Japanese writers. Anthony Thwaite believes a comment such as this is simply a disingenuous ploy to prevent comparisons with the likes of Natsume Soseki and Junichiro Tanizaki. He argues: 'There are distinct Japanese characteristics (such as indirectness) in Ishiguro's work, however much he may disclaim them.'[23] The melancholic pitch of Ishiguro's prose, the formality of the dialogue, the concern with issues of duty and service – all of these seem to indicate an oriental sensibility.

There are other ways, though, of characterising Ishiguro's works. The Japanese author Kenzaburo Oe, recipient of the Nobel Prize in 1994, sees Ishiguro as 'a novelist at the very forefront of English literature.'[24] Robert Clark also foregrounds the English qualities of the writing: 'Ishiguro's techniques are equally those associated with … Jane Austen's representation of her social milieu through the singular and partial consciousness of Emma Woodhouse.'[25] This tendency to concentrate on a limited point of view, usually that of an unreliable narrator, is especially prominent in Ishiguro's first three novels. Another Austen-like feature of these books is the small canvas they portray: the 'little bit (two inches wide) of ivory on which I work with so wide a brush',[26] as one of her letters puts it. Pico Iyer picks up on this when he refers to Ishiguro's 'exquisitely fashioned miniatures, miracles of workmanship and tact that suggest everything through absence and retreat.'[27] Another Western writer Ishiguro is frequently compared to is Henry James. Terrence Rafferty claims that the Jamesian short story 'The Beast in the Jungle' (1903) is a precursor to *The Remains of the Day*.[28] Its narrator, John Marcher, is like Stevens. He spends all his life waiting for a special fate, only to find that his fate is that nothing special ever *does* happen to him. Patrick Parrinder also sees analogies with James when he praises *An Artist of the Floating World* for presenting 'a vignette of a moment of cultural history which is as complete, in its own way, as *Washington Square*'.[29]

One of Ishiguro's main motivations for writing *The Remains of the Day* was to produce a book which was not only about Englishness, but also engaged with recognisable English literary traditions. It succeeded brilliantly in this aim. As David Gurewich maintains, even the title and the opening line strike a recognisable 'classic' note.[30] The phrase 'remains of the day' sounds as if it has always belonged to the language. The opening line's tentative politeness – 'It seems increasingly likely that I really will undertake the expedition that has been preoccupying my imagination now for some days' (*RD*, 3) – could be from a novel a century earlier. Caroline Patey has catalogued elements of picaresque and mock-epic in *The Remains of the Day*: its orderly structure, journey motif, master–servant relationship and plot involving mistaken identities. She also traces elements of diverse genres such as detective fiction, the spy story and the Wessex tale in the novel.[31] The genre it resembles most clearly, however, is the one it parodies: the domestic service farce epitomised by P. G. Wodehouse's 'Jeeves' stories. This was a tactical choice: who, among fictional characters, is more English than Jeeves? Ishiguro admits to undermining the 'jovial butler' myth by using it in a 'slightly twisted and different way'.[32] Where Jeeves is loquacious, Stevens is taciturn; where Stevens is helpless, Jeeves is efficiency itself.

Ishiguro was brought up on the great canon, both English and European, and acknowledges the debt he owes to Fyodor Dostoevsky and Anton Chekhov.[33] From the former he absorbed the exploration of deep psychic dissonances, and from the latter the divining of subterranean currents of emotion. With *The Unconsoled*, Ishiguro's European influences were given free rein. Tom Wilhelmus compared it with the work of Thomas Mann or Thomas Bernhard, artists who were also 'between cultures'.[34] Kafka is present in the long, endless streets and corridors stalked by Ryder; the frustrations he experiences at the hands of petty bureaucracy; and the unceasing requests for the granting of personal favours. There is also a hint of Vladimir Nabokov, particularly his nomadic temperament, in the restlessness of the book. Nabokov lived all his life in a hotel and 'collected' foreign places like a museum curator. 'Nabokov shows us', according to Pico Iyer, 'that if nowhere is home, everywhere is.'[35] This is also the conclusion we are led to when categorising Ishiguro. He seems equally 'at home' in the traditions of Japanese, English and European fiction, and this is what makes him a truly international writer.

The notion that 'everywhere is home' is reiterated in the theoretical nostrums of postmodernism and poststructuralism. These discourses challenge traditional approaches to the analysis of literature and culture by displacing interest away from the centre and towards the periphery. A similar centripetality motors another of these belated post-philosophies, namely postcolonialism. Postcolonial critics such as Edward Said, Homi K. Bhabha, Gayatri Chakravorty Spivak and Abdul R. JanMohamed argue for a multicultural curriculum to examine concepts of ethnicity and alternative history. They question the centrifugal assumptions of Western discourse. They attend to those nations affected by the imperial process (principally in India, Africa and the Middle East), thereby moving away from the usual Anglo-American/European centre. Their key concepts – including 'Orientalism' (Said), 'hybridity' (Bhabha), 'the subaltern' (Spivak), and 'minority discourse' (JanMohamed) – give a voice to those communities who have been silenced in the Western tradition.[36]

Is it justifiable to apply postcolonial ideas to Ishiguro? After all, Japan was never a colony – although it did have colonising ambitions in the 1930s, as *An Artist of the Floating World* amply demonstrates. However, Ishiguro is a writer who believes he is *'stuck on the margins'*,[37] thereby aligning himself with the postcolonial emphasis on the marginal, the liminal, the excluded. Furthermore, Pico Iyer declares that Ishiguro is 'a paradigm of the polycultural order',[38] along with writers such as Ben Okri, Michael Ondaatje, Vikram Seth and Timothy Mo. These writers are at the centre of a new genre of world fiction, one dominated by what Susie O'Brien calls the 'rhetoric of hybridity and polyculturality'.[39]

How feasible is it to group Ishiguro with these other 'international' writers? Bruce King claims that Ishiguro has much in common with the Trinidadian Shiva Naipaul, the Anglo-Indian Salman Rushdie, the Nigerian Buchi Emecheta and the Hong Kong-born Timothy Mo.[40] All five novelists concern themselves with cultural and racial dignity in novels such as Rushdie's *Grimus* (1975), Naipaul's *The Chip-Chip Gatherers* (1973), Emecheta's *The Slave Girl* (1977) and Mo's *An Insular Possession* (1986). Also, they are not afraid to criticise the countries in which they were born both as insiders and Westerners: '[they] help map the post-colonial world by being part of more than one culture.'[41] Others are more sceptical. Kana Oyabu and Steven Connor both feel that Ishiguro does not tackle the colonial mentality or the issue of polycultural identity directly, and that these topics are not within his purview.[42] This does not invalidate postcolonial readings of his work, however. Indeed, there is a whole strand of postcolonial criticism specialising in recording the significant *absence* of such elements in literary works. The benchmark here is Jane Austen's *Mansfield Park* (1814), a book whose tragi-comedy of middle-class manners takes place in a large house subsidised by its owner's colonial investments in the Caribbean. Sir Thomas Bertram's foreign interests is a subject not explicitly taken up by the author. Edward Said corrects this omission in his essay 'Jane Austen and the Empire', by demonstrating that the civilised realm of Mansfield Park is subsidised by the slave-maintained sugar plantations of Antigua.[43]

Ishiguro is rightly suspicious of being lumped with Mo, Emecheta and others simply because he has a foreign-sounding name. But he has other things in common with them. The postcolonial writer, such as Rushdie or Ondaatje, is typically between two worlds and thus produces a hybrid text. Iyer thinks Ishiguro fits this mould. He is 'one of those lucky individuals with one foot on either side of the widening gap between Japan and the world at large'.[44] He is a representative of the 'age of the refugee'. And a refugee is not a bad thing to be according to George Steiner, who believes that being between cultures and identities is a defining characteristic of great writers in the modern era; for example, Kafka, Conrad, James, Nabokov, Joyce, Beckett, Wilde.[45]

The 'in-betweenness' of Ishiguro's work is most evident in *The Remains of the Day*. This book is frequently perceived as a 'stroke of the decolonising pen',[46] for seemingly attacking the imperial pretensions of a fading British Empire. Several critics have delighted in the ambivalence of its cultural critique. Ihab Hassan wonders: 'A Japanese-born writer, living in England since his childhood, writes a novel about the butler of a great English house. Is the result a Japanese vision of England or, more slyly, an English version of Japan? Or is it both and neither, a vision simply of our condition, our world?'[47] Hassan considers the possibility of reading the book as depicting an England that is a mirror-image of Japan. Both countries share an island insularity, and are keen to retain their own native traditions in the face of encroaching globalism. The tale of the butler, and the decline of the nation he represents, could be an oblique myth about the fortunes of Japan. But Hassan is canny enough to recognise that the novel evades such simplifications. Steven Connor also hesitates to state too bluntly that Ishiguro's 'English' novel is really about Japan: 'the uncertainty of a hybrid, or outside-in, rendering of Englishness is made tolerable and coherent by being represented itself as a translation, an opening out of Japanese identity to us for inspection.'[48]

The quandary of weighing the relevancy of the English/Japanese correspondences in *The Remains of the Day* is quagmired further by the distortions of what Edward Said calls 'Orientalism'. In his highly influential book of the same name, Said argues that the West (specifically the English and the French) deliberately constructed the Orient as Europe's 'other' – 'its contrasting image, idea, personality, experience'[49] – in order to legitimate its imperial drives in the East. The rise of the Oriental specialist, who defined his subject in terms of contrastive notions of the Occident, contributed to the process of exoticising the East and extinguishing the similarities between it and the West. The correspondence between the image of the Orient thus constructed and the Orient itself was relatively unimportant. What was crucial was that the image should have an internal coherence, which would render it useful in all manner of aggrandising political, social and cultural activities. In this way 'otherness' is divorced from 'sameness', and displaced on to somebody and somewhere else.

Displacement is a word that often crops up in criticism of Ishiguro's novels. Christopher Bigsby refers to Ishiguro's 'deliberate act of displacement'[50] in setting his first two books in Japan, whilst really writing about values important to his own generation. Similarly, Maya Jaggi states that Ishiguro sees his own lack of cultural equilibrium as 'bound up with displacement.'[51] What is displacement? As might be expected, it is a concept with many different connotations. It is interesting that one of its earliest meanings was 'Removal from an office or dignity; deposition'.[52] In this sense, all of Ishiguro's central protagonists – Etsuko, Ono, Stevens, Ryder and Banks – are displaced in one way or another from their rightful position or context. The standard meaning is the more generalised 'Removal of a thing from its place; putting out of place; shifting, dislocation'. Closely related to this is the sense of 'Removal of a thing by substitution of something else in its place'; replacement, in other words. Less common are specialised uses of the term in geology (a fault in the earth's crust); hydrostatics (the movement of liquid after the immersion or floating of a solid body); pharmacy (extraction by percolation); and physics (the laws of displacement). In all these usages, displacement is an external event, observable and measurable.

However, the most common connotations of displacement, at least in cultural circles, are associated with psychology and engage inner events which cannot be verified. Freud chose this term to designate the dream-process that diverts the attention of the psyche away from potentially damaging material. Fears and forbidden desires are masked by their association with relatively trifling symbols, objects or situations. In this way the significance of the dream is displaced. In waking life, displacement activity is any action performed outside its normal context to deflect stress or anxiety (for example, scratching the head when nervous). So even here there is the eruption of the latent into the manifest. The importance of Freudian displacement to literature is that it encourages the critical gaze to penetrate the surface of the text and look for the substrata of meaning, unconscious avoidances or refigurations of content. The author is no longer at home in the text, which becomes the site for the free-play of language and desire.

Just as psychoanalysis displaces the subject by deprioritising the role of consciousness as the origin of physical and mental behaviour, certain strands of contemporary theory displace the author altogether as the radial centre of significance. As Mark Krupnick asserts, displacement is 'one of the indispensable words … without which post-structuralism could not manage' and 'sums up the spirit of the present age.'[53] Critics such as Roland Barthes and Jacques Derrida move beyond the binary oppositions of conscious/unconscious, presence/absence, writer/reader and so on. They explore the displacements resulting when these hierarchical pairs are reversed, and then dynamite the system in which a particular set of binaries made sense. Deconstruction, then, expresses the joy of displacement, and although the word is not theoretically deployed by Derrida, it is the energy propelling his strategy of decentring. It is also the fuel behind this study. I will show how there is a reversal in Ishiguro's work of the opposition between dignity (being placed, occupying one's position fully) and displacement itself (being dislodged, occupying contradictory or incompatible positions).

The following chapters question Ishiguro's identity as a writer. How Japanese is he? In what ways have the novels and films of both East and West influenced his work? Are his books typical of the realist tradition, or more experimental than has previously been supposed? No definitive answers will be given, but several fields of reference shall be posited in plumbing these issues. It's a long way from the fixities of home as a cultural constant to the Heraclitean fluxes of deconstruction. Yet if it is sometimes 'suicide to be abroad',[54] as Mrs Rooney says in Samuel Beckett's *All That Fall* (1957), staying at home is not always the preferable option. She continues: 'But what is it to be at home, Mr Tyler, what is it to be at home? A lingering dissolution.'

A Pale View of Hills

THINK of Japan. What images come to mind? To the young, it is a place of neon, *manga* comics, microcomputers and *karaoke*. They see it in terms of the futuristic cityscape depicted in Ridley Scott's film *Blade Runner* (1982), itself modelled on modern-day Tokyo. Those of an older generation are more likely to conjure up visions of *kamikaze* pilots, *samurai* swords, pagodas and elegant kimonos. In the first instance, Japan is construed as a kind of hyper-West; in the second, it is foreign and alien, the absolute other of the West. To both young and old, to be Japanese is to be *strange*.

Ruth Benedict was commissioned by the United States government at the end of the Second World War to demystify this strangeness.[1] She characterises this island race as a combination of contradictory opposites, a culture of extreme delicacy (the art of flower-arranging) and unpredictable violence (*harakiri*): 'Both the sword and the chrysanthemum are a part of the picture.'[2]

All of these images are clichés and stereotypes, of course, and have little validity other than as convenient generalisations. Nevertheless, it is surprising to discover just how many conceptions of the Japanese are based upon an 'us' versus 'them' dichotomy. The Japanese are usually perceived as either the exact opposite of the West, or exactly like it.[3] There is little room for middle ground between these polar opposites.

Ishiguro is someone who occupies the middle ground more than most. Born in Japan and raised in Britain, he is at home in neither place. The British, if journalists are anything to go by, have difficulty as seeing him as anything other than Japanese. They conveniently ignore the fact that he has lived in Britain almost all his life and has full United Kingdom citizenship. Conversely, the Japanese cannot see him as anything other than British. When Ishiguro visited Japan in 1989, for the first time since he left as a child, the media portrayed him as representative of someone who had 'lost his Japaneseness'.[4] He spoke only English there, and diplomatically refused to answer questions about Japanese issues.

Whilst Ishiguro is understandably keen to play down the differences between the two cultures, he also wishes to maintain a sense of proper distinction. This ambivalence can be observed in his introduction to two novels by the 1968 Japanese Nobel Prize winner Yasunari Kawabata. Although *Snow Country* (1935) is concerned with the life of a country geisha, and *Thousand Cranes* (1955) revolves around the tea ceremony, Ishiguro asks the reader not to anticipate something 'bafflingly foreign.'[5] There is no reason, he believes, to feel that Japanese behaviour is any different from Western behaviour. The Japanese, at least those found in the novels of Kawabata, are much like anyone else. But whilst these novels cover perfectly normal human concerns – love, hate, pride, jealousy – they require a form of reading unfamiliar to those reared solely on European fictional traditions. Ishiguro advises that Kawabata should be read slowly, to give time for the atmosphere to be savoured, and space for the nuances of the dialogue. If the reader is looking for a gripping plot, they are likely to be disappointed: 'Kawabata's stories are often completely plotless. They are not only plotless, but the pace goes so slowly sometimes it almost stops'.[6] Japanese novels require patience and careful observation to be fully appreciated.

It is hard to resist simultaneously interpreting Ishiguro's comments on how to read Kawabata as diagonal instructions on how to read his own work. After all, his first two novels – *A Pale View of Hills* and *An Artist of the Floating World* – are delivered with the same slow, atmospheric nuances he admires in Kawabata. Similarly, although Ishiguro's fictions encompass a fascinating tangle of emotional and social predicaments, they are not exactly 'page-turners' as far as plot is concerned. Critics were quick to pick up on the distinctly Japanese ambience of these books. Anthony Thwaite believes that *A Pale View of Hills* 'functions brilliantly as a kind of Japanese novel';[7] whilst Geoff Dyer calls the prose in *An Artist of the Floating World* 'clean, unharried and airy; full of inflections and innuendo',[8] like a Japanese watercolour. Gabriele Annan states that the 'elegant bareness [of the first two novels] reminds one of Japanese painting',[9] and it was a frequent strategy among reviewers to compare Ishiguro's style with Japanese art. Terms such as *yugen*[10] ('a suggestive indefiniteness full of mystery and depth') or *mono no aware*[11] ('the sadness of things') were dragooned into action. There is some value in this approach. Ishiguro's early novels are, indeed, mysterious and tinged with the ochre hues of nostalgia and regret, qualities readily associated with a Hiroshige woodblock print of Mount Fuji, or a *haiku* about snowfall by Basho. They also happen to be set in Japan. But the interesting question about Ishiguro's writing is not 'Is it Japanese?' but 'How Japanese is it?' Ishiguro himself maintains that the calm surface of his first two books was simply an expression of his natural voice, and that he 'wasn't trying to write them in an understated, a Japanese way.'[12]

To delve into this question further, this chapter will scrutinise various aspects of the Japaneseness of Ishiguro's *A Pale View of Hills*. It will touch upon the issue of ascribing Japanese qualities to Ishiguro's prose, whilst concentrating on thematic aspects of the novels. In particular, two specific Japanese motifs in *A Pale View of Hills* (ghosts and suicide) shall be examined, as well as the absence of the atomic bomb in its narrative. Throughout I wish to explore how the novel questions the concept of Japaneseness through its images and discourse, beginning with a general look at how Ishiguro represents Japan in his fictions.

A Pale View of Hills has an extremely accomplished structure for a first novel. It tells two main stories, one of which is nested inside the other. The inner story is set in Nagasaki a few years after the war. The atomic bomb has wreaked havoc upon the life of its citizens, as almost everybody has undergone extreme personal loss and material deprivation. It is a world where 'one's own dead children and their sufferings blur with the impact of other people's dislocated lives.'[13] Etsuko, a modest woman trying to come to terms with normality after such abnormal experiences, meets and befriends Sachiko, a woman from a wealthy background now in financial straits. Sachiko's young daughter, Mariko, is psychologically damaged from the horrors she has witnessed during the war. Unlike other girls of her age, she does not go to school, but wanders alone by the wasteground near the river. Sachiko, hoping to escape to the United States with her American lover Frank, is very neglectful of her parental responsibilities. She frequently leaves the child alone in their cold and unlit cottage and carouses with Frank. Despite ample evidence to the contrary, she shrugs off any suggestions that Mariko is unhappy. This section of the plot charts the concern of Etsuko, who is herself pregnant, for the little girl and her mother. The Nagasaki tale is framed as a series of memories recalled by Etsuko during a visit by her daughter, Niki, to her house in England. This outer story takes place several decades after the war, when mother and daughter struggle to repair their relationship after the suicide of Keiko, a child conceived in Japan but raised in England. Keiko became very unhappy as a result of her geographical displacement, and as a teenager locked herself away in her room for days on end. As soon as she was old enough, she left home for some lodgings in Manchester, where her landlady eventually found her hanged. Etsuko cannot rid herself of the guilt she feels about this tragedy, and its pall reawakens memories of Sachiko and Mariko and darkens Niki's stay. The two strands of present and past despair are braided with great dexterity.

The Nagasaki episodes appear to be a convincing depiction of life in Japan after the war, and display several references to aspects of Japanese culture then. To take just one example, in Chapter 7 Etsuko, Sachiko and Mariko gamble at a *kujibiki* stand. This is the Japanese equivalent of a street tombola stall, where the selection of a lucky ticket earns a prize for the holder.

Mariko has her eye on a basket to house her kittens, but after several attempts only succeeds in winning a wooden box, which she decides will serve the same purpose. It is a touching scene, evocative of a way of life fast disappearing under the post-war onslaught of American colonisation. *A Pale View of Hills* reinforces this sense of historical change through several telling details. Mrs Fujiwara – a wealthy woman before the war reduced to being a humble noodle-shop owner after it – confides to her old friend Ogata that 'Young women these days are ... forever talking about washing-machines and American dresses' (*PVH*, 152). Materialism is rampant, and Sachiko is one such young woman who would gladly forsake traditional Japanese customs for a slice of the American pie. Domestic appliances and modish clothes are tokens of a consumerist dream infinitely preferable to the depleted economy of Japan in the 1950s.

These episodes suggest that Ishiguro's novel is seemingly a realistic study of the Japanese society in the wake of its crushing military defeat. It conveys the impression of being a faithful account of the country at that time, despite its lack of social and political substance. How genuine, though, is its Japaneseness? The characters have Japanese names, observe Japanese customs and exist within a Japanese culture, but is this enough to establish its mimetic fidelity? Perhaps the text is disingenuous, and presents a picture of Japan bearing only a circumstantial relation to the actuality. Although sprinkled with apparently authentic historical snapshots, such as the *kujibiki* episode and Mrs Fujiwara's complaint, it could be argued that *A Pale View of Hills* as a whole undermines its claims to authenticity.

One means by which the novel obstructs realist readings is by persistently echoing Giacomo Puccini's *Madam Butterfly* (1904). Both the book and the popular opera take place in Nagasaki, Ishiguro's first home. Sachiko is from a noble family, like Madam Butterfly herself, but has fallen on hard times and wants to sever her ties with Japan and leave for the United States. She is let down by Frank, her equivalent of Madam Butterfly's American lover, the naval officer Lt Benjamin Franklin Pinkerton. Her child, Mariko, is the symbolic parallel of Madam

Butterfly's child, Sorrow (the product of the union with Pinkerton). The inner story and characters of *A Pale View of Hills*, then, can be mapped on to the Puccini tale with some precision. This is important as the opera presents what is plainly an artificial Japan, at several removes from the reality of the country. A great deal of its appeal lies in its exotic costuming, its sets of fake cherry blossoms and sliding rice-paper screens. It rode on the wave of European interest in Japan, following the country's return to the international stage in the 1850s. Along with the prints that influenced the French Impressionists, and musical pieces such as Gilbert and Sullivan's *The Mikado* (1885), Puccini's opera satisfied a Western demand for stock images of an alien and aestheticised Far East.[14] The libretto by Giuseppe Giacosa and Luigi Illica was based on a one-act play produced in 1900 by David Belasco. This was itself inspired by John Luther Long's 1887 fictional version of a purportedly real event observed by his sister, Mrs Correll. *A Pale View of Hills* is thus positioned as a link within a chain of literary reformulations. Its overt intertextual nods towards Puccini hint at the novel's constructedness, preventing the reader from interpreting its depicted world too literally. Despite its tumble-dryers and tombola stalls, the Japan in *A Pale View of Hills* is a displaced Japan, a recreation of an original that probably never existed.

The stereotyped critical responses accorded to both *A Pale View of Hills* and its companion novel, *An Artist of the Floating World*, goaded Ishiguro to consider how his next project could avoid the Japanese pigeonhole. 'I always feel the Japaneseness was a superficial part of my writing', he told Christopher Bigsby, 'something I brought in for reasons of technique.'[15] So his third novel, *The Remains of the Day*, was deliberately set in England and populated by Europeans and Americans, with no Japanese characters. It is narrated by that quintessential Englishman, a butler called Stevens, who devotes his entire life to serving Lord Darlington. His loyalty is misplaced, as Darlington is condemned after the Second World War as a Nazi sympathiser. Furthermore, by devoting himself to his employer Stevens wastes his one chance of private happiness by not returning the affections of his housekeeper, Miss Kenton. The novel was released as a successful film in 1993. Producer Ismail Merchant, director James Ivory and screenwriter Ruth Prawer Jhabvala are a team who have a reputation for producing lavish big-screen adaptations of standard works by stalwart English writers such as E. M. Forster and the nationalised Henry James. *The Remains of the Day* sits well in this company, with its dissection of the nature of Englishness and its values, its stately home setting and its silver salver sheen. Yet even this work did not escape being interpreted with reference to Japaneseness. David Gurewich's comments are representative of the general bias:

> Stevens's insistence on ritual; his stoicism in performing his duties, especially in the face of adversity; his loyalty to his master that conflicts with his humanity – all of these are prominent aspects of the Japanese collective psyche, and Ishiguro imbues his description of Stevens's world with a fine Japanese sensibility.[16]

Gurewich mobilises here the well-known concept of *bushido*. This is the code of the warrior *samurai* class, who became prominent in the Kamakura Period (1185–1333) of medieval Japanese history. Based on Confucian precepts, it elevates loyalty to one's superior as the highest ethical principle. The *samurai* warrior was expected to be self-sacrificing, refined and modest: just like Stevens. Gurewich pursues the Japanese analogy in a different direction when he likens Stevens's punctiliousness to that of an origami-maker,[17] though this is a somewhat less convincing tack. John Rothfork also sees Stevens as a proto-Japanese. He proposes that Ishiguro's first three novels need to be read together to see that *The Remains of the Day* expresses a Buddhist criticism of Confucian ethics.[18] His contrived argument involves a far-fetched comparison between Stevens's inability to banter and the *koan*, or metaphysical puzzle, offered to the Zen Buddhist pupil by his teacher as a vehicle towards enlightenment. There is little mileage in such claims, especially as their proponent's interest in Japanese religious matters appears to be somewhat greater than that of Ishiguro's. Yet even a more perceptive commentator such as Pico Iyer cannot avoid playing the Japanese card when dealing with the implacable Stevens. He writes that 'the unfailing self-surrender that seems so alien, so Japanese to us … [is] alive … in the quiet hills of Oxfordshire.'[19]

The hills of Oxfordshire may well be alive with the sound of Japanese self-surrender for Iyer, but it is far from music to Ishiguro's ears. He is continually puzzled by the currency that stereotypes about Japan and its culture have in the discourse surrounding his work. Generalised talk of this nature leaves too many questions begging, with the cliché of inscrutability dragged out time and time again. Why, Ishiguro wonders, are the Japanese perceived as emotionally restrained? There are some glaring counter-examples: *kabuki* actors and Japanese game-show contestants are not exactly known for their moderate behaviour. Besides, isn't this exactly the way the rest of the world views the English? Here, again, the dichotomy between an East that is the exact opposite of the West, or exactly like it, is rehearsed.

Japanese readings of *The Remains of the Day* are not invalid *per se*. Some useful insights are generated by viewing the novel in this manner. However, the preponderance of such readings threatens to swamp other approaches. Clive Sinclair sums this up very well when he proposes that Japan is not a given for Ishiguro, but it is often all that is taken.[20] So how else, then, can the reader negotiate the Japanese elements of Ishiguro's first three novels? One method is to pay close attention to Ishiguro's comments about his material. He repeatedly refers in interviews to a Japan in his head concocted out of 'a mixture of imagination, memory and speculation.'[21] This Japan is not primarily historical, though it may be accurately located in history. It is a purely functional Japan that serves as the background for Ishiguro's thematic preoccupations. In sum, it is a fictional Japan, and it is as fiction that it deserves to be appraised, rather than as social documentary.

The French theorist Roland Barthes provides a good alternate model for how to assess the Japanese elements of Ishiguro's work. Barthes, who visited Japan in the 1960s, also viewed the country as a 'fictive nation'.[22] Indeed, the first paragraph of

Empire of Signs (1970) pronounces that his book is 'in no way claiming to represent or analyze reality itself'.[23] Instead, he deliberately selects Japan for his semiological meditations because it is so distant, and therefore immune from the familiarity that breeds readerly contempt. By placing himself within a society impenetrable to him, Barthes is better able to look at its language and culture as a series of pure signs without knowable references. He is especially attracted to those artefacts which themselves denote emptiness. These include elaborately wrapped packages concealing the smallest of gifts, and a map of Tokyo with no street names or numbers. At the centre of the wrapping and the map is a space, a suitable symbol for the vacuum of meaning he relished, and which he believed lay at the kernel of every text.

Here, then, is another possible window through which to view the Japan of Ishiguro's first two novels. Ishiguro's Japan, like Barthes', is fictive. It does not represent a world; it is a world in itself. Moreover, it is a world remote from many of its readers, and therefore cannot easily be judged in terms of its representational faithfulness. As a series of pure signs, its importance lies not in *what* it means but in *how* it means. The setting interlocks with the characters, dialogue and plot to produce what Ishiguro would regard as a thematic coherence. Those themes – of home and homelessness, regret, misplaced loyalty, wasted lives, estranged relationships – could have been placed elsewhere in space or time. *A Pale View of Hills* might have been set in the Chilterns, or *An Artist of the Floating World* in Stalinist Russia. This would undoubtedly alter the plausible meanings extractable from the novels. Yet although the *gestalt* of the works would thus be altered, they could still maintain a consistent thematic unity, despite the divergent socio-political implications of these alternative settings. Setting is therefore but one configuration of Japaneseness in Ishiguro's kaleidoscope. The tube can be rotated to display other patterns. To paraphrase Barthes, Ishiguro's Japan is not a country but a system, a system which he calls: Japan.

The critical gaze, then, can be redirected from what Japan

refers to in *A Pale View of Hills* (the way most critics reviewed the novel) to how the text refers to Japan (the Barthesian perspective). This entails a further dislocation of analysis, away from the 'reality' represented by the novel to the illusion of reality produced by the act of representation itself. Interest is thereby channelled away from the obvious markers of Japaneseness (the names, customs, cultural codes), and displaced towards the more chthonic assumptions underlying the image of Japan. This is appropriate as *A Pale View of Hills* is, in many ways, about displacement and occlusion. Several critics have noticed this. Rocío G. Davis asserts that the book 'treats, albeit obliquely, the occasionally tragic effects of displacement'.[24] Gary Corseri agrees: '[it] depicts the incineration of a culture and the disjointed lives of the displaced'.[25] Displacement is present in several senses in the novel. There is the geographical displacement of Etsuko from Japan to England; the cognitive displacement induced by Etsuko's memories; the psychological displacement between herself and Sachiko; and the familial displacement precipitated by the suicide of Keiko.

These displacements are also present in 'A Family Supper',[26] a short story by Ishiguro sharing many of the features of *A Pale View of Hills*. The narrator, who is living in California, returns to Tokyo to visit his father two years after the death of his mother. It appears, although nothing is firmly stated, that he left Japan to be with his American girlfriend – a situation causing a great deal of strain to his parents. The tension is still present as he makes small talk with his father. His sister, Kikuko – who is also contemplating going to America with her boyfriend after she finishes university – arrives. They take a walk in the garden. When they reach an old well, she reminds her brother that as a child he thought it was haunted. The 'ghost', it turned out, was an old woman from the vegetable store taking short cuts through their garden. In the dark, her white kimono and dishevelled hair made her look like a wraith.

There is a spectre of a different kind haunting the narrator and Kikuko in the present. They worry that their father might be on the verge of suicide. Since his business collapsed, he has whiled away his time building plastic battleships and wandering round the large, empty rooms of what was once the family home. He admits: 'This house is too large for a man to live in alone'.[27] Over supper, the conversation turns towards Watanabe, the director of the bankrupt firm, who was so depressed after its failure he murdered his family and then took his own life. This is ominous, as the narrator and Kikuko are eating fish prepared by their father. Could this be *fugu*, the poisonous puffer fish that killed their mother? There is already a mystery surrounding her death, and the photograph of her in a white kimono (which the narrator does not at first recognise) links her with the ghost of the well. The story ends, tantalisingly, without resolving the matter, just as *A Pale View of Hills* ends in mid-air. This is not the only coincidence between the two fictions. The narrator of the short story is displaced geographically from his place of birth, like Etsuko. He has become estranged from his father, like Keiko and Mr Sheringham. Most importantly, both stories contain suicide and ghost motifs.

The treatment of suicide and ghosts in *A Pale View of Hills* is crucial for determining the extent of its Japaneseness, as these themes help mould the milieu of the novel and are ubiquitous in Japanese culture. In the West, suicide is shameful and sinful; yet in the East, it has sometimes been seen as a mark of pride and virtue. This is largely because of the old *samurai* tradition of *seppuku*, or *harakiri* as it is better known. *Harakiri*, which translated literally means 'stomach cutting', is an extremely ritualised form of suicide, and is performed by Cio-Cio-San at the end of *Madam Butterfly*. Ritual self-destruction was also promulgated by the *kamikaze* pilots during the Second World War, as they flew their planes directly into enemy ships without regard for their own lives. This is what the father in 'A Family Supper' refers to as 'the final weapon'.[28] *Yurei* (ghosts) are prominent in many of the legends and myths of Japan, and crop up constantly in its folklore, such as the tales 'The Snow Bride', 'The Robe of Feathers' and 'Willow Wife'.[29] During summer, there are many performances at the theatre and cinema portraying the tormented spirits of betrayed wives returning from beyond the veil to avenge themselves on their husbands. The famous *kabuki* play, *The Ghost Story of Tokaido Yotsuya* by Tsuruya Namboku, has a revenge plot. Ghosts are central to Japan's religions, too. *Obon*, the Buddhist equivalent of All Soul's Day – celebrated between 13 and 16 July or between 13 and 16 August, depending on the area – is one of Japan's most important festivals. The spirits of the dead are invited back into people's homes to enjoy food and offerings laid out for them.[30] *Shinto*, the indigenous religion of Japan, is an animistic philosophy which bridges the world of the living and the dead through a belief in ancestral spirits. It upholds that every animate and inanimate thing possesses its own *kami*, or inner spirit, and these spirits are worshipped at the many shrines dotted around the country.

If Ishiguro's work is to be classified in terms of its Japaneseness, we would expect his treatment of ghosts and suicide in *A Pale View of Hills* to be informed by traces of conventional Japanese topics and symbols. Yet the frame story is more akin to the modern European ghost tale than the Japanese supernatural, and the suicide of Keiko is far from being a straightforward affair. Henry James and M. R. James were both influential in directing the Western ghost genre away from the Gothic excesses (headless monks, medieval castles and the like) of writers such as Horace Walpole and Ann Radcliffe. They introduced average people and settings into their tales, and a greater plausibility. *The Turn of the Screw* (1898) struck the vital note of psychological doubt – are the apparitions real or hallucinations? – which also sounds through *A Pale View of Hills*. This distinguishes Ishiguro's first novel from the literalist fantasy of the Japanese ghost tradition. To illustrate this, I will break down its outer narrative into the five components of the dramatic plot as formulated by Gustav Freytag: initial situation, conflict, complications, climax and resolution.[31]

The beginning of the outer frame story in Chapter 1 sketches out the initial situation. Etsuko is still struggling to come to terms with the suicide of her daughter, Keiko, when Niki, her other daughter now living in London, visits her at the large house in the English countryside. They do not talk about Keiko until the second day, and even then only indirectly (they touch briefly upon why Niki didn't attend the funeral). Despite avoiding the topic, the suicide is continually present: 'although we never dwelt long on the subject of Keiko's death, it was never far away, hovering over us whenever we talked' (*PVH*, 10). So Keiko haunts her sister and mother, though at this stage it is only in a figurative sense.

By Chapter 3, however, there is a hint that the ghost of Keiko is present in a more foreboding way, and its presence provokes conflict between Etsuko and Niki. On the first night, Niki sleeps in her former bedroom, directly opposite Keiko's old room, but the next day asks her mother if she can change to the spare room further away. Keiko's room gives her an 'odd feeling' that chimes with her mother's unease about the 'fanatically guarded domain' (*PVH*, 53) where Keiko withdrew for weeks on end before she left home. Etsuko is angry about the request, but does not reveal to her daughter that 'I, too, had experienced a disturbing feeling about the room opposite' (*PVH*, 53). Instead she displaces her disturbance in two ways. She imagines the room in Manchester where Keiko hung for several days before she was found. Then she attempts to tell Niki about a bad dream she'd had of a little girl on a park swing whom they'd watched the day before. Niki does not respond, but asks again to sleep in the spare room. Communication is breaking down amidst the unsettling aura of the house.

Complications ensue in the next episode of the frame tale in Chapter 6. Etsuko awakes early in the morning on the fifth day of Niki's visit. On the way back from the bathroom, she thinks she hears a sound coming from Keiko's room. She stands still in the hallway for a while, then opens the door. The room 'looked stark in the grayish light' (*PVH*, 88), and is empty apart from a few of Keiko's old belongings. Etsuko feels cold, and so returns to bed. Later in the day, out in the garden, Niki asks her mother about the sounds she heard in the house at around 4:00 a.m. Her mother apologises for disturbing her, and mentions that she'd had that bad dream again. This time they talk further, and it becomes apparent that in her agitated state Etsuko is fusing the little girl on the swing, the suicide of Keiko, and her memories of Mariko.

The climax occurs the following night, in Chapter 11, when Etsuko is awoken at 5:00 a.m. by what seems to be somebody walking past her bed and out of the room. She thinks she is probably imagining things, but gets up to see for herself. The next few sentences render a scene which repeats that of the night before:

> When I opened my door, the light outside was very pale. I stepped further on to the landing and almost by instinct cast a glance down to the far end of the corridor, towards Keiko's door.
>
> Then, for a moment, I was sure I heard a sound come from within Keiko's room, a small clear sound amidst the singing of the birds outside. I stood still, listening, then began to walk towards the door. (*PVH*, 174)

It turns out that it is only the noise of Niki in the kitchen she hears, and not a ghost at all. Etsuko is displacing her anxieties on to the house.

When she goes downstairs, it is her daughter's turn to get a fright. After regaining her composure, Niki informs her mother that she, too, has had bad dreams, but irritatedly refuses to talk about their content. The strain in their relationship is relieved a little in the ensuing conversation. Niki admits that her father (Keiko's step-father) was neglectful towards her sister; Etsuko, for her part, wholly accepts the blame for Keiko's unhappiness, which Niki refuses to allow. So no ghost has materialised, but mother and daughter have begun the process of laying a ghost to rest. The last conversation they have before Niki leaves is about the house, which Etsuko is thinking of selling. The house is no longer a home, and is haunted by memories of Keiko and the past.

The outer frame story plays with the recipe of the paradigmatic European ghost tale, and avoids the supernatural surfeit of the Japanese tradition. There is the gruesome death, the bad dreams, the bumps in the night, the sinister room and, above all, the general atmosphere of unease and uncertainty in the haunted house. Of course, categorising it in this manner is a crudity. Ishiguro's hauntings are more Henry James than M. R. James. He is engaged by the phantoms of memory rather than anything ectoplasmic.

The tact with which Ishiguro handles these hesitations can be discerned in the relation between the outer frame story and a second sequence of ghostly occurrences embedded within the inner framed tale. For convenience, this can also be divided into five Freytagian parts.

The initial situation is laid out in Chapter 1 when Mariko goes missing somewhere in the wasteground near her cottage, and is found by Etsuko near the river. Etsuko tries to be friendly by inviting her back to her house for some cakes. On the next occasion they meet, Mariko refers darkly to a mysterious woman from across the river who also invited her to her house. Etsuko thinks she is remembering their earlier meeting, but the child insists that she is talking about somebody else. This 'other woman' (PVH, 18) visited the night before, when her mother was away. Etsuko assumes that this must have been a babysitter, but Sachiko later discounts this possibility. Mariko voices her claim again at the noodle shop, where Etsuko has obtained work for Sachiko. Whilst the little girl is reprimanded by her mother for being rude to customers, she says that the woman visited her again last night, which only makes Sachiko even more annoyed with her.

In Chapters 3 and 5, a conflict of interpretations arises about the identity of this 'other woman'. Following another incident when Mariko runs away, Sachiko confides to Niki that the 'other woman' is 'not entirely imaginary' but is 'someone Mariko saw once' (PVH, 43) when she was five or six. This was a woman they came across in the ruins of Tokyo:

> There was a canal ... and the woman was kneeling there, up to her elbows in water. A young woman, very thin. I knew something was wrong as soon as I saw her. You see, Etsuko, she turned round and smiled at Mariko. I knew something was wrong and Mariko must have done too because she stopped running. At first I thought the

woman was blind, she had that kind of look, her eyes
didn't seem to actually see anything. Well, she brought
her arms out of the canal and showed us what she'd been
holding under the water. It was a baby. (*PVH*, 74)

The terrible scene is diagrammed precisely: Mariko stands still,
looking at the woman and the baby, whilst Sachiko watches the
three of them from further back.[32] Sachiko goes on to reveal to
Etsuko that a month or so after the drowning, Mariko was
spooked by an old woman who appeared in the doorway of an
abandoned building in which they were sleeping. The little girl
was convinced that it was the same woman who killed her own
baby, even though she had reportedly committed suicide by
cutting her throat in the wake of the infanticide. From then on,
this 'other woman', or ghost, became an obsession of Mariko's
(*PVH*, 74–75).

Further complications ensue. When Etsuko babysits Mariko
at the end of Chapter 5, the little girl again talks about the 'other
woman' and divulges that Sachiko had seen her a few nights ago.
Etsuko is worried, especially as there is a child murderer on the
loose near their district. She becomes frantic when Mariko
escapes yet again in Chapters 6 and 7, and goes out searching by
the river, where she finds her sitting in the grass. A piece of old
rope tangled around Etsuko's ankle frightens the little girl. Is
Mariko scared because she thinks Etsuko is the 'other woman'?
Or does the rope alarm her because of the child murders?

The climax of this inner ghost tale is reached in Chapter 9,
when Etsuko is fooled into believing she sees the 'other woman'.
It happens on a day when Etsuko is unable to rid herself of the
image of one of the child murderer's victims, who was found
hanging from a tree. This overlaps with the disturbing dreams
she has in the outer frame story of the little girl in the park and
Keiko in her Manchester room. Troubled by these grisly
thoughts, she sees a 'thin figure' (*PVH*, 157) walking towards
Mariko's cottage. Confused, she goes across the wasteground to
investigate, and is startled to find an old woman wearing a
'kimono … of a dark sombre colour, the kind normally worn in
mourning' (*PVH*, 158). But this is no ghost: it is Yasuko Kawada,

Sachiko's cousin, who has come straight from a funeral. Brian W. Shaffer connects her with Styx, the river nymph who dwelt at the entrance of Hades in Greek mythology.[33] She is also connected, tangentially, with the Tokyo woman through an association with blindness, as Yasuko tells Etsuko about her sightless father (*PVH*, 161).

It would be misleading to say that this 'other woman' motif resolves satisfactorily, as it culminates at a point of maximum indeterminacy at the end of Chapter 10. Mariko runs away from the cottage again, after witnessing the death of her kittens, and this time Etsuko finds her sitting on the wooden bridge over the river. The little girl tells Etsuko that she doesn't want to go away the following day. When Etsuko begins to reassure Mariko that she'll 'like it over there', the little girl replies: 'I don't want to go away. And I don't like him. He's like a pig' (*PVH*, 172). This seems to be a reference to Frank, Sachiko's American lover, as she has used such terms before about him. Yet Etsuko's response is to become very angry at this and to say that he will be like a new father to her. Why is Etsuko angry? Is there a slippage between Etsuko's memory of this incident and a later, un-reported conversation with Keiko? This would make sense, psychologically, as both Keiko and Mariko were forced by their mothers to go and live in a foreign country.

Then comes the crucial lapse. Although throughout the book there are many parallels between Etsuko's memories of Sachiko/Mariko, and her own situation after the war, the homology is relatively covert. Here, however, the two stories blur into each other when Etsuko says: 'In any case … if you don't like it over there, we can always come back' (*PVH*, 172). Why 'we'? It is Sachiko and Mariko who are supposed to be leaving Japan. To make sure that the reader does not overlook this, or deem it to be a textual error, the collective pronoun recurs four times in the next three sentences: 'If you don't like it over there, we'll come straight back. But we have to try it and see if we like it there. I'm sure we will' (*PVH*, 172). The change of pronoun suggests a displacement of the relation between Etsuko and Keiko on to that of Sachiko and Mariko. Is it Etsuko herself who is the 'other woman' – not just in Mariko's imagination, but in Etsuko's own imaginative projection of herself on to Sachiko? A recurrence of an episode of Chapter 6 indicates that this could well be so. Directly following the exchange about leaving Japan, Mariko is frightened by a piece of rope caught on Etsuko's sandal. This reprises an almost identical moment in the earlier chapter. So the rope literally binds together several different strands of *A Pale View of Hills*: Etsuko's guilt, the dream of the little girl on the swing, the neglect of Mariko and the suicide of Keiko.

Or does it? Give a reader enough rope, and eventually they will hang themselves. This is what happens when Gabriele Annan states that *A Pale View of Hills* contains three suicides: the Tokyo woman, Keiko and – by implication – Mariko. The deaths 'overlay one another like shadows ... on a trebly exposed negative'.[34] Nothing is directly stated in the text about Mariko's suicide, although there is plenty of evidence to show that she is seriously disturbed. She is constantly running away from her mother to spend time alone by the river, and is traumatised by the ghost of the 'other woman'. She has severe mood disturbances, and at different times annoys the customers at Mrs Fujiwara's noodle-shop, insults Sachiko's American lover, eats a live spider and attacks a fat boy on a day out. But no simple judgement can be made about her fate, despite Annan's confidence: Ishiguro leaves the Sachiko/Mariko story unfinished. Etsuko suggests that 'The English are fond of their idea that our race has an instinct for suicide, as if further explanations are unnecessary' (*PVH*, 10). But further explanation *is* necessary to understand the complexity of the textual transference between Keiko and Mariko, and the means by which the story hides itself behind layers of displacements.

In Chapter 7, Etsuko, Sachiko and Mariko go out on a day-trip to the hills of Inasa just outside Nagasaki. They take the cable-car up to a prominent spot where Mariko is able to enjoy the splendid view with the binoculars bought for her by Etsuko. It is after their descent that Mariko wins the wooden box for her kittens at the *kujibiki* stand, the only time in the novel where the characters seem at ease with themselves and each other.

When Niki is preparing to leave Etsuko in Chapter 11 to go back to London, she asks her mother for a photo of Nagasaki to give to a poet friend of hers. Etsuko gives her a picture of the hills of the city from an old calendar. Initially, when Niki asks her what is so special about the photo, Etsuko refuses to answer. But later she reveals that it brings back some very pleasant memories from the day-trip: 'Keiko was happy that day' (*PVH*, 182). Of course, it was Mariko who was on that trip and not Keiko, so once again – as in the bridge encounter between Etsuko and Mariko – there is a displacement between the outer and inner narratives. Moreover, it is a displacement that cannot be easily recuperated to make the text stable. The competing interpretative possibilities keep shifting, like the coloured shapes in a kaleidoscope. Either: (a) Etsuko is confusing different sets of memories; or (b) Etsuko is merging memory and fantasy; or (c) Etsuko is projecting her guilt about forcing Keiko to leave Japan on to her memories of Sachiko in a similar situation; or (d) Etsuko is projecting her guilt about the above on to a *fantasy* of a woman called Sachiko and her child.

Summarising the possibilities in this way cannot possibly do justice to the serpentine coiling of the outer and inner stories. Much of the effect of the novel derives from its sinuous structure, and the seepage between Etsuko's present and her memories of the past. The authorial voice gives no clues as to how to reconcile the incompatible possibilities of interpreting the novel. In this sense, Ishiguro is indeed a ghost writer. He has departed from the text, leaving only a handful of haunting images and a reverberant silence.

A Pale View of Hills is full of silences, omissions and apertures. It is as if the text adheres to the prescription for *haiku* poetry, where the shard is greater than the whole. What is left out is as important as what is kept in. Some critics are not comfortable with the novel's reticence. Paul Bailey, for instance, recognises that the style works largely by inference, but adds that 'at certain points I could have done with something as crude as a fact.'[35] He points out, correctly, that almost nothing is said about Etsuko's second husband, Mr Sheringham. All the reader really gleans about this character is that he was English, a writer, and a poor father. Whilst acknowledging Ishiguro's concision, Bailey worries about the gaps appearing towards the end of the book, especially concerning what happens to Mariko. James Campbell is troubled, too, about the sketchiness of the background details, the anonymity of some of the characters and the vapid dialogue.[36] Are these absences lapses rather than choices? Perhaps Bailey and Campbell have simply misjudged the nature of the silences in the novel. Within the Japanese culture in which the book is set, indirect communication is an important feature of everyday life. The dialogue, far from being vapid, portrays the clipped spoken content of a typical discourse. Its meaning is not simply in the words that are uttered, but in the pauses and prevarications punctuating the exchange.[37] It is a technique which Harold Pinter – who wrote the original, discarded screenplay of *The Remains of the Day* – would surely recognise.

The most important silence in *A Pale View of Hills* is that surrounding the fate of Nagasaki at the end of the Second World War. Although the inner frame tale is set in that city just a few years after its almost total destruction, Etsuko only twice mentions the atomic bomb. The first occasion is right at the beginning of the book, when she outlines where she lived in the early 1950s:

> My husband [Jiro] and I lived in an area to the east of the city, a short tram journey from the centre of town. A river ran near us, and I was once told that before the war a small village had grown up on the riverbank. But then the bomb had fallen and afterwards all that remained were charred ruins. Rebuilding had got under way and in time four concrete buildings had been erected, each containing forty or so separate apartments. Of the four, our block had been built last and it marked the point where the rebuilding programme had come to a halt; between us and the river lay an expanse of wasteground, several acres of dried mud and ditches. Many complained it was a health hazard, and indeed the drainage was appalling. All year round there were craters filled with stagnant water, and in the summer months the mosquitoes became intolerable. From time to

> time officials were to be seen pacing out measurements or
> scribbling down notes, but the months went by and
> nothing was done. (*PVH*, 11)

This is a wonderful paragraph, mainly because of its unwavering
ordinariness. It reads almost as if it were an extract from an estate
agent's memo. The devastation caused by the bomb is mentioned with the same equanimity as the fecklessness of the town-
planning committee.

As the novel progresses, the wasteground gradually assumes
a more sinister role. It is the site of the one remaining pre-war
cottage where Sachiko and Mariko live, and the little girl plays
in its ditches, craters and muddy river banks. Part Two of the
novel opens with a repellent account of how unpleasant the area
became in the summer: 'Much of the earth lay dried and cracked
... insects often caught in one's hair, and there were grubs and
midges visible' (*PVH*, 99). The wasteground develops into a
metaphoric space, as redolent of decay as T. S. Eliot's Waste
Land or F. Scott Fitzgerald's Valley of the Ashes.

The second mention of the bomb occurs in Chapter 8, when
Etsuko takes her father-in-law, Ogata, on a trip to the peace
memorial in the city centre park. The monument there, by
Kitamura Seibo, is ponderously symbolic. Its right hand points
upwards to indicate the nuclear threat, whilst the left hand
makes a gesture of peace. The right leg is folded in a meditative
posture, and the left foot is on the ground ready for action. It
reminds Etsuko – bathetically – of a traffic policeman, and she
confesses that she is unable to 'associate it with what had
occurred that day the bomb had fallen, and those terrible days
which followed' (*PVH*, 137–38). Again, the reference to Nagasaki's
cataclysmic disaster is unemphatic. It is played down even further
by Etsuko's sanguine comment that whenever she recalls that
statue, she is reminded of Ogata's postcard of it rather than the
event it represents.

The constraint of *A Pale View of Hills* about the nuclear
nightmare is in direct contrast to Ishiguro's 'A Strange and
Sometimes Sadness', which places the atomic bomb at the centre
of events.[38] This short story commences with a situation similar

to that of the novel. Yasuko visits the English home of her mother, Machiko. Her mother recalls a strange experience she'd had in Nagasaki during the war involving her friend, also called Yasuko. This friend's fiancé, Nakamura, was away fighting with the Japanese army, and so Yasuko lived with her widowed father, Kinoshita.[39] To keep her company, Machiko would often go walking with Yasuko after work. One night, when they are sitting in the Shingokko gardens, Machiko is startled to see her friend with 'an expression so ghastly it completely distorted her face.'[40] Her eyes were staring and her jaw shaking. Alarmed, Machiko asks her what is wrong, but her friend's face suddenly resumes its usual look of repose. The following day Yasuko, Kinoshita and many thousands of others are killed by the dropping of the atomic bomb on the city. Clearly, Yasuko had some kind of premonition of the catastrophe.

Why, in the light of Ishiguro's bold treatment of this sensitive theme in 'A Strange and Sometimes Sadness', does *A Pale View of Hills* decline to broach the bomb directly? One reason is that at the time of writing the shorter piece, Ishiguro 'hadn't actually thought of it as a story that would be in any way relevant to the nuclear debate.'[41] Michael Wood, however, thinks it is more connected with Etsuko's act of repression: '[The novel is] about drastic denials, and about what happens when the denied material comes back to get you.'[42] There is some truth in this. Etsuko is undoubtedly in denial, not just about Keiko, but also about what she suffered in Nagasaki during the war. When she was first taken in by Ogata she was in such a state of shock that she behaved like a 'mad person' (*PVH*, 58), playing the violin obsessively in the middle of the night. In spite of her experiences, she never once talks about her loss. Instead she alludes vaguely a few times to the 'worst days' (*PVH*, 11) and the 'nightmares of wartime' (*PVH*, 13). Etsuko's need to blank out her past does not account fully, though, for the astonishing absence at the centre of the novel. Nor does it explain the arcane process of how the novel manages to affirm that which is denied. Wood again: 'Almost everything is unspeakable here, and yet it gets spoken.'[43] To understand this paradox better, we need to delve more deeply into the context in which *A Pale View of Hills* can be placed.

Mention Nagasaki to somebody who isn't from Japan, and the chances are that the first thing they will think of is the atomic bomb. For most people, this is all they know about the city. This is hardly surprising as, despite the long and varied history of the Japanese seaport, the bomb has scorched its shadow forever into its landscape and into the conscience of the world at large. Yet to the young Kazuo Ishiguro, born and raised in Nagasaki, the bomb was something unexceptional. Indeed he believed, as children often do, that what was true for him was true for everybody and that every city had its own bomb. It wasn't until he was at primary school in England that he grasped its full significance. An encyclopaedia informed him that only two cities had ever been devastated by the bomb, a fact that led him to feel a 'weird sort of pride.'[44]

The other city was, of course, Hiroshima, a name now synonymous with the atomic bomb itself. It has virtually eclipsed Nagasaki in this regard. After all, it was the first city to be struck, on 6 August 1945, and sustained the greater number of casualties. Many people know that the *Enola Gay* was the plane that dropped the deadly device, but how many can name the aircraft that flew over Nagasaki? Hiroshima is a metonym for the horrors of a nuclear strike; it a codeword, like the Holocaust, for ultimate evil. Many believe that literature should not depict such evils, as this trivialises profound suffering for the sake of entertainment. Nevertheless, Hiroshima is ubiquitous in contemporary fiction. Novels, poems, plays, films, and even comic-books constantly represent the city.

To date, there have been three distinct phases in atomic bomb literature.[45] The first group of writers – Yoko Ota, Tamiki Hara, Shinoe Shoda, Sadako Kurihara and others – faced the problem of trying to represent the unrepresentable. So their work is absorbed with the chasm between imagination and actuality. Those who personally witnessed the conflagration, the *hibakusha* or 'bomb victims', do not necessarily find the task any easier than those who did not. The assumption is, however, that their writings must have greater authenticity. During the second phase, writers such as Yoshie Hotta, Momo Iida, Kenzaburo Oe and Masuji Ibuse widened the canvas to address the historical and political context of the bombings. More recently, Kobo Abe, Makota Oda, Mitsuharu Inoue and others have recast the tragedies of Hiroshima and Nagasaki as part of 'our future as well as our past, a permanent imaginative state of threatened being.'[46] The bombings of Japan are warnings of dangers that lie ahead.

The vast majority of these writings are about Hiroshima, rather than Nagasaki. This is partly because of the reason stated before, namely the fact that Nagasaki was the second city to be bombed. The plane *Bock's Car* struck on 9 August 1945, killing approximately 70,000 people compared to 100,000 in Hiroshima (though by the 1950s the casualties had doubled through the effects of radiation). It was second in another sense, too. The main target of that particular mission was to be Kokura, but this was smothered in smoke following a bomb raid on a neighbouring city.

Chronological accident isn't the only factor at play, however, in determining why Nagasaki is relatively neglected in atomic bomb literature. The city has a very different history from Hiroshima. From 1571 it became an important port for foreign commerce with the rest of Asia and ships from Spain, Portugal and Holland. A sizeable Christian minority grew up there, and they helped import inventions from the West. But in 1639, the Tokugawa Shogunate expelled all foreigners and banned trade with outsiders. For the next two hundred years, a small Dutch trading post on the island of Dejima in Nagasaki Bay was the only point of contact between Japan and the rest of the world, until the reopening of the country in the 1850s established Nagasaki as a major shipbuilding centre. This cosmopolitan history directly affects the way the atom bomb is perceived in literature about Nagasaki. As John Whittier Treat explains, the rage channelled externally in Hiroshima bomb literature is redirected inward in works about Nagasaki.[47] The victims themselves are often blamed for the catastrophe, and the close partnership with the West in the past is seen as somehow being the cause of the retribution. If you add to that the sense of guilt deriving from Nagasaki's persecution of Catholics towards the end of the sixteenth century, you have a potent brew of shame, blame and culpability. You also have the ingredients for an allegorical reading of *A Pale View of Hills*, in which the guilt of Etsuko is aligned with the guilt of Nagasaki as a whole.

Hiroshima, Mary McCarthy declared in 1946, was 'a kind of hole in history'.[48] It may have ended the war, and forestalled even greater bloodshed, but for the first time humankind was capable of obliterating itself from the face of the planet. What is the fitting response to such a calamity? A survivor of Hiroshima, Kijima Katsumi, saw the *Enola Gay* pass overhead and dismissed it nonchalantly as simply another plane. But just seconds later, after white light had seared the city into rubble, 'there were no more words'.[49] No words to describe such utter horror. No words to capture the enormity of such suffering. This is reminiscent of Theodor Adorno's injunction that there should be no more poetry after Auschwitz, and Kurt Vonnegut's dilemma in *Slaughterhouse-Five* (1969) about how to verbalise a massacre. Instead, there is mute incomprehension and a sense of overwhelming meaninglessness. In what way, then, could writers proceed to deal with the event? A stoic silence might be mistaken for an irresponsible refusal to engage with the most pressing problem of our times. Similarly, if the *hibakusha* said nothing they would stand accused of suppressing the truth. As Aunt Emily says to Naomi in *Obasan* (1981), a novel by the Canadian-Japanese writer Joy Kogawa that also deals with the atomic bombings: 'You have to remember ... You are your history. If you cut any of it off you're an amputee ... Denial is gangrene.'[50] It is against this background that the guardedness of the atomic bomb genre should be understood. Like writings about the Holocaust, it is a 'literature of innuendo'.[51] It must speak about the unspeakable, and risk defiling the truth with a mucus of words.

Seen in this wider context, the paucity of comment on the atomic bomb in *A Pale View of Hills* is more explicable. Ishiguro was born almost a decade after the destruction of Nagasaki, and his emigration from Japan imposed a gulf between himself and his original home. He cannot be a spokesman for the unspeakable. And yet, *A Pale View of Hills* somehow succeeds in fulfilling the ideal of crafting a silence more eloquent than words. How is this so?

An appeal to French theorist Pierre Macherey is relevant here: 'In its every particle, the work *manifests*, uncovers, what it cannot say.'[52] He is referring to literary texts in general, but his opinions particularly apply to Ishiguro's novel. The horrors of the bomb are latent in the book's displaced protagonists and anaesthetised prose. It is a very different book from Kogawa's *Obasan*, which eventually breaks the silence by graphically portraying the mutilated limbs and scarred skin of the bomb victims. In Ishiguro's novel, quoting Macherey again, 'What is important in the work is what it does not say.'[53]

The risk is that even without highlighting the bomb directly, simply setting *A Pale View of Hills* in Nagasaki at all is to give the work what Christopher Bigsby calls 'historical resonance, a kind of free ride on the power of history.'[54] Any fiction about the Holocaust or the atomic bomb is open to question, as critics might suspect that the topics were chosen to lend a spurious weight to the project. To prove his integrity, Ishiguro took the unusual step of publishing an article in the *Guardian* which agreed that 'the mere fact of my novel taking place in that city [Nagasaki] was allowing me to achieve an easy kind of global significance'.[55] He thought that reviewers, on the whole, were too 'solemn and respectful, apparently deeming it bad taste to write down a book about that city written by someone actually born there.'[56] This should not deter future writers, he concluded, from tackling such intractable subject matter. Shoddy works will be deemed shoddy, whatever their sensationalist setting, whilst quality writers will manage to make music out of the most mundane matter. And this is precisely what Ishiguro achieves in *A Pale View of Hills*: it is a sonata of common tones and silences, not an opera full of sound and fury. His Japan is more Chopin than Puccini, more absence than presence.

Absence, they say, makes the heart grow fonder. Yet absence in *A Pale View of Hills* – absent fathers, absent daughters, absent bombs – is at the heart of the heart itself. There is little affection in this book, but a great deal of coldness and loss. The absences inscribed in its ghost stories exemplify the uncanny, the term used by Freud to denote the frisson between the frightening and the familiar.[57] The German word for this is *das Unheimlich*, the negation of the 'homely', the disruption of the sense of being 'at home' in the world. In this sense, *A Pale View of Hills* is a study of the unhomeliness and displacements created by a family suicide and a nuclear genocide.

An Artist of the Floating World

MANY images have come to typify Japan in the West: the *samurai* sword, the Zen rock garden, *koto* music and the *Noh* theatre. The most evocative is that of the *geisha*. This refined courtesan, with her lily-white face, cherry-red lips and multi-coloured *kimono,* is the epitome of the eroticised other. It is a misconstrued image, of course. Far from being a prostitute, a *geisha* has many accomplishments, ranging from the arts of dance and song to the etiquettes of conversation and the tea ceremony. Nevertheless, the *geisha* continues to fascinate the occidental public, which might account for the phenomenal success of the bestselling book *Memoirs of a Geisha* (1997).[1] This purports to be a translation by a Professor of Japanese History, Arnold Rusoff, of tape-recorded reminiscences by Nitta Sayuri. Sayuri tells of her rise from the obscure fishing-village of Yoroido to being the mistress of a wealthy patron, thanks to her glorious grey eyes and initiation into the *geisha* culture. The whole thing is a fiction, albeit a meticulously crafted one. Unlike Ishiguro, its actual author (Arthur Golden, an MA in Japanese History from Columbia) did considerable research, and spent ten years delving into the minutiae of the customs and costumes of Japan. He was aided by his talks with Mineko Iwasaki, a contemporary *geisha* in the 1960s and 1970s. The result was so impressive, Columbia Pictures began shooting a film version of the book in 1999, with director Steven Spielberg and Rika Okamoto as Nitta.

Golden's novel, though extremely readable and enjoyable,

presents a somewhat sanitised, inauthentic Japan. The very accuracy of its detail creates an unbelievability. It is a Puccini opera for the modern age, full of melodrama and willowy mistresses. At the opposite extreme is the poetry of Araki Yasusada.[2] When *The American Poetry Review* published a special supplement of his work, a biographical note informed its readers that Yasusada lost his wife and youngest daughter in the Hiroshima atomic blast.[3] Many of his poems bore icy witness to the aftermath of those brutal events of August 1945. They were widely acclaimed as the work of a *hibakusha*, a survivor of the bomb who – again, unlike Ishiguro – writes directly about the subject. One potent aspect of his writing is its refusal to apportion blame. Even 'Mad Daughter and Big Bang: December 25, 1945', where the speaker imagines a nightmarish encounter with his daughter's severed head, is swathed with a level lyricism.[4]

I'll return to Yasusada in due course, but first I wish to peer more closely at this concept of blame. When Ruth Benedict investigated Japanese culture on behalf of the US Office of War Information, she had many puzzles to explain. Why had the Japanese surrendered so gracefully after World War Two? American soldiers were surprised at how friendly the Japanese seemed towards them. Didn't they feel any guilt at being defeated? She concluded that individuals were affected by external sanctions of shame rather than internal factors of guilt. Some thought it was the other way round, and that guilt was the factor motivating the Japanese psyche and its obeisant relation to the group. Takie Sugiyama Lebra resolved this apparent contradiction by suggesting that both shame and guilt were important in the culture as a control mechanism, but that they related to different conceptions of the self.[5] Shame affects the interactional self, and threatens the individual with 'losing face'. Conversely, guilt works upon the inner self, and can corrode self-esteem even in those situations where there is no possibility of the misdeed's disclosure.

Blame, the attribution of an answerable responsibility for a fault or wrongdoing, is what both shame and guilt have in common. This can be verified in *A Pale View of Hills*, where the central question is: who is to blame for the suicide of Keiko? Etsuko is aware that the reason for Niki's visit is to 'reassure me I was not responsible for Niki's death' (*PVH*, 11). The recognition of her blamelessness by her daughter should relieve her of her shame, if she was not actually responsible. Alternatively, the entire Nagasaki narrative can be interpreted as Etsuko's projection of guilt about her parental negligence in bringing Keiko to England from Japan against her wishes. So, is it shame or guilt motivating the mother's examination of conscience? Innocence or inculpation? Memory or fantasy? It is not clear. What is more certain, however, is that Etsuko and that other mother, Sachiko, share twin circumstances. They both have emotionally disturbed daughters; they both are unhappy with traditional gender expectations within marriage; they both see the West as a means of escape. This is why the Nagasaki episodes are, in the words of Thwaite, '[Etsuko's] *own* story, distanced from herself and transposed into Sachiko, so that Mariko and her own dead Keiko are one.'[6]

Towards the end of the frame tale, Niki wonders if it was rather her father, Mr Sheringham, who was responsible for Keiko's death. She states: 'I suppose Dad should have looked after her a bit more, shouldn't he? He ignored her for most of the time. It wasn't fair really' (*PVH*, 175). Etsuko then confesses that she knew all along that Keiko wouldn't be happy in England. Yet she insisted on going ahead with the move, just as Sachiko tried to force Mariko to go to the United States. Niki refuses to accept this version of events: 'You're the last person anyone could blame' (*PVH*, 176). Thus, despite her attempt to bring it out into the open, Etsuko's sense of culpability remains interiorised.

The private guilt of Etsuko is counterpointed with the public shame of Ogata in the sub-plot. Ogata is Etsuko's father-in-law, who cared for her following the war when she was crazy with grief. Several years later he confides to her about a problem connected with his former occupation as a teacher. He has stumbled upon an article in the *New Education Digest*, a professional journal, which argues that he should have lost his post before retirement because of his former nationalist sympathies. The slur is doubly hurtful because it is penned by his son's friend, Shigeo Matsuda, who benefited from Ogata's influence in the past. Ogata finally confronts Matsuda about the article, who will not budge from his views. He accuses Ogata of fostering propaganda and lies to small children, and colluding in the imprisonment of five teachers at Nishizaka in 1938. However, he does concede that 'you shouldn't be blamed for not realizing the true consequences of your actions' (*PVH*, 148). Ogata's public shame, Matsuda suggests, need not impinge upon his inner conscience.

The sub-plot of *A Pale View of Hills*, and its examination of shame and guilt, is displaced on to the centre-stage of *An Artist of the Floating World*. This also investigates the extent to which blame can be attached to somebody whose life is wasted because their 'energies were spent in a misguided direction' (*PVH*, 147). The dilemma of the central character, Masuji Ono, is a refiguration of the plight of Ogata, as he struggles to justify his previous nationalist sympathies in the light of his post-war loss of reputation. Ishiguro frequently returns to the same themes throughout his fictions, teasing them out in different ways.

Another source for the preoccupations of *An Artist of the Floating World* is the short story 'The Summer After the War'.[7] This provides the setting, some of the characters and several of the details of the longer work. Its narrator is a small boy, Ichiro, who visits the war-damaged house of his grandfather, Oji, a former painter. Oji's past fascinates Ichiro, but he is disappointed when he finally gets to see a sample of his grandfather's work. It is a propaganda poster, created for the China campaign of 1937, depicting a *samurai* against the background of the Japanese flag and a nationalistic slogan.[8] During Ichiro's stay, the house receives another guest, an old pupil of Oji's. The two men argue over a letter the visitor requests Oji to write, which would effectively dissociate the pupil from his former master. At stake is the contrasting degree of shame and guilt that the master and his pupil feel about their former nationalist activities. Oji feels there is no need for a man to lie about himself, especially when he did what he did with pride. His ex-colleague, on the other hand, does not wish to be 'burdened down by what happened in the past.'[9] The story ends with the grandfather's sudden illness, following his recognition that the summer after the war marks the start of the autumn of his life.

Many of the components making up the short story reappear, displaced, in the novel. Ichiro and Oji remain two of the main characters, though it is now the latter – renamed Masuji Ono – who narrates.[10] Added to the canvas are Ono's daughters Noriko (the name of a maid in the short story) and Setsuko. The incident over the letter is repeated, as are the details of the propaganda poster. The central thematic strand concerns Ono's swerve of allegiance between incompatible types of artistic activity, and the betrayal of Ono's most gifted pupil, Kuroda. This theme is wreathed with negotiations in the present of the novel surrounding the forthcoming marriage of Noriko.

An Artist of the Floating World is set in the years immediately after Japan's unconditional surrender at the end of the Second World War, a time when the country was experiencing profound changes. The American Occupation, which began in September 1945 and was to last until May 1952, initiated a vast democratisation process. Led by General Douglas MacArthur, the Supreme Commander of the Allied Powers, Japan was transformed through demobilisation of its armed forces, constitutional reform and the removal of prominent nationalists from public office. The Americans hoped to eradicate the raging imperialism that had supported incursions into Manchuria and other parts of south-east Asia in the 1930s under General Tojo's military dictatorship. Tojo himself was under trial for war crimes at the time Ishiguro's novel begins, and his execution in December 1948 is the unspoken background of blame against which Ono's shame and guilt is limned.

Within the space of just one generation, the values of Japanese citizens underwent a volte-face. Before the war, Japan was encouraged to aggressively take its place in the world, through military or any other means. This was partly to revive its economy, which had suffered as a result of the global depression in the 1930s, but also to restore its glorious *samurai* warrior past. After the war, it surprised many when the country accepted defeat with as much vigour as it had once urged victory. Imperialist sympathisers were quickly condemned as 'war criminals'. The best illustration of this U-turn in Ishiguro's book is the fate of the Hirayama boy (*AFW*, 59–61). He is a simpleton who, under the old dispensation, was praised by passers-by for singing snatches of military songs and chanting uplifting slogans in the street. Following the defeat of Japan, he continues to sing the same songs and chant the same slogans, but is beaten up for his impudence. As Brian W. Shaffer intuits, this is a miniaturised version of Ono's own predicament: 'like the Hirayama boy, Ono is exposed as lacking in vision, opportunistic, pandering to crowds and incapable of changing his tune.'[11]

The novel traces the rise and fall of Ono, and his career as a painter from the first decades of the twentieth century through to the early 1950s. Born in Tsuruoka village, Ono's fate is predicted by a wandering priest who warns his parents that the baby has 'a flaw in his nature. A weak streak that would give him a tendency towards slothfulness and deceit' (*AFW*, 45). To circumvent this, when he is twelve Ono is allowed into the reception room of the house for weekly 'business meetings' with his father. This attempt to instil domestic values of honest enterprise is a failure. Three years later, Ono is summoned to the same room for a very different purpose. His father burns his son's paintings and tells him that 'Artists … live in squalor and poverty. They inhabit a world which gives them every temptation to become weak-willed and depraved' (*AFW*, 46). But, as Ono confides to his mother, the only thing his father's drastic actions kindle is his ambition to be a painter. He leaves home, and in 1913 begins an apprenticeship at a studio run by Takeda, which churns out cheap depictions of Japanese subjects. In the 1920s he studies under Seiji Moriyama, and becomes an adherent to the Floating World tradition of Japanese art. The changing political circumstances of the country in the 1930s persuade him to become a propaganda artist for the militant Japanese Emperor. His reformation results in a temporary period of success for Ono, and by the time of the China Crisis in 1937 he is surrounded by acolytes and patriotic banners in his favourite inn, the Migi-Hidari. He is ostracised after the war, however, when the American forces occupy Japan and begin the process of socio-economic liberalisation. Ono now fears exposure as a war criminal, as he had betrayed his most gifted pupil, Kuroda, to the police, and supported a corrupt and defeated regime. The outer narrative of *An Artist of the Floating World* is set several years later, between 1948 and 1950, when Ono has escaped prosecution, but worries that his dubious past will prejudice the wedding negotiations for his daughter, Noriko.

Again, as with *A Pale View of Hills*, the novel is apparently grounded in an accurate environment historically, and on the surface presents a realistic account of Japan before and after the war. For example, during the planning of Noriko's wedding, Ishiguro carefully explains the custom called the *miai*, a feature of the arranged marriages common in Japan until relatively recently. It is traditional for those involved in a possible matrimonial match to hire private investigators to assess the credentials of the couple concerned and their families. If this proves satisfactory, both parties then arrange a formal meeting – the *miai* – at a meal or other social activity. This is sometimes the first occasion when the potential bride and groom get to see each other. Ishiguro handles the build-up to this occasion with great dexterity. Indeed, it is so firmly integrated into the plot that the unwary reader could easily assume that this episode is proof of the novel's credible Japaneseness. However, even here there is a hint of some counterfeiting. The meeting between the Onos and the Saitos takes place in the Kasuga Park Hotel. This was formerly 'amongst the most pleasant of the Western-style hotels', but is now, according to Ono, decorated 'in a somewhat vulgar manner – intended, no doubt, to strike the American clientele … as being charmingly "Japanese"' (*AFW*, 116). Through the large bay windows, there is a grand view down Kasuga Hill toward the city. The room is furnished with a circular table and chairs, and decorated on one wall with a painting by Matsumoto, a former acquaintance of Ono's. The place is not itemised further. So there is a gap between Ono's assertion of its vulgarity and his neglect to spell out why it is so. The reader is free to imagine a plethora of lanterns, sliding screens, *bonsai* trees and colourful fans, as if from a Puccini set. Puccini or not, the Japan of the Kasuga Park Hotel is patently a simulated Japan, a Japan displaced through American expectations.

The significance of the simulation would certainly not escape Malcolm Bradbury, who refers to *An Artist of the Floating World* as 'a work of odd mannerism, a stylised piece of Japonaiserie.'[12] 'Japonaiserie' is a word commonly used in art contexts to refer to a representation of Japan through a cluster of conventionalised signs. It is the opposite of Japaneseness. Japaneseness equals essence, core; Japonaiserie connotes contingence and surface. Bradbury goes on to suggest that in *An Artist of the Floating World*, Ishiguro presents a world that is at more than one remove from the Japan it supposedly represents. It 'feels like a certain kind of Japanese art',[13] but this is misleading. After all, a canvas by a forger such as Tom Keating can 'feel' like a Rembrandt, yet still be a fake. And this is true of *An Artist of the Floating World*, too. The Japan it represents is fake, or – to use a less perjorative term – fictional. Despite the consensus among critics about Ishiguro's style in the book – such as Peter J. Mallett's statement that viewing Ono is 'like looking at a Japanese folding screen that has to be seen from different angles'[14] – certain features of its themes and settings cause us to wonder just how Japanese it is.

The *miai* turns out to be an embarrassment for Ono, as it is here that he finally feels pressured to accept the blame for his former political loyalties. But the response to his revelations is not quite what he had anticipated. Throughout the marriage negotiations he has sought to ensure that things go smoothly, unlike the Miyake affair the year before when Noriko's suitor withdrew for unspecified reasons. Ono strongly suspected that it was his own chequered past and discredited nationalism that led to the breakdown, although he pretended to others that it was the mismatch of social status which was the cause. This time round, Ono has taken the 'precautionary steps' (*AFW*, 49) that he believes Setsuko urged him to take. He has visited past acquaintances to request that they do not betray him if approached by the go-between, Mr Kyo. However, such is his sense of guilt he feels compelled to make a personal confession at the *miai* itself. He pronounces:

> There are some who would say it is people like myself who are responsible for the terrible things that happened to this nation of ours. As far as I am concerned, I freely admit I made many mistakes. I accept that much of what I did was ultimately harmful to our nation, that mine was part of an influence that resulted in untold suffering for our own people. I admit this. You see, Dr Saito, I admit this quite readily. (*AFW*, 123)

What did Ono seek to accomplish by this admission of his guilt? Perhaps his hope was that his honesty would impress Dr Saito, and reassure his potential in-laws that now that everything was out in the open, the marriage could go ahead. Or perhaps Ono thought that the truth was more important than his daughter's marriage prospects, and so risked disengagement with the Saitos through his disclosure and the ensuing public shame. Either way, he could not have predicted the actual outcome, which is one of sheer bewilderment. The Saitos are nonplussed by the outburst and have no idea what Ono means by his utterances. Ono does not fully appreciate the extent of their bafflement until six months later, when Setsuko visits him again. His daughter tells him that Noriko wrote to her after the *miai* expressing surprise and incomprehension at her father's behaviour during the meal, a feeling shared by everyone present. Furthermore, Setsuko denies that she incited Ono to brief his former acquaintances before the marriage investigations. So Ono's confession turns out to be highly inappropriate, and almost comic in its unintended consequences. Far from wrecking the meeting at the Kasuga Park Hotel, his intervention leads to a marked lightening of the atmosphere. Once the ice is broken, the two families get on well together, and the *miai* concludes successfully with a subsequent marriage and, the following year, the news that Noriko is to have her first child.

The *miai* episode is of central importance to *An Artist of the Floating World*. But what does it imply about Ono's blame-worthiness? It can be interpreted in several ways. It could be that Ono's guilt is not registered by the others at the *miai* for the simple reason that he reveals no specific names or crimes. He assumes, almost certainly incorrectly, that Saito is familiar with the propaganda work that he did in support of the militaristic regime immediately before and during the war. He also does not mention the betrayal of his former pupil Kuroda, the unwhole-some facts of which are withheld from the reader, too, until after the *miai*. Given this vagueness, it is little wonder that Ono's listeners are underwhelmed by his revelations. Another option is that Ono has vastly overestimated his importance in the scheme of things. There are many signs that he is a vain, self-serving man who is desperate to be admired by others for having made a contribution to something. When he recalls Shintaro thanking him in 1935 or 1936 for writing a letter of recommend-ation for his younger brother, Yushio, Ono boasts: 'This visit – I must admit it – left me with a certain feeling of achievement. It was one of those moments, in the midst of a busy career allow-ing little chance for stopping and taking stock, which illuminate suddenly just how far one has come' (*AFW*, 21). A similar complacency (the title of one of his most important works) is at play in what Anne Chisholm calls the 'web of shame and anxiety'[15] which Ono has woven in his mind. Despite his efforts to magnify his role in events, ultimately he was just a minor functionary who is now burdened with an inappropriate sense of guilt.

Ono's lifetime achievement is negligible. When he returns to the fields above Mori-san's villa after winning the Shigeta Foundation Award in May 1938, his feeling of triumph is artificial. It is a sunny day, and he intends to address his former master as simply another colleague, whilst flaunting his own success. However, he ends up sitting on the hill eating oranges, indulging in his sense of superiority: 'It was a profound sense of happiness deriving from the conviction that one's efforts have been justified; that the hard work undertaken, the doubts overcome, have all been worthwhile; that one has achieved something of real value and distinction' (*AFW*, 204). The congratulatory tone and lazy self-satisfaction anticipate the voice of Stevens in *The Remains of the Day*, a character who also displaces his shame and guilt in deceptive ways. Yet, ironically, both Ono and Stevens are ordinary men, 'with no special gifts of insight' (*AFW*, 200). It is their fate to live long enough to see all their hopes and ambitions vanish in the wind. All they have left is the floating world of what-might-have-been.

The Floating World, or *ukiyo*, is a Buddhist term that denotes the transience of all things. During the Edo period (1600–1868) it became yoked to the fleeting amusements to be found in urban districts such as Yoshiwara in Edo and Shimibara in Kyoto. In these pleasure quarters courtesans, musicians and prostitutes would ply their trades, freed from the restrictions of the Shogunate. A style of art called *ukiyo-e* developed to depict this mercurial culture. It was distributed in mass-produced wood-block prints by artists such as Hishikawa Moronobu, Masanobu Okumara, Sukenobu Nishikawa; and later Kitagawa Utamaro, Katsushika Hokusai and Ando Hiroshige. They scorned the traditional Chinese-influenced subjects of landscapes and court scenes, and concentrated instead upon the impermanence of everyday life and pursuits. Among the most popular images were those contained in erotic manuals, early comic books and albums of *kabuki* actors. It was a form of art in which canons of artistic norms were violated in the search for new forms of expression. European artists James Whistler, Edgar Degas and Claude Monet were profoundly influenced by the wood-block prints which became available in the West after the opening up of Japan in the middle of the nineteenth century.

Ono becomes a Floating World artist midway through his career, but first he serves an indenture at Master Takeda's Furukawa studio. This is a small room above a restaurant where fifteen artists churn out cheap prints round the clock for sale abroad. There is little artistic merit in what they produce. Indeed, Ono admits that 'the essential point about the sort of things we were commissioned to paint – geishas, cherry trees, swimming carps, temples – was that they look "Japanese" to the foreigners to whom they were shipped out' (*AFW*, 69).[16] After this unrewarding, but gruelling, apprenticeship Ono spends seven years as an artist of the Floating World under the supervision of Seiji Moriyama, or Mori-san, alongside other dedicated painters at a dilapidated country villa in the Wakaba prefecture. The *atelier* system, where painters can work in a community without formal supervision, is a customary aspect of Japanese artistic culture. At the villa the artists are free to paint in their own way, though they are expected to follow the broad path of their *Sensei* or teacher. They are divided into two factions. The 'engineers' work with great speed once they have an idea, like a hyperactive engine driver shovelling coal at a manic pace. The 'backwarders', on the other hand, paint slowly, stepping back from their easels every few minutes to view the canvas (*AFW*, 160–61).

Mori-san is known a 'modern Utamaro' (*AFW*, 140), as he combines traditional *ukiyo-e* subject matter – women combing their hair, or towelling themselves – with European techniques. For instance, his paintings imply depth by subtle gradations of colour, rather than through bold outlines. His emblem is the lantern: 'Mori-san's wish was to evoke a certain melancholy, nocturnal atmosphere around his women … Because of this, it was something of a hallmark of Mori-san's work that a lantern would always figure somewhere in the picture, by implication if not in actuality' (*AFW*, 141). The most gifted pupil at the villa is Sasaki, who acts as an aesthetic policeman by condemning and sometimes confiscating paintings disloyal to his master's principles. Sasaki himself, however, falls foul of Mori-san when he diverges too far along an idiosyncratic path. The other pupils quickly turn against him, and his ignominious dispatch from the community is a forewarning of the dangers of such nonconformity.

The artists spend a great deal of their leisure time at a small teahouse called 'Water Lanterns' and a local archery parlour. This enables them to dip their toes into 'the night-time world of pleasure, entertainment and drink' (*AFW*, 145) which is the focus of their paintings. The villa often plays host to assorted actors, dancers and musicians who revel through the night. It is during one of these wild parties that Ono first expresses misgivings about his direction as an artist. Mori-san finds his favourite pupil skulking alone in a storeroom, and asks him what is the matter. Ono admits that he is perplexed why they spend so much time with such people. The master tells Ono about the consolation an old actor called Gisaburo finds in the Floating World: 'The finest, most fragile beauty an artist can hope to capture drifts within ... pleasure houses after dark' (*AFW*, 150). Mori-san justifies his practice by saying: 'When I am an old man, when I look back over my life and see that I have devoted it to the task of capturing the unique beauty of that world, I believe I will be well satisfied. And no man will make me believe I've wasted my time' (*AFW*, 150–51). This, then, is a very rarefied form of art, engaged with the beauty and tran-sience of the moment, and unaffected by wider concerns. As such, it is inimical to Ono's temperament, which is much more concerned with what might be called things *of* moment rather than things of the moment. It is for these reasons that Ono cannot concur with Mori-san's sentiment that capturing such beauty would be a satisfactory lifetime's achievement. He strives for something more substantial. Yet significantly, even with regard to a crucial point like this, Ono's memory falters. He is unable to remember whether these words were indeed uttered by Mori-san, or by himself when he addressed his own pupils many years later. This is therefore another of those displace-ments so frequent in Ishiguro.

The rift with Mori-san deepens when Ono comes under the spell of Matsuda, a government stooge who recruits artists for the nationalist cause. He shows Ono the poverty in his own city and persuades him that he can only create something of value if he abandons the useless aestheticism of the Floating World style. His arguments are full of expansionist rhetoric: 'We are now a mighty nation, capable of matching any of the Western nations. In the Asian hemisphere, Japan stands like a giant amidst cripples and dwarfs' (*AFW*, 173). This is precisely the kind of language that led to the atrocities at Nanking and elsewhere. Yet to a naive artist eager to make a difference, Matsuda offers a tempting path. So Ono begins to harness his painting in a political direction. Ignited by his conscience, he craves to create 'work of real importance ... that will be a significant contribution to the people of our nation' (*AFW*, 163). He requests privacy at the villa for a new painting, so that he can continue to work on it without interference from the others. His friend, the Tortoise, sneaks a look at the experiment and is appalled. The painting, called 'Complacency', is a crude propaganda piece that shows three boys brandishing sticks in a martial arts pose in poverty-stricken surroundings. Above their heads there is a second image of three well-dressed businessmen, laughing together in a bar. Both images are bordered by the outline of the islands of Japan. The right-hand margin consists of the single word, 'Complacency', whilst the left-hand margin declares: 'But the young are ready to fight for their dignity' (*AFW*, 168).

It is remote from the languid beauty and understatement of the *ukiyo-e* style, and the Tortoise immediately brands Ono a traitor for betraying his master's ideals so flagrantly. Mori-san is less direct in his criticism, but more effective. He meets Ono in a pavilion of the Takami Gardens, and quizzes him about his change of style. He informs Ono that he has seconded several of his canvases, and states 'You seem to be exploring some curious avenues' (*AFW*, 177). He then asks his pupil to let him have some of his other recent paintings in this new style, but Ono demurs. Mori-san makes it plain that if he refuses to comply, then Ono will have to reconsider his future as he will no longer be able to stay at the villa. It is a marvellously measured scene, stratified with various convolutions and ambiguities. Before they talk, Mori-san asks Ono to light all the lanterns around the pavilion, an equivocal gesture as the lantern is the personal symbol of the *Sensei*. Once again, as he recalls the incident, Ono is unsure if it was Mori-san who actually uttered the phrase 'curious avenues', or whether this was something he himself said to Kuroda on a later occasion in the pavilion. It is therefore another displacement, alerting the reader to the possibility that

Ono is projecting his memories of the later encounter on to the earlier one. The situation contains some forcible echoes of other scenes in the book, too, most notably the 'burning paintings' episode in the reception room between Ono and his father. These flickerings and instabilities of memory reflect the wavering nature of the self, as Margaret Scanlan argues:

> This sense that the personal identity with which first-person narrative is usually identified is far from solid, that people might be interchangeable with each other, haunts Ono's narrative ... Confronted with a painful situation, he is likely to abstract it, generalise about it; when he talks about other people, he frequently appears to be talking about himself. This trick, of course, is a familiar psychological defence, but in Ono's case it seems to point to a more fundamental confusion of himself with the people he discusses.[17]

Ono leaves the villa, and sets up an agitprop school, surrounded by acolytes hanging on his every word, at the Migi-Hidari. He becomes a member of the Cultural Committee of the Interior Department and an official adviser to the Committee of Unpatriotic Activities, positions obtained by sycophancy towards the Okada-Shingen society. This organisation is the fictitious equivalent of the real-life Nika Society, a private group of painters who allied themselves with the government control of the arts from 1935. Artists were encouraged to follow social-realist principles in their activities to promote the state. The initiative was led by the minister of education, Genji Matsuda, who is represented in the book by Chishu Matsuda.[18] Under Matsuda's mentorship, Ono even reworks 'Complacency' as 'Eyes to the Horizon', and it becomes one of his most successful posters of the 1930s. This blatant piece of propaganda retains the same visual structure as 'Complacency', but displaces its content. The upper image now depicts three fat, laughing politicians, whilst the lower image shows three soldiers looking towards Asia. Ono's sensibility is coarsening. It reaches its lowest ebb when history repeats itself and Ono betrays his most talented pupil. Police ransack Kuroda's house, burn his paintings, and arrest him. This is presumably on the basis of information given to the authorities by his former master, although this incriminating scene is absent from the text.

The surrendering of Kuroda to the authorities is not the only scene to be excluded from *An Artist of the Floating World*. Indeed, the narrative – which unfolds through the labyrinthine to-and-fro of Ono's shaky recollections – is incomplete, and subject to much selection and distortion. To capture some sense of this liquidity, it is helpful to think of the novel as if it were a film. This is not an arbitrary procedure as the book has many cinematic qualities, as I will now demonstrate.

It is structured into four large parts, each of which has a separate date spanning an eighteen-month period. In a motion-picture, these dates could be displayed as 'intertitles', markers of division that create expectations of progression and change.[19] The opening part of *An Artist of the Floating World*, 'October, 1948', takes up almost half of the book. It focuses on Setsuko's first visit to Ono, and her advice for her father to 'ensure misunderstandings do not arise' (*AFW*, 49) before Noriko's wedding negotiations, which he heeds by visiting Matsuda. 'April, 1949' is about a third of the length of the first part and centres mainly on the *miai* itself and Ono's confession of guilt. 'November, 1949' accounts for about one-third of the book. It records a second visit by Setsuko, where she denies having warned her father, and refutes his claim that Saito knew him well before the war. 'June, 1950', a short coda of just nine pages, concludes the book by describing Ono's last meeting with Matsuda before his friend's death. Within this four-part structure there are seventeen sections, denoted by extra spacings. In a film, these would be called sequences, a group of scenes forming a composite of meaning.[20] They are as follows:

'October, 1948'

1   House auction, Setsuko's first visit, pleasure district. (*AFW*, 7–28)
2   Ichiro plays 'Lone Ranger', draws. (*AFW*, 28–37)
3   Plans for next day. (*AFW*, 37–40)

4 Reception room, 'precautionary steps', 'business meetings'. (*AFW*, 40–50)
5 The Miyake affair. (*AFW*, 50–61)
6 Takeda's studio, 'the Tortoise', Migi-Hidari's. (*AFW*, 61–77)
7 Cinema, Dr Saito and Kuroda. (*AFW*, 77–85)
8 Ono meets Matsuda. (*AFW*, 85–96)

'April, 1949'

9 Quarrel with Shintaro. (*AFW*, 99–104)
10 Build-up to *miai*. (*AFW*, 104–08)
11 Meeting with Kuroda's pupil. (*AFW*, 108–16)
12 The *miai*. (*AFW*, 116–27)

'November, 1949'

13 Setsuko's second visit, Mori-san's villa. (*AFW*, 131–43)
14 The Floating World, storeroom conversation. (*AFW*, 143–55)
15 New directions, the Kuroda betrayal. (*AFW*, 155–84)
16 Supper discussions. (*AFW*, 184–94)

'June, 1950'

17 Matsuda dies. (*AFW*, 197–206)

A movie would separate these sequences from each other via short fade-outs, thus reinforcing their arrangement according to the time-honoured principles of repetition, conflict, variation and resolution.

Continuous with this 'present' chain of events are numerous digressions to the past, outlining Ono's early childhood, his artistic career and the eventual decline of his reputation as a result of his propagandist work. What this brief summary fails to convey is the exquisite intricacy with which the past and present scenes are interlaced. *An Artist of the Floating World* does not emulate the ideal of continuity editing, a standard cinematic practice that renders a narrative seamless and coherent through invisible stitching. Rather, the novel foregrounds its own fault-lines by sudden tremors of space, time, mood and perspective.

The architectonic finesse of Ishiguro can best be demonstrated with a number of terms derived from montage, or the analysis of film editing.

The art of montage arose from the Soviet cinema of the 1920s, and its experiments with the selection, cutting and arrangement of shots. This dialectical process creates a third meaning from the juxtaposition of two adjacent shots and their original meanings. It is associated with the theories of Lev Kuleshov and the films of Sergei Eisenstein. In *Battleship Potemkin* (1925) and *October* (1928), shots collide and collude with each other to generate emergent significations. Many of the editing techniques familiar to film are also used by Ishiguro to create meaning through a montage-like effect of assembling similarities and differences in successive textual scenes.

The most common method of aligning two episodes is the flashback. This breaks chronological continuity by depicting events occurring in the past relative to the 'present' in which the flashback is triggered. It is a subjective, sometimes 'confessional', device that mimics an individual's thought-processes and usually involves an enigma of some kind. In sequence 5 of *An Artist of the Floating World*, for instance, Noriko relates to her father a chance encounter outside the Shimizu department store with Jiro Miyake, her suitor of the previous year. During a pleasant chat, Jiro revealed he was engaged. Noriko was on the verge of asking him why the family had pulled out of their own marriage negotiations, but was reluctant to do so in case she was told that she wasn't pretty enough. This prompts Ono to remember a meeting of his own with Jiro at a tram stop over a year ago, when the marriage negotiations were still ongoing. He recalls a conversation about the suicide of the President of Jiro's company, who gassed himself after two senior employees were dismissed by the Americans after the war. This memory sows a seed of doubt in Ono's mind as he wonders whether it was the views he ventured forth that day about this drastic action that led to Jiro withdrawing from the marriage negotiations. It is a mystery the book never fully dispels. But by embedding Ono's speculation within the context of Noriko's broodings about the Miyakes, the guilt and shame of father and daughter converge. Another more straightforward flashback occurs in sequence 8, when Ono meets Matsuda to obtain his assurances about the forthcoming inquiries. As he waits in the reception room to see his old friend, Ono thinks back almost thirty years to the first time he met Matsuda at Mori-san's villa. There is a drastic contrast between the lean, dandyish persuader of earlier years and the man who has now 'become broken down by ill-health' (*AFW*, 89).

The opposite of a flashback is a flashforward, where events from a later part of the narrative sequence are presented anticipatively. Strictly speaking, this is technically impossible in a tale told by a first-person narrator writing at a dated present, unless it is accomplished by a dream or premonition or some other predictive stratagem. Nevertheless, *An Artist of the Floating World* features some proleptic hops that have the force of flashforwards, by introducing the reader to a character or theme whose significance only later becomes apparent. This is the impact of the scene at the beginning of sequence 7, when Ono recounts a sighting of his protegé, Kuroda, in the first year after the war. It is a rainy day, and his former pupil stands with a broken umbrella staring at some battered buildings. Although this is a memory from Ono's past, the insertion of Kuroda at this point serves to forecast the importance he will play in the story. A different effect is achieved in sequence 15. The story leaps from scene (a), Ono's conversation about his new artistic direction with Mori-san in the lanterned pavilion; to scene (b), a winter's morning some years later when, as a result of Ono's treachery, the police burn Kuroda's paintings and arrest him on the charge of being unpatriotic. Here the flashforward highlights the irony of the betrayed pupil becoming the betraying master.

The flashback and the flashforward are disjunctive interruptions of the plot, transferring attention abruptly to a different locale and/or time-frame. There is a special type of transition in film, however, which can suggest a close relationship between two scenes, even when they belong to disparate spatial and temporal moments. This is called the dissolve, a cinematic equivalent of a comma that superimposes a fade-out over a fade-in, momentarily fusing the two images. A film-director would probably insert a dissolve in sequence 4 of *An Artist of the Floating World*, when Ono invites Setsuko, holding a vase of flowers, into the reception room of his house. The narrative then slips back into Ono's memories of the 'business meetings' in the reception room of his father's house as a teenager, leading to the first 'burning paintings' episode. It then returns to Setsuko arranging the flowers around the Buddhist altar, and the subsequent conversation with her father about securing the silence of Matsuda and Kuroda before they are checked-out by Mr Kyo. Ishiguro thus elides Ono's determination – despite his father's antagonism – to forge a career as an artist, and the long-term consequences of that decision. A dissolve would also be appropriate in sequence 16, when Taro refuses to fully endorse Ono's claim at the family supper that his father knew him well before the war. This would then recede into Ono's earlier talk with Sachiko in Kawabe Park. In this scene, she not only denies that the 'precautionary steps' exchange in sequence 4 ever took place, but also asserts that Dr Saito knew nothing about her father's painterly activities.

As these examples show, Ishiguro's narrative moves nimbly between the past and the present. However, his accounts of Ono's apprenticeship at the Takeda studio in sequence 6 and his stay at Mori-san's villa in sequences 13 and 14 progress in a more linear fashion. In the Takeda sequence, the events of several years are condensed into five short scenes: (a) a general description of the Takeda studio and Ono's attic room; (b) the arrival of his colleague, dubbed 'the Tortoise'; (c) the taunting of the Tortoise by the other artists for his slow painting methods; (d) Ono's defence of the Tortoise; and (e) Ono's meeting with the Tortoise in the Tamagawa grounds when he persuades him to defect to Mori-san's tutelage. Ono's time at Mori-san's villa is also telescoped into two short sequences. Firstly, sequence 13: (a) a description of the villa and the daily life there; (b) the unveiling of a painting by Mori-san; (c) the favouring of Sasaki; and (d) the departure of Sasaki. Secondly, sequence 14: (a) a description of the artists at the villa; (b) an account of their leisure pursuits; (c) information about their parties; and (d) the debate between Mori-san and Ono in the storeroom about Gisaburo and the beauty of the Floating World. The swift movement between these isolated scenes is analogous to cinematic jump cuts, which eliminate dead footage by cutting from one moment or place to another. If a man walks from one end of a large room to another, there is no need to observe his passage across the entire distance. The pace can be quickened by deleting extraneous footage. This is also the rationale of economy motivating Ishiguro's expository passages.

In *An Artist of the Floating World*, the themes of shame, guilt and blame accrue resonance by the accumulation of Ono's experiences. The stage for this psychic drama is the mutating landscape of Japan itself before and after the war, particularly the changes to the pleasure district of Ono's city. There is a cross cut – the linkage of two sets of action happening at different times or places – towards the end of sequence 6. This underlines the decline of the Migi-Hidari bar by displaying it at the height of its popularity and at its lowest ebb. In the first scene, the place is 'boisterous' (*AFW*, 75): waitresses scurry to take drinks to the customers at the tables, whilst pupils circle Ono, eager to receive words of wisdom from their master. It is a time when the bar is 'the spearhead of the new spirit' (*AFW*, 74), as later portrayed in a painting by Kuroda. There is then a flip to the degraded state of the bar after the war, when it is encompassed by ruins, and Mrs Kawakami's only customers are Ono and Shintaro. They propose a futile attempt to 'bring back the old crowd' (*AFW*, 76), a project that seems even more pathetic when Shintaro stops going to the bar in sequence 12. Ono, now the only patron, is 'struck by the thought of how small, shabby and out of place' (*AFW*, 126) the saloon seems.

The symbolic deterioration of the Migi-Hidari is also stressed in the novel by another cinematic tactic, known as the match cut, or the marrying of two shots via some parallel element. The most celebrated instance is the opening of Stanley Kubrick's *2001: A Space Odyssey* (1968). A bone hurled in the air by a prehistoric man segues into a spinning space station, suggesting the advance of technology. There is nothing quite as sweeping as this in *An Artist of the Floating World.* The novel does, however, feature some impressive matching effects, as in the sequence 1 transition between Ono's impressions of the Migi-Hidari bar on his first visit, and the way it appears to him in 1948. It still retains an atmosphere thanks to 'the contrast between the bar counter, lit up by warm, low-hung lights, and the rest of the room, which is in shadow' (*AFW*, 26). Yet outside, there is nothing but war-damaged rubble, puddles and mosquitoes. Where once it was surrounded by other busy establishments and throngs of revellers, now it is as if it were 'in the midst of a graveyard' (*AFW*, 27). The matching of the interior of the bar between the two dates serves to emphasise even more the mismatch between the pleasure district as it once was and the wrecked landscape in the present.

Another deft match is contrived in sequence 14, involving the artworks I touched upon earlier. Matsuda takes Ono on a walk through the destitute shanty district of Nishizuru, in order to impress upon the artist the necessity for him to adopt a politicised aesthetic calling for urgent social action. The sight that stays with Ono is that of three small boys torturing an animal with sticks, which he uses as the central image of his painting 'Complacency'. On his canvas, the figures are dressed in rags like the original boys, and are standing in front of a squalid hut. The look on their faces, however, is no longer criminal, but that of 'samurai warriors ready to fight' as they hold their sticks in 'classic kendo stances' (*AFW*, 168). The image undergoes a further metamorphosis later on, when it becomes the basis for the 'Eyes to the Horizon' painting that gains Ono some notoriety. In this final version, the boys are soldiers, and it is rifles they hold instead of sticks. This series of matching representations therefore charts the regression of Ono's views from humanitarian concern to hostile nationalism.

There are other edits binding together Ishiguro's seemingly discontinuous narrative, which can also be expressed in the language of cinema. An establishing shot is a view, usually long-distance, of a general location for a following scene that allows the audience to orient themselves. If repeated at strategic intervals, it can act as a girding for the rest of the narrative. Such is the case with the scenes at the Bridge of Hesitation, placed at the openings of three of the major parts of the book. So 'October, 1948' draws the reader into the book by asking him or her to imagine that they are climbing a path leading up from the bridge and looking down at Ono's house. 'April, 1949' begins with Ono walking by the bridge at sunset to gaze at the bomb-damaged buildings and reconstruction work. Finally, at the opening of 'June, 1950', Ono walks by the bridge after hearing of Matsuda's death. The Bridge of Hesitation is so-called because it connected the pleasure district with the rest of the city, and was where 'conscience-troubled men … [hovered] between seeking an evening's entertainment and returning home to their wives' (*AFW*, 99). It is also a recurring icon of Ono's own troubled conscience and hesitation, caught as he is between shame and guilt, glory and ignominy, his home and a homelessness of the mind.

The Bridge could be said to span the whole story of *An Artist of the Floating World* with uncertainty. In the same way, the meanings of many individual episodes are altered by their framing within other similar and dissimilar scenes, through the techniques I have outlined. There is one final device to list, one that serves primarily to break and disrupt frames. This is the overlap, a film term denoting a lack of synchrony between the sound from one scene when it bridges into another subsequent scene. So a voiceover rhapsodising about a country meadow on a hot summer's day might continue to talk of grass and sun when the scene changes to a wintry city street. Or a violin, conjuring up a melancholic mood within a scene, might still be playing when the scene cuts to a circus clown with a big red nose. These overlaps disorient the viewer by disturbing the perspective upon the matter at hand. They also provide a template for understanding the numerous misascriptions and blurrings of memory afflicting Ono, particularly those instances when he is unsure as to who said what to whom on which occasion. In sequence 5, for instance, Ono repeats the conversation he had with Miyake when he accidentally bumped into him in the street during Noriko's wedding negotiations. He ends the scene with a verbatim report of Miyake's strong words against the cowards who refuse to admit the mistakes they made during the war. But then Ono wonders: 'Did Miyake really say all that to me that afternoon? Perhaps I am getting his words confused with the sort of thing Suichi will come out and say' (*AFW*, 56). The more he thinks about it, the more certain he is that the words were uttered by somebody else in entirely different circumstances. He then goes on to talk about the day when the ashes of his son, Kenji, were buried. On this occasion, Suichi, his son-in-law, spoke out against cowardice, using the same words which he had previously attributed to Miyake. As in the pairings of summer/winter and sad music/happy clown, an overlap is created between two otherwise unrelated scenes. This solves a problem of transition for Ishiguro, who doesn't like the idea that 'A has to come before B and that B has to come before C because the plot dictates it'.[21] He much prefers to arrange things 'tonally', necessitated by Ono's volatile moods. A similar tonal reframing is induced in sequence 14 at the end of the storeroom conversation with Mori-san. Ono chews over some statements uttered by his master, but then questions the accuracy of his memory, before finally deciding he was right after all:

> It is possible, of course, that Mori-san did not use those exact words. Indeed, on reflection, such phrases sound rather more like the sort of thing I myself would declare to my pupils after we had been drinking a little at the Migi-Hidari … But then again, as I have said, many phrases and expressions which came to be most characteristic of me I actually inherited from Mori-san, and so it is quite possible that those were my teacher's exact words that night, instilled in me by the powerful impression they made on me at the time. (*AFW*, 151)

These extended analogies between editing and the shaping of *An Artist of the Floating World* indicate the importance of film to Ishiguro as a source for ideas on structure. 'Cinema', he once declared, 'is the one area of Japanese 'culture' which I believe has had a direct influence on my writing.'[22] As Fumio Yoshioka notes, and as I have illustrated, the influence of film is generally observable in the techniques of 'cutback, flashback, dissolve, fadeout and overlap'[23] which mould all of his novels. Moreover, Ishiguro's approach to composition is comparable to that of the screenwriter, and is informed by his experience with scripting *A Profile of J. Arthur Mason* (1984) and *The Gourmet* for television. His conscious placement of themes is another reason why it is mistaken to interpret his Japanese settings too literally. They are simply a convenient hinterland for the exploration of certain key issues.

In what other ways does Japanese cinema help mould Ishiguro's fiction? Well, for one thing, he has much in common with Yasujiro Ozu, whose early films such as *I Was Born, but …* (1932), *Passing Fancy* (1933) and *A Story of Floating Weeds* (1934) earned him a reputation as the most Japanese of directors. Ozu's later films – including *Tokyo Story* (1953), *Equinox Flower* (1958) and *An Autumn Afternoon* (1962) – are distinctive due to their simple stories and unorthodox structures. They omit important events; keep significant characters offstage; and spend disproportionate amounts of time on seemingly irrelevant conversations.[24] This is congruent with Ozu's dislike of plot: 'Pictures with obvious plots bore me now. Naturally a film must have some kind of structure or else it's not a film, but I feel that a picture isn't good if it has too much drama.'[25] Ozu's preference for plotlessness clearly aligns him with Ishiguro.

Ishiguro's choice of characters, too, is coloured by Ozu and other directors from the *Shomin-Geki* film genre. These include Yasujiro Shimazu (*Maiden in a Storm*, 1932); Heinosuke Gosho (*Everything That Lives*, 1934); Hiroshi Shimizu (*Children in the Wind*, 1937); and Mikio Naruse (*Mother*, 1952). *Shomin* means 'people like you and me', so the genre is domestic and usually features conflict between parents and children in an extended family setting. It deals with quotidian subjects, such as Ozu's *The Life of an Office Worker* (1929), which is about a man who fails to receive his promised annual bonus. Although essentially realistic in tone, this type of film often has comic overtones and a desentimentalised mix of smiles and tears. The typical hero or heroine is someone who is ready to give up at the intractability of the world, but then finds the strength to continue by compromising with the way things are. They do so with a passive acceptance, and not through the grand emotions of valour and rapture. This concentration on the small victories and defeats of ordinary people as they grapple with their everyday lives is also mirrored in Ishiguro's work.

Shomin-Geki is 'a profound, respectable genre, and distinctively Japanese … [with] a pace which reflects the monotony and melancholy of everyday life',[26] in the words of Ishiguro. This slowness is one of the main characteristics that he has inherited from Japanese films. Gregory Mason clarifies how Ozu often foregrounds apparently irrelevant physical details. A typical scene from his masterpiece *Tokyo Story* will begin by lingering over seemingly inconsequential items such as laundry hanging on a line or the sound of a train in the distance. Then the camera will focus on the main participants of the scene (usually from a low angle), always keeping a respectful distance, never jumping from one shot to the next but remaining inert and watchful. The dialogue will unfold naturally, with many pauses between lines. Ishiguro uses literary equivalents of these resources to 'retard and disperse the impetus of his narratives in order to reveal subtler and surprising aspects of character.'[27] Both the writer and the director infuse a 'de-centering effect'[28] in their tales, displacing the emphasis away from the story and towards the *mise-en-scène*. Draped over the proceedings is a mood of regret and nostalgia, a sense of loss and impermanence.

These features of plot pared to the bone, everyday characters and slowness of pace are particularly marked in *An Artist of the Floating World*, where they are combined with a more European style of editing. They are congenial methods for portraying the associations and elisions of memory and speculation guiding Ono's reflections. For these reasons, Amit Chaudhuri believes *An Artist of the Floating World* is a more natural choice for movie adaptation than *The Remains of the Day*. In an earlier period of cinema – where film was seen as 'an independent visual medium or language'[29] – its fluttering, floating surface would have been ideally suited to presentation on the big screen. By the 1990s, however, when *The Remains of the Day* was produced, there was little demand for the subtle interplay of images. The market model for many films was the costume dramas of television that offered, instead, the glamour of history and painstaking recreation of period detail. The Merchant-Ivory team were quick to adjust to this trend. Their choice of magnificent locations (Powderham Castle as a stand-in for Darlington Hall), and casting of big-name actors to play Stevens (Anthony Hopkins) and Miss Kenton (Emma Thompson), enabled their film of *The Remains of the Day* (1993) to be nominated for eight Oscars.[30] In the opinion of John Ash, however, their movies are 'fundamentally inauthentic' and 'of no interest as *movies*'.[31] They appeal to an ersatz nostalgia for a faded and facsimile past.

Arguably, Steven Spielberg's project of filming *Memoirs of a Geisha* falls into the same category. No matter how big the budget, how magnificent the locations, how stellar the cast, or how painstaking the recreation of historical detail, the core of Japan cannot be captured on celluloid. Inauthenticity seeps out between the sprocket-holes. But what about the works of Yasusada, discussed at the beginning of this chapter? Surely here is something solid and true. Aren't his poems the genuine voice of suffering, a Japan that isn't cosmeticised like Nitta Sayura or Madam Butterfly? The answer, sadly, is no. Yasusada is also an invention, a persona devised in an elaborate hoax by American academic Kent Johnson, possibly in collaboration with others. Once the ruse was revealed, the journals who published the poems subsequently printed disclaimers and apologies, and Wesleyan University Press withdrew from its contract to publish a volume of Yasusada's works. What seemed intolerable about the whole escapade was not only the deception of authorship, but also the irresponsible exploitation of such sensitive subject matter. The atomic bombings continue to be a cause of much shame and guilt for both the Americans and the Japanese.

The Yasusada affair and the ensuing furore crystallise many of the issues relevant to Ishiguro's first two novels: the nature of

Japaneseness and its literary representations; the constitution of national identity and its relation to subjective memory; writerly authority and the misreadings generated by cultural stereotypes. Many of these themes are reiterated in *The Remains of the Day*, but from an English rather than a Japanese angle. The movement away from Japanese subject matter, and the typical images it entails, is an aspect of what could be called Ishiguro's 'dis-orient-ation'.

4

The Remains of the Day

ON 6 September 1997, millions around the world watched the funeral of Princess Diana, the victim of a car crash in Paris two weeks earlier. The response of the British public who gathered in the streets of London to witness the ceremony was unexpected. There was little of the reserve and quiet grief accompanying the death of Lord Mountbatten just a couple of decades earlier. Instead there was an open display of emotion. Thousands wept and threw flowers at the gun-carriage bearing the body. The 'stiff upper lip' was replaced by the 'trembling lower lip'. Ironically, there was considerable controversy surrounding the reaction of the Royal Family, who behaved with classic British decorum by maintaining an air of dignity and carrying on almost as if nothing had happened. Newspapers and the proverbial man on the street clamoured for the Queen to lower her traditional mask and show her human face.

These events connoted a change in the English character, and its perception abroad. Shortly after Diana's funeral, the writer Toru Kuroiwa – author of *The English Way of Life* (1997), a standard reference book in many Japanese universities – gave an interview in which he claimed: 'The backbone of the new class of society is crumbling. This way of life that makes the British is changing. It is sad … I am obliged to say to the British: more tea, more butlers, more gentlemanly golf.'[1] Despite the outdated imagery, many shared Kuroiwa's regret that the past was slipping away. Some blamed these changes on the influence of the media, and its hourly bombardment of every British home with images of alternative (usually Americanised) life-styles. Even Merchant-Ivory movies such as *A Room With a View* (1985), *Maurice* (1987), and *The Remains of the Day* – despite their apparent glorification of the days of tea, butlers and gentlemanly golf – have helped to erode the national character. They are 'profoundly subversive … and provide a continuing and comprehensive critique of the ethic of restraint, repression and the stiff upper lip'.[2]

The novel *The Remains of the Day* is far more subversive than the film, and also indicates a change in the national mood. Ishiguro was eager to escape from the stereotyping of his first two books as Japanese. Consequently, for his next work he deliberately chose a butler, that most English of stock characters, as his central protagonist. Its main theme was not just the potential damage caused by the stiff upper lip, but a questioning of the entire nature of Englishness and its values. This interro-gation is largely absent from the Merchant-Ivory motion-picture. Ishiguro's refocusing made a good deal of sense. After all, there are many similarities between the Japanese and the English. Both peoples are thought to be undemonstrative in their expression of emotions. Their cultures are both obsessed with politeness and etiquette. As island nations, they have both been insulated from many of the foreign influences and invasions that have adulterated countries on the mainlands of Asia and Europe. *The Remains of the Day* moved far beyond these super-ficial similarities, however. Its representation of Englishness in the impeccable Stevens was widely construed as a shock tactic. As Ishiguro wryly joked, *'It's more English than English'*.[3] Patey designates this as the 'Japanese-writer-more-English-than-the-English' stance, and it quickly became a cliché for reviewers to see Stevens as the 'English-butler- [who is] more-English-butler-than-any-English-butler'.[4]

So, much to Ishiguro's consternation, his attempt to avoid stereotyping was itself quickly stereotyped. Steven Connor shared his apprehensions. Although, in his opinion, it is beyond dispute that Englishness is analysed in the novel, he is worried that critics such as Gabriele Annan, Claude Habib and Pico Iyer insist upon reading the book as yet another dissection of Japan-eseness: 'For Ishiguro's butler is so English that he could be Japanese, in his finely calibrated sense of rank, his attention to minutiae, his perfectionism and his eagerness to please; his pride is his subservience, and his home is only in the past'.[5] But this refusal to see Ishiguro and his work as anything other than Japanese is, Connor believes, an act of 'cultural repatriation'.[6]

Japanese readings of Ishiguro's fictions are not illegitimate, as I established earlier, but should be placed alongside other interpretations. So as well as seeing Stevens as a Japanese in disguise, it should also be recognised that he follows a long tradition of butlers who are meant to represent the best of British virtue. Avatars of such unflappable decorum from past literature include Lane in Oscar Wilde's *The Importance of Being Earnest* (1895); Crichton in J. M. Barrie's *The Admirable Crichton* (1902); Bullivant in Ivy Compton-Burnett's *Manservant and Maidservant* (1947); and, the best-known parody of the type, P. G. Wode-house's Jeeves.[7] Ishiguro builds on this lineage in *The Remains of the Day*. Indeed, Ihab Hassan believes that he 'surpasses that tradition; more precisely, he perfects it and subverts it at the same time.'[8] A good example of such subversion is the 1923 conference episode. Terrence Rafferty compares these 'forty pages of brilliantly stage-managed dark farce'[9] directly with Wodehouse, and shows how in this sequence Stevens is, in effect, the parody of a parody. He is as reticent as Jeeves is garrulous; as gauche as Jeeves is resourceful. If Stevens resembles Jeeves, he also has more than a touch of T. S. Eliot's J. Alfred Prufrock about him, with his pomposities and perplexities. 'Like Prufrock', as Norman Page comments, 'he [Stevens] has been not Prince Hamlet but an attendant lord'.[10] William Hutchings lists the 'Prufrockian traits' of Stevens: he is 'unvaryingly deferential, meticulous, and ... glad to be "of use"'.[11] Prufrock is, in many ways, a comic character like Jeeves, but he has also a tragic dimension that is missing in Wodehouse and present in Stevens. As Anthony Thwaite observes, 'Ishiguro's Prufrock is a memorable portrait of futility.'[12]

The choice of butler as the representative of Englishness for

Ishiguro's third novel was not a haphazard one. He had already experimented with the idea in his television play *A Profile of Arthur J. Mason*.[13] This satellite study for *The Remains of the Day* spotlights a butler, Mason, who is in the service of Sir James Reid. Unusually, Mason has become a major literary celebrity following the publication of his novel, *The August Passage*. The book remained in manuscript form for almost forty years before it was 'discovered' by the agent Mortimer Crane, a friend of Reid's. Ishiguro's play is shot in the style of an arts documentary, as television reporter Anna investigates the background of the writing butler. She is sure there must be a tension between Mason's career of service and his artistic ambitions. The butler, however, does not appear to be perturbed. He is quite happy with his duties as a servant: 'I've long ceased to think of it as a job. It's who I am, it's what I do, it's what I've always done, and it's what I always intend to do. It's a responsible, dignified, thoroughly honourable occupation'.[14] Mason claims to have no qualms that his novel was not published far earlier. However, a different picture emerges from the extracts of the book he reads out, and from what he reveals to Anna about the circumstances of its composition. It was written in the aftermath of the Second World War, when Arthur and his wife Mary were employed at a house near Ashford. This was a time when a new spirit of equality was in the air, the England of the Welfare State and education reforms, and they both thought it would be 'very undignified'[15] to continue working for much longer as servants. Mason's novel was supposed to be their chance to better themselves. So intriguingly, *The August Passage* seems to be about dignity and the nature of Englishness, and reflects aspects of Mason's predicament. In the passage Mason recites for the camera, a character named Kathrine is attempting to persuade her manservant partner to leave domestic servitude in an English stately home for the limitless opportunities of the United States. But her husband is resigned and pessimistic: 'It's our fate to be English through and through. Until England changes, nothing will ever change for the likes of us'.[16] Nothing changes for Mason and his wife, either, as the novel was consigned to the bottom drawer for many years. They never managed to escape from their domestic servitude, and in time the marriage was annulled. The butler therefore became resigned to his role, and many of the scenes from Anna's documentary show Arthur engaged in typical daily pursuits. He dresses Sir James; serves food and high tea; polishes the silver in the dining room; and dusts the family portraits in the corridor of the cottage.

The butler/writer and his relation to English values anticipate the concerns of *The Remains of the Day*. Like Mason, Stevens operates as more than just a domestic servant. He fulfils a metaphorical purpose, as Ishiguro explained: 'I chose the figure deliberately because that's what I think I am, and I think most of us are: we're just butlers.'[17] The average person is a butler in that the most he or she can do with their life is to use their small talents to serve higher interests, a theme central to *An Artist of the Floating World*. This figurative use of the butler was misunderstood by several commentators who thought the book was a work of social realism and so bemoaned certain historical inaccuracies in *The Remains of the Day*. A letter to *The Times* complained that port would never be handed round by a butler after dinner, but would be circulated clockwise by the dining gentlemen.[18] Philip Howard is scornful of this charge: 'as literary criticism, this was as sensible as judging that *Hamlet* was a bad play because its account of court etiquette at Elsinore in the Dark Ages is inaccurate in some details'.[19] Others were sceptical that a butler would think at all about the state of the nation and spend his spare time in the pantry;[20] or thought that it was a 'gross sociological error'[21] to have Jewish maids in an English country house before the arrival of the first German refugees. These quibbles betray what Ishiguro feels to be a major misreading of his intentions. He has declared several times that accurately recreating historical situations does not particularly interest him: 'My main purpose in writing these books ... [isn't] to explain what a specific point in history was like.'[22] He does not dismiss the novelist's obligation to create a plausible background. But this is sketched in later, after the themes and ideas have already been chosen. He compares this process of looking for a suitable backdrop to 'the way that a film director might search for locations, for a script he had already written.'[23] In other words, he exercises the art of placement. These insights about his *modus operandi* are especially pertinent to interpreting *The Remains of the Day*. Ishiguro does not intend the England he presents there to be a historically accurate portrait. Indeed, it is a 'mythic England … the kind of England that is often used by the heritage or nostalgia industry to sell tablecloths or teacups.'[24]

How does Stevens epitomise this mythic England? Terrence Rafferty affirms, rather vaguely, that 'he is intended to *represent* something about the English soul'.[25] Joseph Coates is more specific when he says that the butler is 'the consummate imperial Englishman on the eve of extinction'.[26] Both would agree with Steven Connor, who points out the parallels between Stevens and 'the sense of Englishness as a whole.'[27] But what *is* Englishness? Of what does it consist? Can it be characterised without resort to cliché? According to Coates, it signifies a certain emotional repression, a love of hierarchy, a complacent self-belief and a respect for the country's history. Few would bicker at this list of conventional traits. It should never be forgotten, however, that a national identity has many facets, and cannot be reduced to a single formula. Englishness is constructed out of many overlapping myths and images, from the legends of King Arthur to the 'Cool Britannia' of the 1990s. It is more accurate to speak of 'Englishnesses', especially as England has been a multicultural country for some decades.

Stevens has no time for such wishy-washy pluralism, and is very precise in his own mind about what constitutes the essence of Englishness. Much of the novel follows Stevens's ruminations on his identity, and the car trip he takes to the West Country is also a journey into his English sense of self. Temporarily abstracted from his home at Darlington Hall, the environment where he has spent most of his adult life, he is free to ponder his place in the larger scheme of things. Not long after he has left familiar landscape, he takes a break to stretch his legs on the side of a hill. There he meets a local, who advises the butler to follow a nearby footpath in order to see 'a nice little spot … you won't get a better view in the whole of England' (*RD*, 25). Stevens climbs the hill, and is rewarded with a splendid sight:

> What I saw was principally field upon field rolling off into the far distance. The land rose and fell gently, and the fields were bordered by hedges and trees. There were dots in some of the distant fields which I assumed to be sheep. To my right, almost on the horizon, I thought I could see the square tower of a church. (*RD*, 26)

The description is minimalist and stripped of adjectives. The view could be anywhere in England, which makes it all the more curious why the local should rate it as the best view in the country. Yet there is an impressive negative power in this image. It is parenthesised by the 'slight sense of alarm' (*RD*, 24) Stevens feels at leaving Darlington Hall behind, and the 'flush of anticipation' (*RD*, 26) he experiences for the journey ahead. The power is similar to that expressed by Roland Barthes when he scanned the Japanese landscape: it produces itself 'in a pure significance, abrupt, empty, like a fracture'.[28] Steven Connor develops this point further when he considers Stevens's later reflection on the qualities of the landscape. He argues that Stevens praises the view for being identical with itself, reserved, demure. Its greatness, which the butler declares is indicative of the greatness of Britain itself, lies in its tacit plenitude.[29] As Stevens puts it:

> I would say that it is the very *lack* of obvious drama or spectacle that sets the beauty of our land apart. What is pertinent is the calmness of that beauty, its sense of restraint. It is as though the land knows of its own beauty, of its own greatness, and feels no need to shout it. In comparison, the sorts of sights offered in such places as Africa or America, though undoubtedly very exciting, strike the objective viewer as inferior on account of their unseemly demonstrativeness. (*RD*, 29)

The 'objective viewer' appealed to here is anything but: he is English, white, associated with the upper class, a nationalist and imperialist prone to bouts of self-glorifying hyperbole – in short, he is Stevens himself.

Stevens's musings about the greatness of the English land-scape lead him to a related question: what is a 'great' butler? He is careful to distinguish this from the issue of *who* is a great butler. This is a contingent question open to debate. Some would immediately point to his peers Mr Marshall and Mr Lane as exemplars of the field, whilst others might extol the dubitable talents of Mr Jack Neighbours. In either case, the inquiry would yield little in the way of 'genuine interest' (*RD*, 31). Stevens is concerned with the essence of greatness in butlers, not its secondary characteristics. To this end, he looks towards the pro-nouncements of the Hayes Society. This (fictitious) professional organisation flourished in the 1920s and early 1930s, and prided itself on admitting only the highest quality of butler into its ranks. It kept its membership exclusive by applying élitist criteria for enrolment. One of its prerequisites is that applicants must be attached to a distinguished household. This means, in effect, that they must be butlers for the landed gentry or for other prominent members of society. The houses of business-men or the *nouveaux riches* do not count: they are far too vulgar.

Stevens takes considerable pride in being fortunate enough to serve in Darlington Hall, the distinguished household of Lord Darlington, as this fits the Hayes Society's expectations. The butler delineates at length the position of the stately home in the political structure of international relations by contrasting a 'ladder' metaphor with a 'wheel' metaphor (*RD*, 115). His father's generation saw the world as a hierarchical ladder, with Royalty at the top and those with titleless wealth at the bottom. Stevens's generation, however, picture the world as a wheel with con-centric rings of influence. Close to the centre, or 'the great hub of things' (*RD*, 227), are those country houses where grand decisions affecting global matters are reached before ratification by the official sources of power. Through this metaphor Stevens is able to sustain the self-delusion that his life of service to the distinguished household is also 'an undeniable contribution to the future well-being of the empire' (*RD*, 114).[30] Darlington

Hall's decline after the Second World War is thus symptomatic of the weakening of British colonial rule. The reduction in staff – from almost thirty at its height in the 1930s, to just four in the 1950s (Stevens, Mrs Clements, Rosemary and Agnes) – tells its own tale about the fall of Empire. Small wonder that Stevens is eager to implement a new 'staff plan' (*RD*, 9).

Besides an attachment to a distinguished household, the Hayes Society specified another condition for a butler to be admitted into its restricted fold. This requirement is so important for Stevens, he has committed it to memory: 'the most crucial criterion is that the applicant be possessed of a dignity in keeping with his position. No applicant will satisfy requirements, whatever his level of accomplishments otherwise, if seen to fall short in this respect' (*RD*, 33). Stevens not only learns this by heart, he takes it to heart, and it becomes his main barometer for self-esteem. To be English is to be great, like the landscape; to be great, is to possess dignity; and dignity is epitomised by the great butlers:

> It is sometimes said that butlers only truly exist in England. Other countries, whatever title is actually used, have only manservants. I tend to believe this is true. Continentals are unable to be butlers because they are as a breed incapable of the emotional restraint which only the English race is capable of … In a word, 'dignity' is beyond such persons. We English have an important advantage over foreigners in this respect and it is for this reason that when you think of a great butler, he is bound, almost by definition, to be an Englishman. (*RD*, 43)

Although entirely reprehensible, as a creed it is at least candid. This somewhat xenophobic pronouncement leaves further questions begging, however: such as what *is* dignity, and why does Stevens feel that he possesses it? To answer these questions, it is necessary to find out more about what dignity means to Stevens, and how he makes himself 'at home' with that concept. Then it will be possible to outline how Stevens's self-conception is displaced through denials and lies. Lastly, by examining the butler's relationship with Miss Kenton and his strategies of emotional avoidance, we can ascertain whether Stevens's English-ness has been a help or a hindrance in his life.

Dignity has four common meanings: (1) 'The quality of being worthy or honourable; worthiness, worth, nobleness, excellence'; (2) 'Honourable or high estate, position, or estima-tion; honour; degree of estimation, rank'; (3) 'An honourable office, rank, or title; a high official or titular position'; and (4) 'Nobility or befitting elevation of aspect, manner, or style; becoming or fit stateliness.'[31] Of these alternatives, (1) and (4) come closest to approximating what Stevens means by the term. Dignity, for Stevens, is largely a matter of reserve and aplomb in the pursuit of butlering excellence. (2) and (3) are applicable, also, if we bear in mind the importance for Stevens of the butler within the distinguished household, and his belief that he is at the pinnacle of his profession.

Stevens provides an ostensive definition of dignity by relay-ing three anecdotes about his father. In his prime as a butler, Stevens, Sr 'was indeed the embodiment of "dignity"' (RD, 34) in his son's eyes.[32] The first anecdote is a tall tale his father used to tell involving a butler in India who manages to serve dinner on time, despite having to shoot a tiger in the dining room. When the room is cleared, he assures his master that 'there will be no discernible traces left of the recent occurrence' (RD, 36). A worthy deed done with becoming stateliness. The second anecdote takes place during a motoring trip as Stevens, Sr chauffeurs two drunken gentlemen. When they insult his employer, he silently – but effectively – rebukes them, and even manages to secure an apology. A noble act, which defends his employer's honour. The last anecdote illustrates the extent to which Stevens's father was willing to subordinate personal feelings in the interest of pro-fessional duty. His son, Leonard, died as a result of an inept military manoeuvre during the Boer War. Ten years later, when the General responsible for this tragic loss of life visits the employer of Stevens, Sr, the butler suppresses his indignation by acting as his valet and providing service 'to the usual standards' (RD, 41).

Stevens aspires to the impossibly high (yet apparently

usual) standards of his father by maintaining his dignity under extremely trying circumstances. The most notable instance of this is during the 1923 conference. Although his father is dying upstairs after a severe stroke, Stevens continues to serve the guests in the smoking room. He passes round the port, indulges the ill-at-ease Reginald Cardinal in some comforting small talk, and even attends to the sore feet of a belligerent French diplomat. By normal yardsticks, the butler's priorities seem perversely awry, but he manages to recast his behaviour as a professional victory:

> if you consider the pressures contingent on me that night, you may not think I delude myself unduly if I go so far as to suggest that I did perhaps display, in the face of everything, at least in some modest degree a 'dignity' worthy of someone like Mr Marshall – or come to that, my father. Indeed, why should I deny it? For all its sad associations, whenever I recall that evening today, I find I do so with a large sense of triumph. (*RD*, 110)

A similar sublimation takes place on a later occasion. Stevens forgoes the opportunity to dissuade Miss Kenton from marrying Mr Benn in order to attend to Lord Darlington and his guests, Herr Ribbentrop and the Prime Minister. It would have taken only a few minutes of the butler's time to say the right words and sway his housekeeper to reconsider. Instead, he dutifully waits outside the dining room ready to be called to provide refreshments for the VIPs, even though Lord Darlington had dismissed him for the night, and Miss Kenton is crying upstairs. Once again, he hides his personal concerns in a fog of self-congratulation:

> as I continued to stand there, a curious thing began to take place; that is to say, a deep feeling of triumph started to well up within me ... I had, after all, just come through an extremely trying evening, throughout which I had managed to preserve a 'dignity in keeping with my position' – and had done so, moreover, in a manner even my father might have been proud of. (*RD*, 227)

So again dignity prevails, and the butler has risen to his father's great heights. But is Stevens's sense of professional triumph simply a displacement of his personal loss in these two instances? The natural response of the reader is to feel abhorrence at the butler's apparent lack of empathy. In most people's eyes, the death of a parent or the loss of a potential marriage partner should take precedence over an employee's prosaic duties. A different perspective is opened up, though, if the question of dignity is approached laterally. Edward de Bono defines dignity spatially in *The Happiness Purpose* (1977). He states that 'A man has dignity *when his image of his own self-space coincides with his real self-space.*'[33] Self-space is the part of a life-space that can be coped with easily. Life-space is the sum of pressures and expectations with which a person is confronted. Happiness, in this system, is attained when the self-space and life-space coincide. Dignity is achieved if the self is able to handle comfortably the demands that are placed upon it.

Now Stevens is convinced that he has indeed achieved dignity in the professional realm. In the trials presented by the conference and the meeting of the VIPs, he has proved himself more than capable of meeting both his own expectations and those of others. The problem is, however, that the image he has of his own self-space in the private sphere is disjunctive with his real self-space. He simply discounts his obligations as a son and as a potential husband. Or, more to the point, he tries to displace these private obligations elsewhere and treat them as interruptions to his public duty. Tries, but fails. As he serves his guests in the smoking room with his father dying upstairs, he twice denies to Reginald Cardinal that he is feeling unwell. When Lord Darlington spots tears in Stevens's eyes, the butler pretends it is the excess sweat of a hard-working day. On the later occasion of the visit of the politicians, Cardinal (who is now a journalist sniffing for a scoop) again asks Stevens how he is bearing up. The butler once more denies his own stressful state.

Denial and displacement of his real feelings are essential if Stevens is to become a butler through and through. 'The great butlers', he announces, 'are great by virtue of their ability to inhabit their professional role and inhabit it to the utmost' (*RD*, 42–43). The word 'inhabit' is telling: the great butler is at home in the part he plays. It *is* home to him, not a temporary lodging. He cannot cast his role aside 'as though it were nothing more than a pantomime costume' (*RD*, 169). Stevens's habitation of his role occupies almost the whole of his self-space: 'it came to be a … matter indeed of dignity, that I did not appear in anything less than my full and proper role' (*RD*, 169). If we take these words of Stevens at their face value, it would appear that his commitment to being a butler has an almost existential fervour. He has made a leap of faith by immersing himself in his profession. Moreover, he has sustained the butler façade even at times of extreme personal anguish. But how authentic is Stevens? Whilst few can quibble at his capacity for butlering – his Prufrockian meticulousness and Jeevesian ingeniousness – his protestations of belief in his professional being sound hollow, precisely because they are so pleading and overwrought. He is always conscious of himself as a butler, therefore he is never able to be natural and spontaneous in his vocation. Like Ono in *An Artist of the Floating World*, Stevens believes that he has acted throughout his life in good faith. But the phrase itself contains a built-in contradiction. If he was a genuine, faithful butler he wouldn't be 'acting' at all. He would simply *be* a butler.

By aligning himself with Lord Darlington, a decision that he deems to be 'loyalty *intelligently* bestowed', Stevens seeks to make this Englishman's home *his* castle. Yet, when it becomes apparent through hindsight that this commitment has unpleasant ideological repercussions, Stevens refuses to accept responsibility for his decision. He appeals: 'How can one possibly be held to blame in any sense because, say, the passage of time has shown that Lord Darlington's efforts were misguided, even foolish?' (*RD*, 201). The recourse to the I-was-only-obeying-orders attitude is what Jean-Paul Sartre designates as 'bad faith'. It is surely no accident that Sartre's well-known illustration of bad faith in *Being and Nothingness* (1943) is a waiter in a café who is only playing at being a waiter, and is unable to simply *be* one.[34] Analogously, Stevens – impressive though his performance is – can only play at being a butler.

Much of Stevens's bad faith is revealed by his habitual lies, to others and to himself, which expose the gap between his self-space and life-space. An example of deceiving others occurs during the hush-hush rendezvous of Ribbentrop, the Prime Minister and Lord Darlington. They are holding secret talks about establishing a *rapprochement* between Britain and Nazi Germany. Reginald Cardinal arrives at Darlington Hall, after a tip-off about the important meeting. He asks Stevens what is going on, but the butler pretends that he doesn't know. He feigns ignorance in order to be discreet. Yet in this instance – given that Stevens is well aware of the mounting criticisms his employer has received for brokering such liaisons – valour would be the better part of discretion. An example of self-deception is Stevens's reflection upon the embarrassing incident when Miss Kenton catches him in his pantry reading a sentimental romance novel. He kids himself with the improbable excuse that perusing such books was 'an extremely efficient way to maintain and develop one's command of the English language' (*RD*, 167). It is as if he needs to convince himself that he has no emotional life, and that any leisure time that comes his way will be devoted to improving his professional capacities.

Not only does he deceive others and himself, but Stevens is also often fully aware that he is telling lies, thus compounding his inauthenticity. He almost accidentally tells the truth when he confesses that he 'did at times gain an incidental enjoyment' (*RD*, 168) from the kind of romance book Miss Kenton caught him reading. He is also unrepentant about why he does so: 'I have chosen to tell white lies[35] ... as the simplest means of avoiding unpleasantness' (*RD*, 126). This last insight is gained at Mortimer's Pond, Dorset. He is meditating about an incident earlier in the day when his car overheated, and he stopped by a large Victorian house to obtain assistance. Luckily, a chauffeur was able to help him by putting some water in the radiator. Whilst chatting, the chauffeur asks Stevens where he worked. Stevens admits to being a butler at Darlington Hall, but strenuously denies ever serving Lord Darlington. At the pond, Stevens ponders why he told this lie, and is reminded of a similar event from a few months ago. On this earlier occasion, he was showing the American couple Mr and Mrs Wakefield around Darlington Hall, when they asked him what it was like working for Lord Darlington (*RD*, 122–24). Again, he denied any association with his former employer.[36] Later on his new employer, Mr Farraday, quizzes Stevens about this deception: 'I mean to say, Stevens, this *is* a genuine old English house, isn't it? That's what I paid for. And you're a genuine old-fashioned English butler, not just some waiter pretending to be one. You're the real thing, aren't you? That's what I wanted, isn't that what I have?' (*RD*, 124). Note the evocation of the Sartrean waiter here, and its connotations of inauthenticity. The third time that Stevens acts duplicitously in relation to his employer occurs when his car breaks down again, this time at Moscombe, near Tavistock. He is offered a room for the night at the Taylors' cottage, where the villagers mistake the butler for a gentleman. Stevens is happy to play along with the charade, and fails to dispel their false impressions. So when Mr Andrews asks him if he has had anything to do with politics, Stevens replies 'Not directly as such … More so before the war perhaps' (*RD*, 187). He evades further questions with more equivocations, but becomes carried away when talking about his impressions of Winston Churchill and Anthony Eden. He has, of course, met these prominent people at Darlington Hall, though not quite in the circumstances envisaged by the villagers. He caps his reminiscences with a theatrical metaphor, by agreeing that it was a 'great privilege, after all, to have been given a part to play, however small, on the world's stage' (*RD*, 188). Prufrock couldn't have put it better.

So Stevens denies Lord Darlington three times – to the Wakefields, the helpful chauffeur and the Moscombe villagers – just as Christ is denied three times in the Bible story. Salman Rushdie picked up on this allusion when he calls Stevens a 'cut-price St. Peter'.[37] What Rushdie didn't notice, however, are the related intertextual jokes about the crowing of cocks that recur

throughout the text. In a bantering exchange towards the beginning of the novel, Farraday asks his butler: 'I suppose it wasn't
you making that crowing noise this morning, Stevens?' To
which Stevens replies, knowing that the sound was made by
some passing gypsies, 'More like swallows than crows, I would
have said, sir. From the migratory aspect' (*RD*, 16). Much later,
when Stevens is about to spend the night at the Coach and
Horses inn at Taunton, the customers predict that he'll be
woken up early in the morning by the sound of the landlord and
his wife arguing. Stevens, who has been practising his bantering
skills for professional reasons, attempts a witticism: 'A local
variation on the cock crow, no doubt' (*RD*, 130). They are not
amused. These allusions to the Gospels substantiate that much
of *The Remains of the Day* is about denial and its corrosive
consequences, a theme linking the novel with *A Pale View of
Hills* and *An Artist of the Floating World*. In the words of Galen
Strawson, the book 'records the accumulating costs of silence;
the way denial spreads its effects, establishing complex diver-
sionary circuitry in the mind.'[38] Stevens wishes to deny his past.
Yet he cannot accept that his time at Darlington Hall was wasted,
or that Lord Darlington was anything other than a benign,
misguided employer worthy of his service. It is because of these
incompatible drives that the novel is 'rich with the contortions it
is possible to go through to rationalize past errors.'[39]

To maintain cognitive consistency, Stevens has to wriggle
and squirm his way out of awkward situations when he is away
from home. In the conversation with the Moscombe villagers,
the butler – whom they believe to be a distinguished visitor – is
asked to identify the mark of a gentleman. This gives Stevens
the opportunity to air some of his views about greatness and
Englishness, and he asserts that dignity is the crucial quality
distinguishing a gentleman from the mass. He is unable to
elaborate, however, as he is interrupted by Harry Smith, a local
socialist. Smith declares: 'Dignity isn't just something gentlemen have. Dignity's something every man and woman in this
country can strive for and get' (*RD*, 185–86). This was why the
war was fought, he goes on to argue, to avoid the world

becoming a place with millions of slaves ruled by a few masters. Unsurprisingly, Stevens does not agree with Smith's democratic definition of dignity, although he does not voice his objections in public. The following day, when local doctor Carlisle drives Stevens back to his Ford with some petrol, they pick up the topic again. Carlisle, who by this time has guessed that Stevens is a butler and not a gentleman, asks him outright about what he thinks dignity is. The butler, relieved at no longer having to pretend, replies laconically: 'It's rather a hard thing to explain in a few words, sir ... But I suspect it comes down to not removing one's clothes in public' (*RD*, 210).

The imagery of clothing is profuse in *The Remains of the Day*. Stevens compares inhabiting his role as a butler with wearing a suit. He declares that 'the great butlers ... wear their professionalism as a decent gentleman will wear his suit'; continentals, on the other hand, 'are like a man who will, at the slightest provocation, tear off his suit and shirt and run about screaming' (*RD*, 43). It is in keeping, therefore, that when he prepares for his West Country motoring trip he wishes to be suitably attired. He wonders 'what sorts of costume[40] were appropriate on such a journey' (*RD*, 10). He has several items to choose from: suits from Lord Darlington and Lord Chalmers, and a lounge suit given to him by Sir Edward Blair in the early 1930s. Thanks to his splendid dress and his dignified demeanour, he is often mistaken for a gentleman during his travels. The landlady at the guest-house in Salisbury believes him to be 'a rather grand visitor' (*RD*, 26). The chauffeur who fixes his car thinks that Stevens is 'a really posh geezer' (*RD*, 119). Virtually the entire village of Moscombe feels privileged to have 'a gentleman like yourself' (*RD*, 183) visit their locality.

Because of these mistaken apprehensions, Stevens undergoes a displacement of identity. No longer the servant, he is perceived as the master. Such masquerading was not uncommon among domestic staff, according to Pamela Horn: 'The social aspirations of some of the vainer men-servants made them vulnerable to the temptation of impersonation, as did the opportunity for gain that this might also bestow.'[41] Stevens even refers to this phenomenon himself when he runs through a list of famous servants from his past, and mentions 'Mr Wilkinson, valet-butler to Mr John Campbell, with his well-known repertoire of impersonations of prominent gentlemen' (RD, 18). There is no suggestion, however, that Stevens is hoping to gain anything – other than a few minutes of reflected glory – by being taken for a gentleman. In fact, as M. Griffiths observes, 'he is never more lost and dis-located than when ... he takes on the persona of Darlington'.[42] So why does he deceive himself and allow others to be deceived? The answer can only be that Stevens's car journey has precipitated an acute identity crisis. For some time before the trip he has questioned his investment in the role of butler. Now that an American has taken over Darlington Hall, the manservant is little more than an exhibit in a museum. Even his daily duties have deteriorated to the extent that he is now making the kind of errors for which he excused his father in his advanced years. Additionally, the disgrace into which Lord Darlington fell after the Second World War due to a tabloid newspaper exposé means that Stevens's entire life has been devoted to an unworthy cause. The butler suddenly finds himself to be a displaced person.

Stevens struggles to hold on to his sense of self at Mortimer's Pond by redefining what he means by greatness in his profession. He adds a further stipulation to the Hayes Society's criteria of dignity and attachment to a distinguished household, namely the display of loyalty to a worthy master: 'A "great" butler can only be, surely, one who can point to his years of service and say that he has applied his talents to serving a great gentleman – and through the latter, to serving humanity' (RD, 117). Stevens served Lord Darlington for thirty-five years because he realised at a certain stage of his career that 'This employer embodies all that I find noble and admirable' (RD, 200). He placed his trust in his master, believing that a butler can recognise worthiness when he sees it, even if he is ignorant of the wider political matters in which his employer is engaged. There is something enticing about Stevens's logic here. Without doubt, it is noble and admirable to serve a just cause. Of course, in the final analysis Lord Darlington's sympathies were foolishly directed to unjust Nazi recipients. But does this entail, given Stevens's ignorance of the political sphere, that his own loyalty to his master was misguided? His singleminded devotion makes sense from the Japanese perspective. Chie Nakane, author of *Japanese Society* – a foremost study in the field – asserts that the saying 'No man can serve two masters' is the 'golden rule of Japanese ethics'[43] and is observed wholeheartedly. The notion of devotedness to one's superiors is deeply ingrained in the English psyche, too. The medieval knight was expected to serve his military commander and, through the chivalric code, the lady he championed.[44] One of the rarer meanings of the word 'dignity' is to be found in astrology. There it denotes the increased influence and virtue gained by a planet on account of its benevolent alignment with other planets and aspects of the zodiac. By aligning himself with Lord Darlington, it is indeed Stevens's aim to achieve dignity in this sense.

Does Lord Darlington deserve Stevens's dedication? The answer to this depends largely on how we weigh his gentlemanliness against his flawed political judgement. That Lord Darlington was a gentleman is clear, and he upholds an ideal that is evergreen throughout the history of English society: 'It is impossible to think of the character of England without thinking also of the character of the gentleman.'[45] And what is the crucial component of the character of the English gentleman? Character itself; good conduct; modesty. Such were the attributes of great English gentlemen such as Sir Walter Raleigh, Sir Philip Sidney and Lord Montgomery. Also necessary is a cultivated amateurism, especially in political affairs, as professionalism reeks of proclivity. Lord Darlington certainly meets these criteria. He is, as the phrase goes, a decent chap. *The Remains of the Day*, however, implicitly challenges the efficacy of these traits in a world that is in the hands of unscrupulous politicians. Darlington's insistence on maintaining a sense of decency towards a defeated enemy looks decidedly outdated in an era when the technology of modern warfare threatens mass destruction. He regrets that the Germans, especially Herr Bremann, suffer considerably from the harsh reparations imposed by the Allies after the First World War. But while his empathy is laudable, his ideology is laughable. Hence the contradictions in his claim that 'We [himself and Bremann] treated each other decently over six months of shelling each other. He was a gentleman doing his job and I bore him no malice' (RD, 73). Similarly, Darlington's reserve and understatement are no assets for the purposes of negotiation. At the 1923 conference, the forthrightness of the American, Lewis, and the cunning of the Frenchman, Dupont, drown out his quiet English pleas for honour and mutual tolerance.

From the outside, Stevens's untiring devotion to duty – at the expense of his own welfare – can appear almost monstrous in its inflexibility. Yet the butler is persuasive and presents a plausible set of ethical motivations for his actions (plausible, that is, within his own admittedly limited moral horizons). He argues that his service to Lord Darlington was guided by loyalty and trust, and that his employer's dalliance with Nazi Germany was his own business. A butler's task is to serve high tea, polish the silver and dust the family portraits, not to 'meddle in the great affairs of the nation' (RD, 199). It is unreasonable to expect a servant to criticise his employer, especially in matters which are not of his concern: 'Throughout the years I served him, it was he and he alone who weighed up evidence and judged it best to proceed in the way he did, while I simply confined myself, quite properly, to affairs within my own professional realm' (RD, 201). There is some substance to Stevens's claim that it wasn't his employer's fault that things turned out as they did. For a start, Lord Darlington was not the only one in the 1930s who believed that the best way to avoid another worldwide conflict was to contain the aggression of Germany by granting concessions.[46] Appeasement was British government policy right up to 1938 and Neville Chamberlain's infamous Munich agreement. Many top-rank Germans, including Hitler, were pro-British at the time, and neither Stevens nor Lord Darlington could possibly have known about the brutal annexations and exterminations the Nazis were to unleash. Also, it is easy to construct

counterfactual hypotheses to put Stevens's devotion to Darlington in a new light. How would we feel, for instance, if his self-
abnegation had been in the service of a Winston Churchill? Or
to a Lord Darlington who refused to have anything to do with a
belligerent Nazi state? In these circumstances, his life would
seem worthy and well spent, and yet his actions and beliefs
would be the same.

The quandary of how to evaluate Stevens is rendered even
more problematic if we accept an orientalised reading of the
novel. From a Japanese point of view, the whole concept of self-
space is different from that of the West. The very word for 'self'
in Japanese, *jibun*, signifies 'self-part'. That is to say, it does not
refer to an isolated, sovereign ego, but to a personal integer
within a larger whole.[47] The individual's self-space is positioned
in various vertical groupings and relationships, where loyalty to
one's superior (whether it be in the family or in business) is a
paramount virtue.[48] If Stevens is interpreted in this context,
then his actions (or failure to act in some circumstances) can be
construed much less negatively. For instance, the critics Anthony
Thwaite and Hermione Lee see analogies between the butler and
the heroic *ronin* of Japanese legend. The 'Tale of the Forty-seven
Ronin' tells of the loyalty and selflessness of a group of *samurai*
who were left masterless following the death of Lord Asano
Naganori. They obtained revenge in 1703 by killing the court
official, Kira Yoshinaka, responsible for their master's death.
The Edo shogunate decreed that all but one of their number, the
eldest, should commit *harakiri* – which they dutifully performed.
Their grave is still revered today, and their story is commonly
cited as distilling the Japanese spirit – just as the bravery at
Agincourt is often invoked as an index of Englishness. Judged by
these standards, Stevens's conduct seems admirable, even though
the consequences of his actions are abhorrent.

Whatever the verdict on Stevens and his gentlemanly
impersonations, there is no doubting the bravura of the ventri-
loquism in *The Remains of the Day* as a whole. Hermione Lee
congratulated the novel for its 'extraordinary act of mimicry, [it
is] an impeccably professional miming of the thoughts of an

impeccable professional.'[49] Ishiguro's reproduction of the timbre and tenor of 'butlerspeak'[50] does indeed seem effortless. What makes the feat even more distinctive is that it is the mime of a mime. Stevens impersonates a diction, register and style that is not his own. In his seminal essay 'Of Mimicry and Man', postcolonial critic Homi K. Bhabha proposes that colonisers desire the mimicry of the colonised to feel comfortable with an 'other' who is almost the same, but not quite.[51] Although the coloniser/colonised relation does not pertain in this case, it can be mapped on to the class imbalance existing between Lord Darlington and Stevens. The butler mimics a language above his station to create the impression of being the 'gentlemen's gentleman'. Yet despite his general fluency in the language of his superiors, there is something absurd about Stevens's speech. He strives too hard to be formal and correct, especially in his vocabulary; for example, 'Southern Africa' (*RD*, 41) and 'Association Football' (*RD*, 18). The strain is also there in the syntax, which is alternately stiff and slithery. A random sentence can illustrate this: 'When he [the landlord] inquired whether I had dined, I asked him to serve me with a sandwich in my room, which proved a perfectly satisfactory option as far as supper was concerned' (*RD*, 129). Much of the last clause is redundant, and could be replaced with a simple 'which proved satisfactory'. Stevens makes such errors because he is speaking a displaced language, a discourse that is not his own. Patterns of speech innate in Lord Darlington have to be acquired by Stevens, and continually reinforced. The result is the butler's 'plonking but catching, sub-Jeevesian, PC Plod Witness Box English.'[52] Like a constable in court, Stevens cannot talk with ease because his mouth is full of words. After the war, his 'superannuatedly genteel'[53] expressions are even more out of place.

The pressure on Stevens to pretend that he is complicit with the class he serves is one reason why he speaks English as if it were a foreign language. But there is another factor. This is connected with the butler's attempt to maintain a self-space in which all traces of a personal life have been extinguished. The dictates of his profession, which values unobtrusiveness to the point of imperceptibility, dampen what is already a subdued temperament. The result is an extreme periphrasis. A good illustration of this is a comic episode arising during the 1923 conference. Stevens's preparations for this event are so demanding, there is 'little room for any "beating about the bush"' (*RD*, 78). He therefore solves the problem of his father's increasing frailty by giving him a trolley to push around Darlington Hall. Once the conference is in full progress, Stevens's time becomes even more precious. He is therefore somewhat taxed when Lord Darlington requests a special favour. Darlington wants the butler to inform Reginald Cardinal of the 'facts of life'. An embarrassing task at the best of times; even more so when the addressee is twenty-three. After some deliberation, Stevens approaches Cardinal when he is alone in the library. His attempt to broach the prickly topic is amusingly inept: 'Sir David wishes you to know, sir, that ladies and gentlemen differ in several key respects' (*RD*, 84). The butler has a second opportunity to tackle Cardinal when he finds him walking in the garden. Again, however, Stevens beats about the bush – a rhododendron bush, to be specific, from which he suddenly emerges to catch the young man unawares. Despite the advantage of surprise, he still cannot quite come to the point, and gestures haplessly to some nearby geese and the 'glories of nature' (*RD*, 90).

Stevens's euphemisms and circumlocutions form a 'linguistic mask'.[54] This mask hides his feelings, and his inward self, behind the façade of the fastidious valet. It is a false face he has fashioned over many years, but it is far from perfect. A great deal of the pathos of the novel lies in the reader's recognition of the clumsy skull beneath the capable skin.

From time to time the mask slips, to reveal a much less even Stevens. In the Prologue of *The Remains of the Day*, the butler's kerfuffle about the inadequate staff-plan is a smoke-screen. It hides the real reason why he agrees with Farraday's suggestion of a motoring trip to the West Country: namely, to visit Miss Kenton, and reignite their relationship. The former housekeeper at Darlington Hall is the only person in the book who is able to pierce the butler's shield of dignity. Shortly after joining the staff of the stately home in the 1920s, Miss Kenton tries to enrich and expand Stevens's self-space, only to be continually rebuffed. Gabriele Annan portrays their relationship in unflattering terms: 'if porcupines had a mating dance it would look like this.'[55] At first they communicate purely as professionals, but then Miss Kenton approaches Stevens more personally by bringing him some flowers to brighten up his parlour. He curtly informs her that 'this is not a room of entertainment' (RD, 52). From this point on they begin to have many arguments. These are ostensibly about petty work matters – a dust-pan left carelessly in the hall, a misplaced ornament – but underlying them is an emotional tension. Miss Kenton thinks, fairly, that Stevens's father is too old for the job; Stevens counter-attacks by continually fussing, unfairly, about the housekeeper's own shortcomings. This antagonism culminates in a falling-out with each other during the 1923 conference, when they resort to communication by written notes. A further major spat erupts in the 1930s, when they disagree over Lord Darlington's prejudiced dismissal of two Jewish maids. Miss Kenton is incensed at losing good staff on dubious moral grounds, whilst Stevens predictably (and unthinkingly) sides with his master. Later, when Lord Darlington himself admits that what he had done was wrong, Stevens insinuates that he was as upset about the dismissal of the maids as the housekeeper. Miss Kenton is irate: 'Why, Mr Stevens, why, why, why do you always have to *pretend*' (RD, 154). A good question, which the butler cannot answer. He merely laughs, and makes a sheepish exit.

It is exchanges such as this that have led to charges that Stevens is 'emotionally deaf'[56] or 'made of cardboard'.[57] Whilst it is true that the butler's life lacks personal amplitude, it is going too far to say that he has no feelings. There are several moments when the mask of composure slips to reveal the human face beneath. He is visibly upset, although he tries to hide it, when his father dies and when he learns of Miss Kenton's acceptance of her acquaintance's marriage proposal. And during the romance book incident, when Stevens and Miss Kenton come closest to revealing their feelings for each other, he is aware of an intensity: 'suddenly the atmosphere underwent a peculiar change – almost as though the two of us had been suddenly thrust on to some other plane of being altogether' (*RD*, 166–67). Despite their many skirmishes, the butler and the housekeeper establish a rapport. They even meet occasionally to share some cocoa at the end of a long hard day. Stevens, of course, views this ritual as 'overwhelmingly professional in tone' (*RD*, 147) and not in the least bit social. By this time Miss Kenton is unmistakably in love with Stevens, though the butler does not realise this until many years after she has left Darlington Hall. This is her tragedy. It is even later when Stevens comes to understand that he was in love with her. That is his.

Towards the end of the book, Stevens meets Miss Kenton, or Mrs Benn as she has been for many years, in the tea lounge of the Rose Garden Hotel at Little Compton. Now that the former housekeeper is about to become a grandmother, she concedes that for a long time she was unhappy in her marriage. She even tells him that she sometimes thinks she made a mistake leaving her job for her husband, and might have been better off with Stevens. However, she then goes on to say: 'One can't be forever dwelling on what might have been. One should realize one has as good as most, perhaps better, and be grateful' (*RD*, 239). She is content to make the most of what remains of her day. It is at this point that Stevens's façade crumbles and he is left emotionally exposed: 'Indeed – why should I not admit it? – at that moment, my heart was breaking' (*RD*, 239). Significantly, though, he only admits it to himself, and not to Miss Kenton.[58] Yet, ironically, for once his reservoir of reserve serves him well. If he said what he really felt to Miss Kenton, at this minute to midnight, it would in all likelihood devastate her. And for what? She has a grandchild to look forward to. All he can offer her is more cocoa and dust-pans. Instead, he displays a little of the dignity he has aspired to for so long, and does the gentlemanly thing by reassuring her:

> 'You're very correct, Mrs Benn. As you say, it is too late to turn back the clock. Indeed, I would not be able to rest if I thought such ideas were the cause of unhappiness for you

and your husband. We must each of us, as you point out, be grateful for what we *do* have. And from what you tell me, Mrs Benn, you have reason to be contented. (*RD*, 239)

So Stevens, at last, shows some empathy. He has stepped out of his shrunken self-space to inhale the heady air of somebody else's life-space. And like Ono in *An Artist of the Floating World*, he realises that 'there is certainly a satisfaction and dignity to be gained in coming to terms with the mistakes one has made in the course of one's life' (*AFW*, 124–25). After this final meeting with Miss Kenton/Mrs Benn, Stevens concludes his journey with a visit to the seaside town of Weymouth. There, sitting on a pier bench, he has a chance to reconcile himself with his professional mistakes when he talks with a stranger. A crowd has gathered to see the lights come on, and the man – an ex-butler himself – tells Stevens that 'for a great many people, the evening was the best part of the day' (*RD*, 240). They chat amiably for a while about matters of service, but then Stevens – tired and confused after his long motoring trip – breaks down and unburdens himself about his errant employer:

Lord Darlington wasn't a bad man. He wasn't a bad man at all. And at least he had the privilege of being able to say at the end of his life that he made his own mistakes. His lordship was a courageous man. He chose a certain path in life, it proved to be a misguided one, but there, he chose it, he can say that at least. As for myself, I cannot even claim that. You see, I *trusted*. I trusted in his lordship's wisdom. All those years I served him, I trusted I was doing something worthwhile. I can't even say I made my own mistakes. Really – one has to ask oneself – what dignity is there in that? (*RD*, 243)

This is an illumination for Stevens, a recognition that he has wasted his life by blindly trusting his superior. Such loyalty, he now sees, is undignified if it is not nourished by vigilant self-examination and self-respect. Not long after this conversation there is a literal illumination when the pier lights are switched on, and Stevens determines to 'try to make the best of what remains of my day' (*RD*, 244). Even in the midst of his epiphany, however, he reasserts his old view that retainers such as himself must resign themselves to fates determined by their masters. Old butlers never die; they can only stand and wait. The outcome of the book, then, is ambivalent. On the one hand, what lies in store for Stevens in the future is simply 'work, work and more work' (*RD*, 237) at Darlington Hall. It's who he is, it's what he does, it's what he's always done, and it's what he always intends to do. Worse still, he will be working for an employer who treats the stately home as a theme-park rather than as a hub of world affairs. On the other hand, Stevens has had his moment of *anagnorisis*. He has felt the heart beating beneath the black tail-coat, and is ready to return home to banter with Mr Farraday.

So what has Stevens learnt from his journey? He understands now that dignity is nothing without empathy. He realises that dignity is not just a matter of knowing one's place, but of feeling congruent with the self in whatever place one happens to be. It is therefore the contrary of displacement, where the self is insecure when removed from its moorings. And what is empathy? Empathy is the ability to put one's self in the place of the other.

On 13 June 1956, when the last British troops left the Suez Canal zone – an event marking the definitive decline of the Empire – an Army spokesman said the departure was made 'quietly and with dignity'.[59] Perhaps this was the last occasion when dignity was held to be an unquestioned national virtue. This is also the summer when Stevens undertakes his motoring trip. Yet, as Salman Rushdie observed, the crisis is not mentioned explicitly at all in the novel, 'even though the Suez débâcle marked the end of a certain kind of Britain whose passing is a subject of the novel'.[60] Are we therefore entitled to read the novel in terms of something that it does not discuss? It is tempting to do so, especially when we compare the absence of references to Suez in *The Remains of the Day* to the absence of references to the atomic bomb in *A Pale View of Hills*. Both are 'doughnut novels', as Joseph Coates puts it. Not only are they 'about people whose lives have a hole in the center – lives whose meaning is defined by events that do *not* occur';[61] they are also set in periods when historically important events *have* occurred, but are not mentioned.

If *The Remains of the Day* is seen as an allegory of the decline of the British Empire, then it can be interpreted both pessimistically and optimistically. Stevens's failure is a fable on the passing of a certain conception of Englishness; but it is a death many would not wish to mourn. On a more personal level, Stevens's reevaluation of himself and his life leaves him in a rather bleak situation, alone on a bench at a pier in Weymouth. Yet at least he is now willing to acknowledge the human warmth he has avoided for so long. So what remains? The vestiges of a dead Empire, or the chance to make amends? In the words of McLandburgh Wilson:

> Twixt the optimist and the pessimist
> The difference is droll;
> The optimist sees the doughnut,
> But the pessimist sees the hole.[62]

The Unconsoled

ISHIGURO'S first three novels explore similar territory: the essence of national identity; the relation of the individual to significant historical events; the search for excellence in one's chosen career; the possibility that a life can be wasted through a change in external circumstance. These issues arise out of the struggles of a first-person narrator to come to terms with his or her past. Inevitably, then, the novels are all engaged with memory. And memory, by its very nature, is uncertain, quivering, subject to erasures and displacements. As Etsuko says towards the end of her own recollections in *A Pale View of Hills*: 'Memory, I realise, can be an unreliable thing; often it is heavily coloured by the circumstances in which one remembers, and no doubt this applies to certain of the recollections I have gathered here' (*PVH*, 156).

Indeed, memory is so unreliable in *A Pale View of Hills* that the reader cannot be certain that Sachiko and Mariko existed at all. They may be part of a fantasy projected by a mentally disturbed Etsuko to absolve herself of blame for neglect of her own child, Keiko. The clues to this interpretation, apart from the obvious parallels between herself and Sachiko, lie in various inconsistencies that pepper the text. For instance, in the space of a couple of pages Etsuko contradicts herself about when she first approached Setsuko to express concern about Mariko. She prefaces her recounting of the incident by referring to 'one afternoon' (*PVH*, 13) when she saw Sachiko near the housing precinct. After her conversation, however, she says: 'The river that morning was still quite high and flowing swiftly after the rainy season a few weeks earlier' (*PVH*, 16). There are other inconsistencies: does Etsuko visit Sachiko at Mrs Fujiwara's noodle shop in the afternoon (*PVH*, 23) or morning (*PVH*, 26)? Why does she express contradictory opinions of Frank on the same day? (*PVH*, 69 and 81).[1] The answer can only be because her memory is unreliable, a fact with which she readily agrees: 'It is possible that my memory of these events will have grown hazy with time, that things did not happen in quite the way they came back to me today' (*PVH*, 41).

Hazy, unreliable memories bedevil Masuji Ono, too, in *An Artist of the Floating World*. Like Etsuko, he concedes that 'with repeated telling … accounts begin to take on a life of their own' (*AFW*, 72). Unlike Etsuko, however, Ono tends to place too much trust in his recollections, even when there is ample evidence to disprove his version of events. The litmus test is his insistence that he knew Dr Saito, his daughter Noriko's father-in-law, for over sixteen years. More importantly, he swears that Saito knew him and was aware of his reputation as an important artist. Setsuko, his eldest daughter, directly challenges this, and avows that 'Dr Saito was never so familiar with Father's career' (*AFW*, 193). She bases this on the refusal of Saito's son, Taro, to substantiate Ono's claim. The importance of this dispute is that it casts doubt upon the validity of some of Ono's other claims, particularly those in which his guilty past is at stake. He swears that Setsuko advised him to take some preventative measures before Noriko's marriage negotiations. That is why he visited Kuroda and Matsuda, to obtain their assurances that they would not let him down if approached by a private investigator. She denies it. His uncertainty about whether his former associates will cooperate results in his own garbled confession at the *miai* itself, which baffles those present. Ono cannot even be sure about his own past, and manipulates his recollections to feed his bloated sense of self-importance. As Nigel Hunt says, 'We … see with Ono … that memory is always subject to reinterpretation… we cannot help but feel that the "floating world" – the world which breathes and expires with the change of light – is our world.'[2]

The Remains of the Day is Ishiguro's most sophisticated treatment of the vagaries and vanities of memory, as its protagonist both represses the past and seeks to rewrite it. At one point he expresses disdain for those butlers who train themselves to answer random questions like a 'Memory Man at the music hall' (*RD*, 35). When he himself is tested in this manner by three of Lord Darlington's guests, he replies to each question: 'I'm very sorry, sir ... but I am unable to be of assistance on this matter' (*RD*, 195). Refusing to memorise trivia is one thing; selective recall about the turning-points of his own life is something else altogether. Yet time and time again, the butler distorts the truth. Whilst recounting an argument with Miss Kenton about mistakes made by his father in the course of his daily duties, Stevens attributes the following statement to his housekeeper: 'These errors may be trivial in themselves ... but you must yourself realize their larger significance' (*RD*, 59). On further reflection, however, he believes that Miss Kenton would not have spoken so forthrightly that day, and that it was Lord Darlington who uttered those words about his father. This error, though trivial in itself, has a larger significance. It causes the reader to wonder about the extent of Stevens's collusion in his misremembered past. Is he deliberately falsifying events to himself to minimise his sense of culpability in wasting his life? The answer is probably yes, as is illustrated by another displaced memory connected with Miss Kenton. The butler recalls standing in a corridor outside Miss Kenton's room after she has heard about the death of her aunt. Although convinced that his housekeeper is crying, he is afraid to knock and express his sympathy. Later, whilst driving in Cornwall, he dwells again upon the image of himself standing outside that door, 'transfixed by indecision' (*RD*, 212), and reconsiders when this circumstance happened. It transpires that the memory belongs to a different occasion altogether, to the night when the Prime Minister and Ribbentrop visited Lord Darlington. This is also the evening when Miss Kenton informed Stevens that she had accepted a proposal of marriage from her acquaintance, Mr Benn. Stevens – absorbed solely with the momentous events of state taking place upstairs – gives a brusque response to the housekeeper's news. Towards the end of the evening, Stevens passes Miss Kenton's room, and it is then that he is convinced that she is crying. He fails to knock, and thereby abandons all possibility of a future relationship with Miss Kenton by failing to empathise with her at a moment of need. What this displacement of memory shows is Stevens's avoidance of emotional responsibility. He transposes his personal neglect in a matter of the heart (his unwillingness to reassure Miss Kenton about her marital decision) to a situation where the housekeeper has been upset by an external cause (the death of her aunt). By juggling between the two occasions, he is able to displace his regret at not saying something to 'ease her burden a little' (RD, 177).

The Unconsoled differs greatly in some respects from Ishiguro's previous three novels, and in it the theme of memory is managed very differently. Bad experiences from the past are no longer repressed – as they are by Etsuko, Ono and Stevens – but erupt into the consciousness of the central protagonist and are projected outwards into his circumstances. The plot is this: Ryder, an internationally acclaimed concert pianist, is the victim of an inexplicable amnesia. He arrives on a Tuesday at an unnamed town, somewhere in the heart of Europe, without a schedule. But this is not just another venue on his tour: it is the home of his partner, Sophie, and child, Boris, facts that have curiously slipped his mind. The book charts the myriad inter-ruptions to his preparations for a concert on the following Thursday evening by a populace who are convinced that Ryder will be able to rejuvenate the city's declining fortunes. It also follows the disintegration of his family life, and their failure to find a place called home. As if in compensation for his bad fortune and deficiencies of memory, Ryder is blessed with unusual extrasensory perceptions. He overhears conversations well out of listening range; has knowledge of other people's actions when not present; and can access the memories, fantasies and thoughts of other people.[3] Take Stephan's first visit to Miss Collins in Chapter 5. Although Ryder remains outside in the car, he is able to describe the interior of the building at the back of the drawing room, the chat which takes place there, and even the inner dispositions of the two speakers.

What is happening here? To grasp how it meshes with the logic of *The Unconsoled* as a whole, I will examine the dream-like distortions of events, space and time in the novel, with particular reference to Freud's concept of displacement. Then I will consider how the book displaces Ryder's anxieties on to the musicians he meets in the town and his significant others. Lastly, I will look at the text as fantasy and as a postmodernist work, to elucidate how it apes the elisions and projections of dreams for its unique mixing of memory and desire.

Whilst telling their stories, the memories of Ishiguro's unreliable first-person narrators display many mergings and meanderings. Digressions and evasions are frequent, and their narratives link episodes with the hidden cunning of a free-associative analysis. The novels invite psychoanalytical readings, and many of Freud's classic ideas – particularly that of displacement – are relevant for grappling with their intricacies. Displacement has a specific benefit within Freudian dream theory. It serves to allay emotional anxiety by substituting one idea or object or person for another within the sequence of fantasised events. It does this in two ways, according to Freud. Firstly, a latent element is substituted by something not directly connected with itself. This is almost a form of allusion. Secondly, the item of psychic importance is transferred from a serious element to a trivial one, thus defamiliarising the dream and producing an off-centre effect.[4] Those aspects of the dream remembered and recounted by the patient (the manifest content) conceal a deeper, hidden meaning (the latent content), which is recovered by the analyst. Dreams are therefore like literary texts: they must be interpreted on several levels. The analyst, like the critic, looks specifically at the operations that conceal meaning through symbolisation. Displacement is one such activity. The other main one is condensation, Freud's term for the scrambling of several elements into a single overdetermined entity. The literary equivalent of displacement and condensation are the figures of speech called metonymy and metaphor.

Daily experience divulges many displacement phenomena. Freud refers to the spinster or bachelor who transfers their emotions to animals or hobbies; the lover who finds bliss in a lingering clasp of hands; and the soldier who gives his life for a flag. All of these are easily understood within their various social settings. When displacements occur in dreams, however, they are less easy to decode. Freud explains the dreamwork of displacement by disentangling a young woman's dream of a butcher and a cook. He shows, with his singular ingenuity, how the dream has its origin in the verbal events of daily life, which are distorted and decontextualised. He concludes that this dream, whose manifest content appears to be about a trite shopping expedition, hides a latent distrust of the process of psycho-analysis itself. The essential insight Freud gathers from this is that the 'dream is, as it were, centred elsewhere; its content is arranged about elements which do not constitute the central point of the dream-thoughts.'[5] With this in mind, we can return to Ishiguro's *The Unconsoled* to try to make some sense of its own decentredness and dismemberments, and its revolt against Aristotelian notions of unity.

A dreamlike sequence acts as the climax of Part One of *The Unconsoled*. Ryder is asleep in his hotel room when Hoffman phones him and asks to see him urgently in the lobby. Ryder goes down in his dressing-gown, and the officious hotel manager persuades him to attend a late-night reception – unprepared as he is – in a large house across town. The guests do not seem to notice that Ryder is still wearing his night clothes, nor do they take any particular interest in the musician. They are all more concerned with the recent death of Brodsky's dog, a subject inspiring a number of bizarre, impromptu eulogies by various citizens of the town. The moment comes when Ryder is expected to make a contribution to the proceedings. He climbs on to his chair, making sure that his dressing-gown is fastened, then delivers his opening line: 'Collapsing curtain rails! Poisoned rodents! Misprinted score sheets!' (*U*, 145). This turns out to be his speech in its entirety, for he is then distracted by Miss Collins, who engages him in a lengthy private conversation. The following day, despite his poor performance, Ryder's speech is greeted by Hoffman with rapturous praise: 'Ah, that was such a marvellously witty address! The whole town is talking of nothing else this morning!' (*U*, 155). This episode displays many of the features associated with dreams. There are the outlandish, illogical events, such as the visit to a reception in the middle of the night, and the exaggerated grief about the dog. Then there is Ryder's fear of public exposure, signalled by the wearing of the dressing-gown, which is undercut by the neglect he receives at the function. And there is a noticeable degree of wish-fulfilment in the success of Ryder's eight-word speech.

Such dreamlike features occur throughout the novel and undermine its stability. Whilst preparing the book, Ishiguro wrote a series of short stories that were not intended for publication but were 'dry-runs' for the displaced world he was creating. Some of the episodes retain this feel of being self-contained set-pieces. Here are three examples. In Chapter 23, after two days of interruptions and postponements, Ryder is finally able to prepare for his piano performance when Hoffman shows him to a practice room. Unfortunately, the space is nothing other than a toilet cubicle into which a piano has been squeezed. Ryder complains to Hoffman about the inadequacy of this arrangement, and so is taken to a hut in the country – but this is little more than an undecorated garden shed (*U*, 356). In Chapter 25, Ryder meets Brodsky in the town cemetery, and the pianist is recognised by a man attending a funeral. He is invited to join the ceremony, and quickly becomes the main point of interest among the other mourners. Somebody even hands Ryder a piece of cake and a peppermint, as the open grave is forgotten. In Chapter 30, Brodsky and his bike are caught up in a serious car accident not long before the Thursday night concert, at which he is scheduled to make his own crucial musical comeback. A doctor at the scene decides that his leg must be amputated, and uses an old hacksaw found in somebody's car boot for the operation. Undeterred by the loss of a limb, Brodsky later hobbles out on to the stage with the help of an ironing-board as crutch. There is a level of surreality in these events which recalls the work of Max

Ernst or Max Wall. The collage of toilets, peppermints and hacksaws is far removed from what was assumed to be the social and historical fidelity of Ishiguro's first three novels. This is a narrative that cannot be naturalised, without recourse to the topsy-turvy twists of dreams.

One of the most prominent dream elements of *The Unconsoled*, as the toilet cubicle episode demonstrates, is the displacement of space. The unnamed town through which Ryder wanders has the sinister narrow alleys of a painting by Giorgio di Chirico and the impossible geography of a print by M. C. Escher. Ryder is permanently lost in its loops and windings, and is continually asking for directions. In Chapter 4, when Ryder and Boris are following Sophie back to their apartment, they end up in the countryside, waiting for a bus that is never likely to arrive. In Chapter 17, the musician asks a car park attendant how to find the Karwinsky Gallery, and is instructed to follow a red car that has just set off there. He tails the car through miles and miles of open fields, then round numerous hair pin bends as he climbs mountainous terrain. The journey takes so long he is obliged to stop at a service station for refreshments. Afterwards, he manages to spot the red car again. He then drives through 'vast expanses of farmland' (*U*, 257) before finally arriving at the Gallery, only to discover that it is the same building where he had attended the reception the night before with Hoffman. Furthermore, it turns out to be next door to the hotel where he is staying.

The Unconsoled is full of such excursions that collapse back in on themselves. As Pico Iyer states, the novel traces 'an odd, sepulchral, maze-like journey through a nameless European country with no point of reference save the North Road, the South Road, the Old Town.'[6] Valentine Cunningham refers to the 'deterring labyrinth'[7] of the town. Like most mazes and labyrinths, the town has many circularities and dead ends. When Ryder visits his old apartment with Boris in Chapter 15 to retrieve a toy, they end up wandering round and round the vast walkways of the immense high-rise housing estate. Ryder suspects that it is 'perfectly possible that we could walk in circles indefinitely' (*U*, 212). This echoes his endless rotation around the guests at the first reception, none of whom seemed to recognise him or think his dressing-gown unusual. The book even ends in a loop, with Ryder orbiting round the O-shaped suburbs of the town on a circular tram. There is at least one episode where Ryder comes to a complete dead end. In Chapter 26, after Hoffman has dropped him off from his car near the concert hall, the musician is lost and dawdles down a street blocked off by a brick wall across its entire breadth. There are no openings. A woman emerging from a gift-shop explains that the obstruction is a folly that has become a tourist attraction. Ryder is furious, and vents his anger: 'if I may say so, this wall is quite typical of this town. Utterly preposterous obstacles everywhere' (*U*, 388). He considers using the wall as a symbol in his important speech to the townsfolk later that evening. If it is a symbol, it is a displaced one. As with the case of Stevens and the rhododendron bush in *The Remains of the Day*, an idiom is squeezed to the point where it almost becomes literal. Ryder is indeed, at this point, virtually banging his head against a brick wall.

Although the novel is set in a town somewhere in continental Europe, Ryder's English past continually displaces his present environment. When he moves into his hotel room at the very beginning of the novel, he is struck by a strong feeling of familiarity: 'The room I was now in, I realised, was the very room that had served as my bedroom during the two years my parents and I had lived at my aunt's house on the borders of England and Wales' (*U*, 16). In Chapter 15, when he peers into the lounge of his old apartment in the high-rise estate he visits with Boris, he realises that it is the same as the Manchester parlour from his childhood. The buildings and landscape keep melting into something else, in a Daliesque way. Similarly, although the town is populated with people bearing non-Anglo-Saxon names (Karl Pedersen, Per Gustavsson, Horst Jannings and so on), Ryder nevertheless keeps coming across old English friends. Geoffrey Saunders, whom he hasn't seen since schooldays, emerges from one of the city's numerous blind alleys in Chapter 4. Boarding a tram in the town in Chapter 12, Ryder is surprised to discover that the ticket-inspector is Fiona Roberts, a girl from his Worcestershire primary school. The central European state is palpably a displaced England of his memory and imagination.

These distortions of space in *The Unconsoled* disorient the reader as well as Ryder. In many ways, Ryder is himself a kind of reader, struggling to make sense of the text in which he is trapped. It is a text in which time is dislocated, too. Temporal compression is showcased very early on in the book, when Ryder takes the hotel elevator up to his room with Gustav. The elderly porter gives the musician a long disquisition on the job of portering and his special rules for handling luggage. This occupies four pages. Ryder then notices that Miss Stratmann is also in the lift, and talks with her about his schedule for almost another three pages. Eventually the elevator reaches its destination, having travelled a distance that can only be incommensurate with the time it took to get there. Conversely, the elasticity of time is at work in Chapter 11, when Ryder meets some journalists who wish to take some photographs of the musician. Ryder sits Boris down in a café with a cake, and promises him: 'Okay, I won't be long … I'll just go and see these people, then come right back' (*U*, 165). He does not return until Chapter 14. In between he overhears a conspiratorial confab between the two journalists; poses for some photographs immediately outside the restaurant; takes a lengthy tram-ride into the countryside; climbs a steep hill to the Sattler Building, where more photographs are taken; introduces himself to Christoff, who leads him back down the hill to his car; and witnesses a sustained dispute at a small roadside greasy spoon between Christoff and fellow musicians about 'the circular dynamic in Kazan' (*U*, 201) and other compositional matters. The same 'circular dynamic' informs Ishiguro's text. Ryder escapes from the chaos of the café through a small door into the kitchen, and then clambers through a broom cupboard leading him back to the café from where he first started. Boris greets Ryder with a laconic 'Where've you been? … You've been ages' (*U*, 204). Never before has this familiar children's whinge rung more truly.

The dreamlike quality of *The Unconsoled* has not escaped the notice of many reviewers and critics. Michael Wood observes that each of the three main sections of the novel begins with Ryder waking up after sleeping. He asks: 'Is the entire book perhaps a version of one of those dreams in which you keep dreaming you are awake?'[8] Or is it, rather, an extended metaphor for anxiety? Linda Simon combines both ideas when she suggests that the novel 'reads like a long, very long, anxiety dream; in this case, the anxiety of contemporary culture about the ability of art to offer enlightenment and consolation.'[9]

Contemporary culture? Art? Enlightenment? How are these connected with Ryder's nightmare? The displacements of events, space and time dealt with so far are not sufficient in themselves to uncover this broader interpretation. They are simply the manifest symptoms of a latent anxiety. That is why the next step is to inspect the displacements between the main characters in the novel, to see if this underlying anxiety can be excavated. I will consider first the other musicians in the novel, to see how they reflect aspects (actual or potential) of Ryder's own artistic identity. Then I will look at Ryder's private life, to see how the disturbances in his family keep his relationships homeless and hesitant.

Each of the musicians of the town – Stephan, Hoffman, Christoff and Brodsky – represents displaced versions of Ryder as he has been in the past or as he may be in the future. Stephan is a portrait of the frustrated artist as a young man; whilst his father, Hoffman, portrays the artist manqué as an old man. Christoff is the artist who has been rejected by the community; whereas Brodsky personifies the artist attempting to become reconciled with his audience.

The centrality of music to the citizens of the town is exemplified by Hoffman's tale, told to Ryder at length in Chapter 24. They are driving to the practice hut in the middle of the country, and the hotel manager regales the musician with the story of his tense marriage. His wife, Christine, was born into a gifted family of poets and other artists, and so their courtship was nurtured by long talks about their mutual love of music. After he had proposed to her, Christine visited him in his small digs near the canal and, as there was no piano in sight, asked him where he composed his music. Hoffman realised at once that his fianceé had mistakenly thought he was a musician. Rather than run the risk of breaking the engagement by correcting her misapprehension, he lied to her by saying that he had decided to take a two-year break from composing. The deception puts the marriage under a terrible strain, despite the fact that the subject was never raised again. Over the years, Hoffman panders to Christine's every whim about the arts, but withers under what he assumes to be her resentment at his inadequacy. Things come to a head many years later, at a reception for visiting composer Jan Piotrowski. Hoffman finds out from Piotrowski that his wife loves the poems of Baudelaire, a passion previously concealed from him. His shame at his ignorance of his wife's intimate thoughts deepens further when he sees her provide a cushion for Piotrowski's back as he sits on the sofa. He confesses to Ryder (in words parodying Stevens in *The Remains of the Day*) that 'when I saw it, I felt my heart breaking. It was a movement so full of natural respect, a desire to be solicitous, to please in a small way. That little action, it revealed a whole realm of her heart she kept tightly closed to me' (*U*, 352).

For twenty-two years Hoffman has been convinced that his wife will leave him, even though she shows no signs of doing so. When their son, Stephan, was born, Hoffman invested all his ambitions in the possibility that his child might become the gifted musician he had never been:

And then of course, there was always the one hope. There was the one hope, which perhaps explains how I've managed to keep her so long. That hope is now dead, has been dead for a good few years already, but you see, for a while, there was this one, single hope. I refer, of course, to our son, Stephan. If he'd been different, if he'd been blessed with at least some of the gifts her side of the family possess in such abundance! For a few years, we both hoped. In our separate ways, we both watched Stephan and hoped. We sent him to piano lessons, we watched him carefully, we

> hoped against hope. We strained to hear some spark that
> was never there, oh, we listened so hard, each for our
> different reasons, we wanted so much to hear something,
> but it was never there ... (*U*, 353)

Ironically, Ryder is very impressed by Stephan's talents – as are
the people of the town when he finally gets to perform in front
of them – but this does not convince Hoffman and his wife.
Their hope is dead, and is not revived at the Thursday night
concert. After leaving the concert hall in disgust whilst his son
is still playing, Hoffman bumps into Ryder in the foyer. He
holds up his wife's albums of press cuttings on the musician
which he had asked him to peruse several days earlier. Christine
is furious that he does this without her permission, and Hoffman
breaks down beneath her tirade. He makes a long speech in
which he exhorts her to 'Leave me. Find someone worthy of
you. A Kosminsky, a Hallier, a Ryder, a Leonhardt' (*U*, 507).
He then strikes his forehead dramatically, and falls weeping on
his knees. Christine holds out her hand as if to stroke his head
tenderly, but then withdraws it. There is no consolation for
Hoffman. As Shaffer divines, 'like the Ryder-Sophie relationship,
the Hoffman-Christine relationship is fraught with masochism
and miscommunication, and is dysfunctional in the extreme.'[10]
What's more, their rejection of Stephan seems to parallel Ryder's
own childhood experiences with his parents. No matter how
hard he tries to please them, they can never be satisfied.

The Hoffman marriage has close affinities with the relationship between Brodsky and Miss Collins, and Brodsky has
many things in common with Ryder. He is a musician with
tastes that lean towards the modern; a man with high ideals for
his art; and a partner in a relationship buckling under the
pressure of his aesthetic calling. Unlike Ryder, he has lost
respect from the citizens of the town, and for many years has
wallowed in a state of drunken self-pity. It is possible to see
Brodsky as an image of what Ryder might become in later years
– a Ghost-of-Ryder-Future, as it were.[11] Brodsky is also a kind of
Captain Ahab, appearing in the novel at a late stage (Chapter 22)
after much rumour and anticipation. Like Herman Melville's

hero, he is obsessed with both the loss of his leg and the capturing of his Moby Dick (a.k.a. Miss Collins). The first time Brodsky meets Ryder, in Miss Collins's front parlour, he talks about his wound. At first Ryder thinks he means a 'wound of the heart' (*U*, 308), as he knows that Brodsky has been separated from Miss Collins for many years and wants desperately to get back together with her. But Brodsky discloses that he was badly injured in Russia many years previously, and has been in physical pain ever since.[12] The wound is a pivotal factor linking Brodsky to Ryder. When Ryder asks him if Miss Collins has the power to heal his wound, Brodsky replies 'She'll be like the music. A consolation. A wonderful consolation. That's all I ask now. A consolation. But heal the wound?' and shakes his head (*U*, 313). This establishes an indelible association between love, art and consolation that becomes piquant towards the end of the novel. Brodsky, against all the odds, manages to conduct the orchestra at the Thursday night concert. He is hoping by his heroic act to win back the respect of the citizens of the town and, what is more important to him, to regain the love of Miss Collins. However, despite his Herculean efforts, he collapses on stage. When Miss Collins comes to his aid, he urges her to embrace him in front of the audience to show that they are reunited. She cannot bring herself to do this, but gently takes his hand. Brodsky starts talking about the pain of his wound, at which point Miss Collins flies into a rage. She tells him that she hates him for wasting her life, and that the wound is the only thing he has ever loved: 'Me, the music, we're neither of us anything more to you than mistresses you seek consolation from. You'll always go back to your real love. To that wound!' (*U*, 498). Moreover, she tells him that the wound is nothing special, and that many other people have carried on with much worse. Her final parting-shot is that he is nothing but a charlatan, and was never really a true musician at all. After this crushing blow, Ryder makes a puny attempt to console Brodsky by telling him that his music was magnificent – but this hardly matters now. There is no consolation for Brodsky.

Brodsky's relationship with Miss Collins and his music is a

displacement of Ryder's own marriage and commitment to art. In both cases, the triangular situation creates tensions that cannot be sustained. It is easy to imagine Ryder falling into the same alcoholic decrepitude as Brodsky after the split in the final chapter with Sophie and Boris. Indeed, there are some hints that Ryder may already be on a downward spiral through drink. When he visits his old apartment in the high-rise estate, a neighbour moans about the couple who used to live there. He says they were always arguing, largely because the male partner drank heavily and was away from home a lot through his work. Ryder is very upset that Boris has to listen to 'this sort of talk' (*U*, 216) and draws his son away. The obscure logic of *The Unconsoled* is such that it is quite possible that the neighbour is really referring to Ryder himself. The musician's shame at his own behaviour is displaced, dreamily, on to someone else.

Brodsky enlists Ryder in his campaign to win back the love of Miss Collins, and he is one of many of the citizens of the town to take advantage of the pianist. From the moment Ryder arrives, he is beset by requests and demands from others. Hoffman wants Ryder to look at his wife's albums of photo-cuttings. Stephan would like Ryder to listen to him play piano. Gustav asks him to speak to Sophie on his behalf to clear up a disagreement that has led to years of silence between them. As Tim Rayment remarks: 'The demands seem urgent and worthwhile: to help a husband please his emotionally faraway wife, to help a young man please his mother, to help lots of decent, entreating people, many of whom are trying to meet the needs of someone else.'[13] Before long, however, Ryder finds himself totally swamped and his schedule in tatters as he accedes to more and more favours.

To comprehend Ryder's predicament, it is worth recalling the de Bono concepts of 'life-space' and 'self-space' applied earlier to Stevens. Another term for life-space is 'demand-space', as it consists of the total set of expectations accompanying the role of the individual within a family, at work, and in society. Nested in this large circle is a smaller zone, the self-space, which can also be called the 'coping-space'. In this area, the individual can cope with ease and without effort across a range of activities. The well-being of a person depends upon the balance between his or her coping-space and demand-space, otherwise known as the cope/demand ratio. A small gap between the coping-space and the demand-space will be perceived as an opportunity to expand and grow. A large gap between the two spaces, however, will be felt as a pressure. With Ryder, the cope/demand ratio has become imbalanced. Although accustomed to extending his self-space to meet new demands both emotionally and artistically, he is stretched too far throughout the novel. Eventually in Chapter 30, after arduous attempts to suppress his anger, he snaps. He yells at Sophie: 'Look ... you don't seem to realise just how much pressure is on me now. Do you suppose this is easy for me? I've very little time left now and I've still not had a second to inspect the concert hall. Instead there are all these other things people expect me to do' (*U*, 444). Ryder's problem is that he cannot say no. Like Stevens, he is far too willing to serve others above himself. His main priorities should be his family and his preparations for the concert, but he is unable to turn down the demands of the people he meets. Pico Iyer expresses this succinctly when he writes that the novel is about 'being put out and put upon – and about putting on a face of obliging acquiescence.'[14] Ryder cannot cope with the demands foisted upon him, and so his life-space suffocates his self-space.

The condition of taking on burdens that cannot be coped with is displaced symbolically on to Gustav, Ryder's father-in-law. At the beginning of *The Unconsoled*, the porter deliberately carries more luggage than he can comfortably handle and refuses to put it down once he is inside the elevator. He then launches into a long justification of this onerous practice to a bemused Ryder. Gustav's 'philosophy' of bag-carrying is ritually re-enacted in the Porter's Dance at the Hungarian Café in Chapter 22. Responding to the encouraging chants of his fellow porters, he leaps on to a table and begins to caper with a heavy suitcase on one shoulder. A second suitcase filled with wooden chopping-boards is also incorporated into the routine. The ultimate test, however, comes when he substitutes the first suitcase for a golfing-bag containing an engine from a motor bike or speedboat. Even this leaden object becomes part of the dance, although only Ryder and Boris are able to see that Gustav is in pain from his exertions.

Gustav's grimace during the dance is the first indication of the elderly porter's ailing health, and heralds his eventual death. In Chapter 29, he falls ill. Ryder is told that he was found unconscious in the washroom, standing over a sink gripped with such force that his fingers had to be prised off the porcelain. The description of this scene has close parallels with the passage in *The Remains of the Day* when Stevens's father takes a stroke. Gustav is placed on a mattress inside a small dressing room, and when he regains consciousness he asks to speak to Ryder urgently. The elderly porter wishes to make one last request. At first, Ryder thinks it is connected with saying a word or two in favour of the porter fraternity at his big speech scheduled for later that night before the concert performance. But then he realises that Gustav wants Ryder to approach Sophie to help break their many years of silence. Unfortunately, despite his best intentions, Ryder is unable to keep his promises. As usual, he is deflected by the concerns of others. When he eventually phones Sophie to tell her the bad news about her father, he somehow neglects to bring up the delicate matter of their non-communication. Moreover, after the shambles of the concert – where the audience had left before he had the chance to perform – he finds out that Gustav's dying words were to ask if Ryder had mentioned the porters' cause in his speech. The speech, like the concert, was never delivered.

Because they have not been on speaking terms for so long, Gustav has not acted like a father to Sophie (even though he has kept regularly in touch with Boris). Similarly, Ryder's long tours have kept him away from home for long periods, and prevented him from carrying out his fatherly duties. This motif of absent fathers sounds throughout Ishiguro's work. In *A Pale View of Hills*, 'real fathers are rarely seen or in most cases replaced by fatherly figures or step-fathers.'[15] Etsuko is made fatherless by the atomic bomb, and adopts her father-in-law Ogata as a surrogate parent; Sachiko never saw much of her father; Mariko lost her father in the war; and both Keiko and Niki are separated from their respective fathers through divorce and death. In *An Artist of the Floating World*, Ono soon becomes alienated from his father after differences about his career aspirations. His own parental authority is diminished after the war when his daughters Setsuko and Noriko marry and move away. In *The Remains of the Day*, Stevens confesses that he rarely spoke to his father, and when they did it was out of domestic necessity and 'took place in an atmosphere of mutual embarrassment' (*RD*, 64). On his deathbed, Stevens, Sr says he hopes he has been a good father, as Stevens has been a good son. The younger butler cannot respond, even on this occasion, with simple words of comfort. In *When We Were Orphans*, Banks's father – an employee of Butterfield and Swires, a trading company that profits from the opium trade in the East – disappears in Shanghai under suspicious circumstances. Banks grows up convinced that his father has been abducted after making a brave stand against the iniquity of his employers. The truth, however, as he finds out many years later, is far more banal. His father, unable to meet the expectations of the beautiful wife he idolised, ran off with a mistress to Hong Kong and died of typhoid within two years.

Estrangement between father and son is rife in the relationship between Ryder and Boris. They cannot communicate with each other in a family way. It is not as if they have nothing in common. Both of them share an interest in football, hence Ryder's recurrent thoughts about a World Cup match between Germany and Holland, and Boris's obsession with the 'Number Nine' figure from a table-top soccer game. Yet they never talk about this topic together.[16] There is a touching moment in the last scene of the novel when the electrician on the tram tries to cheer Ryder up by suggesting that they chat about football. Is this the kind of friendly small-talk that would have brought the musician closer to his son? Then there is the pathos of the dog-eared handyman's manual which Ryder buys for Boris at the cinema. Although the book is clearly an unsuitable present for a child, and is chosen without any thought or care, the young boy feigns fascination with the gift: 'I really like this book ... It shows you everything' (*U*, 471). As Cynthia F. Wong tartly notes, 'What the manual cannot show, of course, is how to unite this fragmented family'.[17]

Further evidence that all is not well in Ryder's personal life can be found in Boris's fantasy in Chapter 15 about fighting off a large number of assailants in the street. How Ryder has access to these inner thoughts is not explained, but Boris's internal monologue reveals a great deal about his own insecurity as he delivers a long speech to the bruised and battered thugs:

> There's no sense in this fighting. You must all have had homes once. Mothers and fathers. Perhaps brothers and sisters. I want you to understand what's happening. These attacks of yours, your continual terrorising of our apartment, has meant that my mother is crying all the time. She's always tense and irritable, and this means she often tells me off for no reason. It also means Papa has to go away for long periods, sometimes abroad, which mother doesn't like. (*U*, 220–1)[18]

The fantasy concludes, when the thugs have learnt their lesson, with Boris returning to the apartment where his parents greet him as a hero. Sophie cooks him a special meal, whilst Ryder plays a board game with him. This ideal vision of a happy family evening at home almost becomes real. It is invoked in Chapter 18 by Sophie as a means of persuading Boris to endure the reception at the Karwinsky Gallery. She dangles the meal and the board game and the possibility of talking about football as a bribe to placate her son: 'It'll be a marvellous evening, just the three of us' (*U*, 265). But such humdrum domestic bliss is unattainable for Ryder, Sophie and Boris, except in the young boy's daydreams. They finally arrive at the apartment after their ordeal at the Gallery, and slowly Ryder begins to remember the 'distinctly familiar' surroundings (*U*, 284) of his own home. As Sophie prepares the food, Ryder reads a newspaper. When Boris tries to cajole him into playing the board game as promised, Ryder continues to ignore him. Finally, Boris loses heart and decides that he is too tired to play. Sophie attempts to salvage the atmosphere by giving him the DIY manual which Ryder had bought for him at the cinema. Even though it falls apart in his hands when he opens it, the little boy makes gratified comments about the gift such as 'There's a special sort of brush you can get for putting up wallpaper' (*U*, 287). Sophie begins to play the board game with Boris, but Ryder becomes annoyed and inwardly castigates his wife: 'it was not even as though she had particularly excelled herself with the cooking' (*U*, 288). Where are the sausage kebabs? The hard-boiled eggs? The strawberry Swiss rolls? His criticism about the cooking is a displacement of the anger he feels at what he sees as Sophie's earlier disruptions to his schedule. He leaves early, the night in ruins. Home – at least in the Ryder household – is not so sweet.

Nor, it would seem, was home very sweet for Ryder as a child. Boris is a Ghost-of-Ryder-Past, and there are several flashbacks in the novel disclosing the solitariness and emptiness of the musician's own childhood. When he first meets Fiona Roberts working as a ticket-inspector on the tram, he recalls a memory from his distant Worcestershire upbringing. The two of them sat beneath their dining-room table 'hide-out', and talked about marriage. Fiona said that when she grew up she would have a large family – 'Five children at least' (*U*, 171) – and she would cook supper for them every night. The young Ryder responded in return that he would never marry because he liked being lonely. Prophetic words. This prompts another buried memory about the 'training sessions' he used to have as a child. These consisted of the impulse to run home whenever he felt panicky or in need of parental comfort. He would stand rigid under an oak tree, trying to master his emotions. At the end of the 'hide-out' flashback, Fiona reassures Ryder that 'when *you* get married, it needn't be like it is with your mum and dad. It won't be like that all the time. They only argue when … when special things happen' (*U*, 172). There is a hint about what this special thing might be in Ryder's case when Fiona's mother tells her that he is too young to know what everybody else knows. Is it that Ryder is not his father's son? If so, this is also possibly true of Ryder and Boris, another instance of the present displacing the past.

Even though Ryder has established himself as a world-renowned pianist, his relationship with his parents is still fraught with anxiety and an overeagerness to please. They have never seen him in action, and he is worried about the preparations for their visit to the nameless town where they are due to see him perform for the first time. Trude and Inge, members of the Women's Arts and Cultural Foundation, are supposed to look after them. But Ryder has a disturbing vision of his parents arriving in the town with nobody to meet them or carry their cases. He means to look into the arrangements himself, but is constantly deflected by the demands of others. Much later on in Chapter 26, when Hoffman drives him back to the town for the concert from the country hut, he expresses his concern about his parents again. Hoffman reassures him by conjuring up an image of their stylish arrival at the concert hall in a horse and carriage. Ryder is so entranced by this wishful thinking that in Chapter 30 he has an auditory hallucination of 'the beat of hooves, a rhythmic jingling, the rattle of a wooden vehicle' (*U*, 435–36), which heralds – or so he wants to believe – the arrival of his parents.

Ryder's dilemma is that he cannot decide where his true commitments lie, and he is pulled in many different directions at once. This is especially true when it comes to choosing between the demands of his own family, Sophie and Boris, and his parents. At a crucial juncture in Chapter 33, he opts for the latter. Sophie, reconciled with her dying father, asks Ryder to stay with her and Boris in the dressing room in which the failing porter lies. Ryder, overcome with stress, leaves the scene pleading 'My parents, don't you see? My parents will be arriving at any moment! There's a thousand things I have to do!' (*U*, 475). Yet even on this occasion of apparent iron determination, Ryder is distracted from his purpose by other matters, and doesn't get to make enquiries about his parents until some time has passed. He finally gets to see Miss Stratmann again in Chapter 36 for the first time since the elevator incident. In her large office, she informs him that his parents cannot be found in the town. Ryder breaks down and sobs. The onslaught of outside demands has shattered his coping-space. He whines like a child that he was sure his parents would come to see him perform this time: 'They must be here somewhere … I could hear them coming, their horse and carriage. I heard them, they must be here, surely, it's not unreasonable' (*U*, 512). Miss Stratmann tries to console Ryder by assuring him that his parents *have* visited the town once before, many years ago. She pulls down on a roller a massive colour photo of the hotel where they stayed: it looks like 'the sort of fairy-tale castle built by mad kings in the last century' (*U*, 515). This soothes his fears, inexplicably, but not for long. He has other things to worry about, now that his marriage is disintegrating rapidly.

The relationship between Ryder and Sophie is complex. She is, at times, his consoler, but can only offer him false consolations. When Ryder phones her from the scene of Brodsky's accident in Chapter 30, for instance, she calms him down by guaranteeing that everything will be fine on the night at the concert. They go on to indulge in their shared fantasy of finding a new home together where all their problems will be solved. Ryder, on the other hand, refuses to console Sophie. He even fails to recognise that she is in need of consolation, despite hearing Gustav's story in Chapter 7 of how the porter failed to comfort his distraught daughter in her childhood following the death of her pet hamster.

After the concert is over and Ryder finds out that Gustav is dead, he sees Sophie and Boris walking away from the Conservatory. He hurries after them, knowing that this could be the last chance for them to be together as a family. This leads to the most poignant scene in the whole novel. Ryder catches up with Sophie and Boris on the tram and sees them hugging each other:

> They were still in a deep embrace, their eyes closed. Patches of sunlight were drifting over their arms and shoulders. There was at that moment something so private about their comforting of each other that it seemed impossible for me even to intrude. And as I went on gazing at them, I began to feel, for all their obvious distress, a strange sense of envy. I moved a little closer until I could feel the very texture of their embrace. (*U*, 531)

Emotionally, this is a displacement of the embrace which Miss Collins refused to give Brodsky at the end of the concert. When Ryder tries to offer his condolences, he receives a devastating retort from Sophie: 'Leave us. You were always on the outside of our love. Now look at you. On the outside of our grief too. Leave us. Go away' (*U*, 532). The rejection is made even more stinging when she responds to Boris's protests by saying that Ryder will never love him like a true father. This is not the first time that it has been implied that Ryder is not Boris's genetic father.[19] Ryder makes a last-ditch appeal to Boris as the little boy leaves the tram with his mother. He asks him to remember the bus ride they made together to the artificial lake in Chapter 15, when the other passengers had given him sweets and fussed over him. It is the one moment of pure happiness which Ryder has spent with his son over the past few days. But it is too late. Sophie and Boris leave the tram. There is no consolation for Ryder.

So, virtually every character in the novel is looking to be consoled, either by loved ones, through the satisfaction of a demand or in the pursuit of a valued activity. Yet it is the fate of the citizens of this nameless town to remain unconsoled, unsatisfied, and unceasingly chasing goals they cannot reach. What is the reader to make of this lamentable state of affairs? Is it tenable to suggest that the adversities of Ryder, his family and his fellow musicians are a displacement of Ishiguro's own frustrations in relation to his life and art? A Freudian would certainly think so, especially as Ishiguro has spoken in interviews in terms almost identical to those used by Brodsky:

> Writing is a kind of consolation or a therapy … The best writing comes out of a situation where I think the artist or writer has to some extent come to terms with the fact that it is too late. The wound has come, and it hasn't healed, but it's not going to get any worse; yet, the wound is there. It's a kind of consolation that the world isn't quite the way you wanted it but you can somehow reorder it or try and come to terms with it by actually creating your own world and own version of it.[20]

But to say that therefore Ishiguro is Brodsky, because he

expresses himself in terms similar to one of his characters, is too simplistic. It does not take into account the self-conscious deployment of Freudian dream theory in the book. As Ishiguro reveals, 'I used dream as a model. The people Ryder encounters are appropriated by him to work out part of his past.'[21] The town is therefore a projection of Ryder's unconscious. It is impertinent, and improper, to go any further. Does this mean that we can read *The Unconsoled* as Ryder's dream? Is it an updated version of James Joyce's *Finnegans Wake* (1939)? This would be one way of recuperating the novel as a work of realism. But the text is trickier than that. The narration is refracted through what can only be called an omniscient/limited first-/third-person point of view, and resists easy focalisation. Ryder is not dreaming within his life; he is living within a dream. Whose dream it is, is not clear.

If the novel is not a work of realism, and not distorted autobiography, to which genre does it belong? Fantastic literature allows the bending of normal fictional 'rules' and suspends the reader's disbelief when impossible events occur. This might, then, account for the book's distortions of events, space, time and its displacements between characters. There are definitely traces of Jonathan Swift's classic fantasy, *Gulliver's Travels* (1726), in the novel. These crop up in the squabbles of the citizens over Lilliputian matters; for example, the dispute 'concerning ringed harmonies' (*U*, 196) with Christoff at the roadside café, and their belief that an outsider can arbitrate their problems. There are also correspondences with Lewis Carroll's *Alice's Adventures in Wonderland* (1865) in the maniacal dialogues between Ryder and his petitioners, and the broom-cupboard-rabbit-holes through which the musician is forever disappearing. Unlike Alice, however, Ryder is 'totally passive'[22] and 'falls in with the nonsequiturial stance of the citizens'.[23] He lacks the little girl's curiosity, and accepts his Wonderland blithely.

Another fantasist Ishiguro has been compared to regarding *The Unconsoled* is Franz Kafka. This is perhaps more accurate than comparisons with Swift and Carroll, given the undercurrents of black humour linking these two modern writers. The parallels are many. Ryder and Josef K. in *The Trial* are in societies that sift like sand beneath waves, and swept away by a tide of demands. The world they attempt to negotiate is by turns comic and threatening. Postponement is their only certainty. The atmosphere is drenched with dreams. Ultimately, however, the critical consensus seems to be that *The Unconsoled* falls short of Kafka's high accomplishments. Michael Wood believes that the work is too diffuse to have the pressure of Kafkaesque fable. Ned Rorem observes that the situation of the novel is 'Kafka in reverse',[24] substituting a prominent musician for a protagonist of lowly status. Amit Chaudhuri agrees that *The Unconsoled* has many superficial similarities with the Czech modernist – especially in its depiction of 'the official subordinate who, though seemingly significant, has the hidden power … to keep you from entering the room you have been waiting to enter.'[25] What he thinks is lacking, however, is the presence of an allegorical social critique. In its place is 'a sort of revenge on the increasingly intractable and Kafkaesque world of publishers and the publishing market'.[26]

Despite the influence of Swift, Carroll and Kafka, *The Unconsoled* doesn't feel like a fantasy. Its world is not without rules, but rather is governed by an unspoken set of quirks. Ryder may well forget that he is married or turn up at a reception in his dressing gown, but there is never a possibility that he will change size or meet white rabbits with watches. Perhaps, then, the novel should be classified in a different way. According to Valentine Cunningham, with this book Ishiguro joins the 'Oh-Dear-Me-No-the-Novel-Doesn't-Tell-a-Story lot, the cheese-paring Kafka-Borges-Calvino-Handke tendency.'[27] He goes on to predict that 'It'll be on a university syllabus before you can say Tristram Shandy.'[28] Although Cunningham's tone is disparaging, there is a good case for taking up his suggestion that *The Unconsoled* can be viewed through a postmodern lens. Postmodernist fiction is defined by its temporal disorder, its disregard of linear narrative, its mingling of fictional forms, and its experiments with language – all of which are to be found abundantly in Ishiguro's novel. Cunningham's mention of

Laurence Sterne's *Tristram Shandy* (1759–67) is apposite, if only because of the oddities both books contain. Some of the most striking anomalies can be found in Chapter 9, when Ryder and Sophie attend a cinema near the hotel to watch a late-night movie. The theatre is packed with local dignitaries, many of whom are casually playing cards. Before the film begins, Ryder buys the tattered DIY manual for Boris from a woman with a tray selling confectionaries. The film showing is *2001: A Space Odyssey*. It inexplicably stars Clint Eastwood stalking the corridors of a spaceship with a gun, and Yul Brynner testing his speed on the draw by clapping hands in front of him. A careless reviewer thought this was an 'editorial oversight'.[29] It is, of course, nothing of the kind, but is symptomatic of the postmodernist 'inconsequentiality which marks every scene in this book'.[30]

This inconsequentiality results in a flouting of realist conventions, as Bradbury confirms:

> Every door and window opens out onto exception. Days go on longer than they should, the rules of place don't work (British characters keep appearing strangely), no appointment or journey ever goes as planned … Fiction's basic laws are also constantly broken. Ryder knows things he shouldn't, entering rooms he hasn't been in or the minds of characters he doesn't know.[31]

We can add some more items to this list of postmodernist inconsistencies. The musician's perceptions fluctuate between telepathy and an empty-headed unawareness. In the elevator with Gustav, it is quite a while before he notices that Miss Stratmann is also present (*U*, 9). Later, when he meets Sophie outside the hotel, he fails to see immediately that she is carrying a large brown paper package containing an overcoat (*U*, 91). The emotional tone of the novel veers dramatically between extremes, too. There is a weight of pain and regret in the story that is lightened by the imperturbability of the central character. At the very end of the book, Ryder recovers from Sophie's devastating and irretractable rejection of him by having some breakfast on the tram. 'Things had not, after all, gone so badly'

(*U*, 534) he muses, as he tucks into his croissants, somehow ignoring the countless catastrophes that had befallen him and others throughout his stay in the town.

Ryder, as his name implies, rides through his life, perpetually moving somewhere else, unable to find the stasis of home. And he is still riding at the end of the novel. He remains sobbing on the tram after his wife and son have left him. An electrician tries to cheer him up by offering empty optimistic phrases (much like the ex-butler on the Weymouth pier bench with Stevens in *The Remains of the Day*). Ryder fills his plate, and seeks solace in the thought that 'Whatever disappointments this city had brought, there was no doubting that my presence had been greatly appreciated' (*U*, 534). But this is as hollow as the judgement Ono makes about Sugimura in *An Artist of the Floating World*: 'For his failure [to transform the city] was quite unlike the undignified failures of most ordinary lives ... If one has failed only where others have not had the courage or will to try, there is a consolation – indeed, a deep satisfaction – to be gained from this observation when looking back over one's life' (*AFW*, 134). Consolation? Deep satisfaction? Or shallow self-deception? As Tamsin Todd writes, contrasting the nostalgia in Vladimir Nabokov's novels with Ryder's false comfort: 'What's terrifying about this stark portrayal of displacement is that it feels true. *The Unconsoled* reveals nostalgia of the Nabokovian brand to be mere literary conceit; in reality, there's little comfort for the displaced.'[32]

To sum up, *The Unconsoled* is an experimental work, successfully utilising several dream techniques to skew its narrative, and incorporating aspects of postmodernism, fantasy and realism. Ishiguro is not fully at home in any one of these genres, and falls between them. As he declared in an interview with Allan Vorda, he prefers to 'move away from realism ... not so much into out-and-out fantasy', but towards 'us[ing] the landscape that you do know in a metaphorical way'.[33] This is evident in *A Pale View of Hills*, where Nagasaki is represented as a mood rather than as a concrete place. The Japanese setting is made even metaphorical in *An Artist of the Floating World* by the device of deliberately not naming the city in which it takes place. The England of *The Remains of the Day* was praised for its recognisable authenticity and presence, yet it conforms to 'heritage' stereotypes and is severely underdescribed. It, too, operates subtly on an analogical level. Perhaps, then, *The Unconsoled* is not so different from Ishiguro's previous novels after all. It is the culmination of his desire to close in on '*some strange, weird territory*'[34] that is 'somewhere between straight realism and … out-and-out fabulism'.[35] This fuzzy space of his fictions has the texture and timbre of memory – it is uncertain, quivering, and subject to erasures and displacements.

Critical overview and conclusion

BEFORE surveying critical responses to Ishiguro's fiction, let us return to a scene from *An Artist of the Floating World*. Mori-san has left the merrymaking of musicians and actors at his villa to enjoy the night air, and spots a light amidst the surrounding darkness. He discovers that it is his pupil, Masuji Ono, hiding in the storeroom. He makes his way towards Ono, who perceives that 'As he did so, the lantern in his hand caused shadows to move all around us' (*AFW*, 147). Critical interpretation, according to Pierre Macherey, is like this lantern: it may well illuminate, but it also creates dancing shadows, flickering forms insubstantial next to the radiance of the work itself. At best, criticism might bring to light some hidden aspects of the discourse of the work, but it can also diminish the text and reduce its range of meanings.

The critic must therefore, states Macherey, emphasise the 'juxtaposition and conflict of several meanings' in the book, to expose its 'radical otherness'.[1] But this brings with it another pitfall: the perils of overinterpretation. Again, this can be illustrated by an episode from Ishiguro, this time *The Remains of the Day*. Towards the beginning of the book, Stevens reads Miss Kenton's letter and is certain that she wishes to return to Darlington Hall. By the time he reaches Salisbury, he recognises that 'she does not at any point in her letter state explicitly her desire to return' (*RD*, 48). Nevertheless, the butler concludes that his ex-housekeeper is deeply nostalgic about her former home. After rereading the letter in Taunton, Stevens admits that there is no evidence to warrant the conclusion he has reached, and when he is in Moscombe he realises that his inferences have been unwise.[2] He has read meanings into her words that were simply not there. Some critics might say this does not matter: there are no limits to how a text can be understood. But there *are* limits, contextual ones, to the usefulness or appropriateness of any one particular strand of interpretation.

One of the interpretative limits in relation to Ishiguro's work is the paucity of critical response to his short stories and television plays. Understandably, interest has fallen predominantly upon his novels. But what can be gleaned about these other writings? Ishiguro's short stories fall into two categories: exercises in style, arising from the University of East Anglia Creative Writing course he took, and satellite studies for his novels. In the former category are 'Waiting for J'[3] and 'Getting Poisoned'.[4] The first is a somewhat Borgesian suspense in which a young artist awaits the ghost of a friend he has murdered. They made a pact in their youth, and vowed to kill each other when they reached forty. What is immediately striking about this story is its reliance upon sheer plot, a feature largely absent from Ishiguro's longer fictions. As Clive Sinclair writes: 'It wasn't brilliant. I can't remember where it was set, but it certainly wasn't Japan.'[5] Equally lacking in brilliance (and also not set in Japan) is 'Getting Poisoned', a diary fiction in which the narrating child is neglected by his mother during the summer holidays. Mum is too wrapped up in her new boyfriend, John, to see that her son's cruel games will lead to a fatality.[6] This is Ishiguro-as-Ian-McEwan – a novelist whose works such as *The Cement Garden* (1978) often flirt with the macabre – and the attempt to be contemporary in tone jars somewhat with his later work. Ishiguro admits, 'I was consciously experimenting then. Just the challenge of, say, writing in diary form or in the present tense could actually be enough justification for writing a story. That kind of thing wouldn't sustain my interest now.'[7]

Much more accomplished are the short stories which fall into the other category, the sketches containing themes, characters or situations explored in greater depth by the novels.

Again, these have been largely overlooked by the critics, despite being included in several prominent anthologies. Yet, as we have seen in the previous chapters, 'A Strange and Sometimes Sadness', 'Summer After the War', and 'A Family Supper' offer fascinating glimpses into the gestation of ideas Ishiguro developed further elsewhere. The same is also true of his two television plays, *A Profile of J. Arthur Mason* and *The Gourmet*.

These minor pieces by Ishiguro are not considered in Brian W. Shaffer's otherwise excellent *Understanding Kazuo Ishiguro* (1998), the first full-length study of his work. He analyses *A Pale View of Hills* principally in relation to Etsuko's rationalisation of her parental neglect, and makes some telling local observations. He sees intertextual analogies between the novel and James Joyce's 'Eveline' from *Dubliners* (1914). In this short story, the female protagonist dreams of escaping from her dreary surroundings with the aid of a sailor called Frank (the same name as Sachiko's would-be rescuer). Less plausible is Shaffer's proposal that the initials of Sachiko and Mariko (S and M) are a clue to their sado-masochistic relationship. He considers Ono's defence mechanisms in *An Artist of the Floating World*, commenting astutely on his breaks with authority figures and how he 'prostitutes his art to the fascist regime'.[8] Another Joycean comparison is indicated in Shaffer's chapter on *The Remains of the Day*, this time with 'The Dead'. Gabriel Conroy, and his wish to renew his life by visiting the West of Ireland, is a precursor to Stevens and his West Country motoring trip. Shaffer is particularly sharp on the symbiosis between the butler's sexual and political repressions. The most impressive chapter is the one on *The Unconsoled*, which subdivides the main characters into three sets of triangular relationships: Ryder–Sophie–Boris, Brodsky–Miss Collins–Bruno and Hoffman–Christine–Stephan. Although Shaffer acknowledges that the novel is a 'clear change of tone, direction and scope',[9] he also recognises its continuities with Ishiguro's earlier novels.

Cynthia F. Wong's *Kazuo Ishiguro* (2000) applies the aesthetics of reception and reader-response theory associated with Georges Poulet and Wolfgang Iser to Ishiguro's fiction. The result is an exact and penetrative account of the complex negotiations enacted in each text between author, narrator and reader. She locates Ishiguro firmly within the context of international writing, and demonstrates how in his work thematic considerations take precedence over historical and social reference. Wong explores the domestic dislocations Ishiguro's narrators suffer, and the limits and conditions of the self-deceptions by which they seek to preserve their dignity and stability. One of her most powerful insights is that the mirroring of Etsuko and Sachiko in *A Pale View of Hills* correlates with Etsuko's dual functions of 'homodiegetic' and 'extradiegetic' narration.[10] In other words, the projection of her own predicament on to those of somebody else can be explained by the fact that she is both inside and outside the stories she tells. The same is true of Masuji Ono in *An Artist of the Floating World,* whose paranoia and pride suspends him between denying and admitting his 'self-inflicted wounding'.[11] It is only when he is passing comments on others, such as Mori-san, that we can intuit indirect judgement about himself. Stevens also wavers between concealment and disclosure in *The Remains of the Day*, and his 'false expansion of self'[12] is accomplished by idealising a father with whom, in reality, he had little in common. In *The Unconsoled,* Ryder's attempts to reach understanding 'appear more elusive than those of the earlier narrators, because, ironically, his problems are more ordinary than theirs.'[13] The setting in which the musician gathers his chaotic recollections is not tagged to grave issues of atomic devastation or the consequences of national aggrandisement/appeasement. Yet, by struggling to clarify his state of unknowing, he is ineluctably kin to Etsuko, Ono and Stevens. What distinguishes his story from that of the others is that there is no longer the possibility of an 'extradiegetic' dimension. Like other 'contemporary nomads'[14] of the postmodern world, Ryder must find what significance he can in the meaningless drift of things.

The first three books – *A Pale View of Hills, An Artist of the Floating World* and *The Remains of the Day* – share many things in common with Ishiguro's minor works. They prioritise texture over plot, and deal with a controlled repertoire of themes. They are full of family resemblances, and Ishiguro once described them as 'three attempts to write the same book.'[15] Each of these novels has first-person narrations in which the unreliabilities of memory and self-deception are well to the fore. The plot of *An Artist of the Floating World* arose from the sub-plot of *A Pale View of Hills*: a Japanese patriot – lauded for his views before the war, but vilified after it – seeks to restore his social esteem. Ono and Ogata might have very different temperaments, but their tangles are variations on a theme. Similarly, *The Remains of the Day* is like an alternative English 'remix' (to use a term from popular music) of attitudes and situations present in *An Artist of the Floating World*. Ishiguro even joked that his third book could well be called *The Butler of the Floating World*.[16] Because of these generative links, it makes sense to think of Ishiguro's first three novels as an informal trilogy. Another pattern becomes evident, however, when we add *The Unconsoled* to the list. This fourth novel reprises and parodies many of the themes of *The Remains of the Day*: the obtuseness of blind duty; the hazards of polite acquiescence; and the indignity of struggling to appear dignified in undignifying situations. As Pico Iyer proposes, 'the book is a natural extension, and grand amplification [of the earlier novel] … presenting us with a whole world made up of Stevenses'.[17] Ishiguro's first four novels, then, can be grouped together in a 1–2, 2–3, 3–4 formation, with each succeeding novel resembling most the book preceding it.[18] This is natural, as an author is bound to be most influenced by his or her last book. It also replicates, though, a distinctive attribute of Ishiguro's stylistic technique: sequent repetition-with-variation. Transitions between episodes in the novels often depend upon a memory, the content or context of which is revised after a digression, thus sparking another train of thought. It is a very musical method, and has probably emerged from Ishiguro's early fascination with writing popular songs.[19]

This theme-and-variation technique is also detectable in the titles of Ishiguro's novels, as Hermione Lee has spotted. Each of the titles is difficult to remember exactly. Is it *Pale View of Hills* or *A Pale View of Hills*? Or even *A Pale View of the Hills*? Is it *The Artist of the Floating World* or *An Artist of the Floating World*? *Remains of the Day* or *The Remains of the Day*? The definite or indefinite articles make a difference. This pernicketiness is also noticeable, she suggests, in the openings of the three novels, each of which 'give off a puzzling and contingent air'.[20] Etsuko, Ono and Stevens begin their narratives with an equivocation. The name 'Niki' in *A Pale View of Hills*, Etsuko believes, belongs to neither East or West. It is a hybrid, like the girl herself. As Lee states: '[It] tells us that a short name – like a short novel – need not be an "abbreviation" … a lightweight version of something larger', but an 'exact expression' of what it denotes.[21] Ono's Bridge of Hesitation at the beginning of *An Artist of the Floating World* is an emblem of his own indecision. At the start of *The Remains of the Day*, Stevens is undecided as to whether or not he should take the motoring trip to the West Country suggested by his employer. So the three openings are like three attempts to write the same introduction. Even the settings of the trilogy are permutated, as Lee also points out. *A Pale View of Hills* takes place in England and Japan; *An Artist of the Floating World* in Japan; and *The Remains of the Day* in England.

At the start of Part Two of *A Pale View of Hills*, Etsuko mentions that during the summer when she befriended Sachiko, she would gaze emptily at the 'pale outline of hills' (*PVH*, 99) visible from her apartment window on clear days. These are the hills of Inasa, just outside of Nagasaki, where she spends a pleasant day in Chapter 7 on the cable-cars with Sachiko and Mariko. Many years later, at the end of her visit, Niki asks her mother for a photograph of Nagasaki, so Etsuko gives her a calendar image of the view of the harbour from the hills. Niki wonders why this photograph is significant. Etsuko tells her about the day on the cable-cars, and remembers that Keiko was happy that day. The displacement of Mariko by Keiko is an important indication that Etsuko's memories of Sachiko are really self-referring. This accords with Ishiguro's summary of what he was trying to do in this novel:

the whole narrative strategy of the book was about how someone ends up talking about things they cannot face directly through other people's stories. I was trying to explore that type of language, how people use the language of self-deception and self-protection ... it's really Etsuko talking about herself.[22]

The title of *A Pale View of Hills*, then, is a succinct expression of how the novel works as a whole through indirect association and suggestion. It hangs together via what Francis King calls 'a shimmering, all but invisible net of images linked to each other by filaments at once tenuous and immensely strong.'[23] Not every critic was happy with this tenuousness of structure. Ishiguro himself felt that he may have fumbled the pronoun-merging scene on the bridge a little. Few could argue, though, that for a first novel this was a work of exceptional grace and clarity. Jonathan Spence, reviewing the book in *New Society*, called it 'a beautiful and dense novel, gliding from level to level of consciousness';[24] Fumio Yoshioka admired its 'stunning simplicity both in style and storyline';[25] whilst Cynthia F. Wong, in an essay prior to her monograph on Ishiguro, convincingly applied to the text several recondite theoretical ideas (from Maurice Blanchot and Gérard Genette) about speech and speechlessness.[26] Several critics picked up on the understated aspect of Ishiguro's writing. To Pico Iyer, this is 'an ink-wash elusiveness, an ellipticism almost violent in its reticence';[27] to Allan Massie, an 'exquisite precison';[28] Penelope Lively prefers to call it 'stylistic negativism'.[29]

References to the novel's simplicity were often associated with stereotypical notions of Japaneseness. Francis King, for instance, said *A Pale View of Hills* was 'typically Japanese in its compression, its reticence and in its exclusion of all details not absolutely essential to its theme.'[30] He continues by stating that it felt like an early work by Shusaku Endo or Yasunari Kawabata. Ishiguro has praised the latter's careful pairing of setting and event, and the general impression of 'sparseness ... [and] subdued, natural colours'[31] in his work, so perhaps there is some credence in King's claims.

Compression, reticence, sparseness – these terms capture the essence of Ishiguro's fictions also, and it is no coincidence that much of this language is implicated with the discourses of visual art. Bruce King thinks that the gestural elegance of Ishiguro's style is 'similar to the deft brushwork of Japanese paintings';[32] Malcolm Bradbury affirms that 'every instant of the verbal composition feels like a certain kind of Japanese art';[33] whilst Gabriele Annan finds Ishiguro's descriptions 'as factual and plain as a Morandi still life'.[34]

Certain passages in *An Artist of the Floating World* appear to reflect back upon their own fictional techniques through analogies with painting. Mori-san – the only artist in the novel who isn't compromised by money or politics – is said to modernise the methods of *ukiyo-e* artist Utamaro. Utamaro represented everyday subjects – usually pleasure district women – engaged in trivial activities, such as fastening a *kimono* or gazing into a mirror. Mori-san continues this tradition by portraying such women in soft hues, although he modernises his subjects by defining shape through contrasts of light and shade and blocks of colour, rather than using bold outlines. His paintings strive to 'capture the feel of lantern light' (*AFW*, 141), even in those situations where a lantern is not present. This is equivalent to how Ishiguro 'paints' his main character in *An Artist of the Floating World*. Ono is depicted from unusual angles, like the Mori-san painting in which a kneeling woman is seen from a low point of view. Ono is not delineated in bold outlines, but rather his self is figured against contrasting social backgrounds. This nebulous characterisation is analysed in Margaret Scanlan's 'Mistaken Identities: First-Person Narration in Kazuo Ishiguro', where she probes the unstable, decentred self of Ono and his unreliable memory. Charles Sarvan goes further in 'Floating Signifiers and *An Artist of the Floating World*', and reads the entire novel as a study of absences and deferments: 'The narrative has no confident, authoritative centre, and in a deconstructed text, many things remain elusive to the eavesdropping reader.'[35] He uses the ideas of French psychoanalyst Jacques Lacan about the fluidity of the signifier to show how Ono's statements are never verifiable, and cannot even be grounded in a fixed set of social values. Malcolm Bradbury in 'The Floating World' draws attention to the way that the story 'hides behind itself, forcing the reader persistently to unlock it'.[36] The novel, all three would concur, is an enigma like Leonardo da Vinci's *Mona Lisa*.

This enigmatic quality helped *An Artist of the Floating World* win the Whitbread Novel Award in 1986.[37] The prize, administered by the Booksellers Association of Great Britain and Ireland, is for the best work of fiction in any one year written by a resident of those countries. This was a splendid achievement for a second novel, and is one of several prizes and awards received by Ishiguro. His first novel, *A Pale View of Hills*, won the Winifred Holtby Prize in 1983. In the same year he was nominated as one of the Best Young British Novelists alongside such writers as Salman Rushdie, Graham Swift, Pat Barker and Maggie Gee. Ten years later he was still young enough to be nominated in a second list of the Best Young British Novelists, the only writer to appear twice in this way. Other writers on this list included Louis de Bernières, Caryl Phillips and Will Self.

When Ishiguro was nominated for the Booker Prize in 1989 with *The Remains of the Day*, he faced stiff competition from the strong shortlist.[38] But the panel had no hesitation in awarding the prize to Ishiguro. The chair, David Lodge, explained the decision when he called the novel 'a cunningly structured and beautifully paced performance … [which] renders with humour and pathos a memorable character and explores the large, vexed themes of class, tradition and duty.'[39] Malcolm Bradbury later suggested that Ishiguro helped the British novel on to the international stage and out of the provincial rut of the 1950s and 1960s, precisely by engaging with such capacious themes. Winning the Booker Prize, Britain's most prestigious literary award, was a tremendous boost for Ishiguro's writing career. It gave him a wider public profile, a heftier bank account, and ensured that his next book would be eagerly awaited. Shortly after nomination for the shortlist, though, he outlined the scope of his ambition. Prizes, he implied, are fine as a promotional tool and honour the recipient. But the serious writer has deeper concerns.[40]

In Ishiguro's Booker acceptance speech at the Guildhall in London, he addressed one such issue. He stated that 'It would be improper not to remember Salman Rushdie this evening and think about the alarming situation and plight in which he finds himself.'[41] It was earlier that year (February 1989) that the Ayatollah Khomeini had issued the *fatwa* decree against Rushdie for the alleged blasphemy of *The Satanic Verses*. Rushdie is an important writer to consider alongside Ishiguro. In fact, Ishiguro believes that a great deal of his own success stemmed from the 1981 Booker Prize award to *Midnight's Children*, after which 'everyone was suddenly looking for other Rushdies.'[42] Ishiguro, with his Japanese name and his first two novels set in Japan, conformed to publisher's requirements of an international author whose books were situated in the limbo between two cultures. Rushdie is very eloquent about his own condition of 'in-betweeness' or homelessness. In his essay 'Imaginary Homelands', he details how writers in the same position as himself – 'exiles or immigrants or expatriates'[43] – feel the need to reclaim their past, even if it means suffering the fate of Lot's wife in the Bible and being turned into pillars of salt. The backward gazes of Ishiguro and Rushdie are markers of the difficulties of such cultural schizophrenia. The countries they look back to are reimagined spaces, where – as Rushdie formulates it in a phrase reminding us of Stevens – 'shards of memory acquired greater status, greater resonance because they were *remains*'.[44]

Rushdie favourably reviewed *The Remains of the Day*. He praised it for not being afraid to pose 'Big Questions'[45] about the nature of Englishness, greatness and dignity, and for asking them with a combination of humour and incisiveness. As Ishiguro himself confesses, his own style is 'almost the antithesis of Rushdie's',[46] but this did not prevent Rushdie from admiring the almost imperceptible perturbations breathing over the placid surface of the book. He acknowledged the generic nods to Wodehouse in the novel, whilst recognising that it is a 'brilliant subversion of the fictional modes from which it at first seems to descend.'[47]

On the whole, the reviewers of *The Remains of the Day* shared Rushdie's enthusiasm for the novel. Joseph Coates thought it was 'an ineffably sad and beautiful piece of work – a tragedy in the form of a comedy of manners';[48] Galen Strawson admired it as a 'very finely nuanced and at times humorous study of repression';[49] and Lawrence Graver dubbed it 'a dream of a book … a profound and heart-rending study of personality, class and culture.'[50] It is a work which appeals across the spectrum, and unsurprisingly the book has attracted considerable critical scrutiny. In 'The Crisis of the Social Subject in the Contemporary English Novel', Daniela Carpi looks closely at the construction of the butler's self, and places it in the context of the broader cultural uncertainty about subjectivity. She asserts that 'some of the key words to understand the postmodern situation [and Stevens] are … the terms uncertainty, "homelessness", fragmentation'.[51] She makes a brief, but fertile, comparison between Stevens and the butler/servant figure in Rose Tremain's *Sadler's Birthday* (1976). Caroline Patey's 'When Ishiguro Visits the West Country: An Essay on *The Remains of the Day*' is an ambitious and occasionally erratic attempt to discuss the novel in terms of its literary forebears (including Henry Fielding and Thomas Hardy), and the vertigo of modern linguistic theory. She feels that Ishiguro's fictions are 'best understood through the double cultural affiliation of their author, or rather his double non-affiliation.'[52] '*The Remains of the Day*: Kazuo Ishiguro's Sonnet on His Blindness'[53] by Rocío G. Davis uncovers some surprising parallels between Ishiguro's novel and Milton's poem. Kathleen Wall's '*The Remains of the Day* and Its Challenges to Theories of Unreliable Narration'[54] anatomises some of the more experimental aspects of the text, particularly its extension of first-person diegetic uncertainty. Terrence Rafferty paid Ishiguro a handsome compliment, when he wrote that it is 'a novel that feels as if it had been written by some wily literary veteran, a distinguished old warrior who has decided, as his life and career wind down, to show the slovenly young a thing or two about the power of traditional craftsmanship.'[55] The same review, however, goes on to express some reservations about what he feels to be Ishiguro's emotional manipulativeness and predictable plotting: 'The glycerin tear is placed so artfully on the stoic cheek ... [The novel] always travels a well-marked route ("Epiphany – 200pp."), and it's a well-worn route, too.'[56] David Gurewich agrees, and he thought that the calculation of the plot followed the timing of a writer for television.[57] These reservations were, to some extent, shared by Ishiguro himself. He admits that by the time he came to write *The Remains of the Day*, his technique had become so polished that he could predict 'at the smallest detail, line by line, a reader's response. A laugh here. Sad here. Here they will start to suspect Steven's [sic] honesty with himself.'[58] To avoid relying upon a successful formula, Ishiguro determined to make his next book very different. This would prevent him from getting to a situation where he could say 'well, we've been here before, let's take method 489 off the shelf and apply it here.'[59]

There have been other dissenting voices about the merits of *The Remains of the Day*. Michael Wood thinks the novel is 'overrated'[60] and lacks the misty suggestiveness of the Japanese novels. He has problems with the character of Stevens, too, and finds his repressiveness suppressive. Martin Dodsworth is dismissively frank and insists that *The Remains of the Day* shows 'the limitations of his [Ishiguro's] art'; Stevens is nothing more than a 'music-hall parody of atrophied feeling, self-importance and abasement'; and the representation of Lewis, the American delegate at the 1923 conference, is 'unbelievably crude and so ineffectual.'[61] Gabriele Annan concludes that the novel is 'too much a *roman à thèse* ... Compared to his astounding narrative sophistication, Ishiguro's message seems quite banal: Be less Japanese, less bent on dignity, less false to yourself and others, less restrained and controlled.'[62]

The most sustained critique of the novel, though, is by Susie O'Brien. In 'Serving a New World Order: Postcolonial Politics in Kazuo Ishiguro's *The Remains of the Day*',[63] she concedes the undoubted literary merits of the book, but challenges the ethical status of the Booker Prize itself by inspecting the background of its sponsors. She describes how the Booker company began in the early nineteenth century by operating sugar plantations in Demerara, Guyana. It used cheap labour to grow and gather the product and then shipped it to England for distribution and sale. It was forced to return to the United Kingdom in 1966, when Guyana attained independence. Through diversification, it became the leading food wholesaler in the British Isles, and established the Booker Prize in 1969. According to O'Brien, this was both a public relations exercise and a siphon for taxable excess profits. Her main discomfort lies with the contradiction of a company historically imbricated with colonialism awarding a prize to a writer whose book is seemingly anti-colonial in spirit. Furthermore, she is suspicious of the way in which Ishiguro is promoted as an 'international' writer. She claims that 'What remains concealed in the story of World Fiction [the genre label commonly attached to Ishiguro's books] is the *continuation*, in the realm of American publishing, of a colonial narrative of desire for an exotic other to satisfy a jaded empire's craving for novelty.'[64] What O'Brien doesn't take into account, however, is Ishiguro's own ambivalence about the internationalist label. He feels he has little in common with the writers with which he is usually grouped. However, because his novels are published in over two dozen languages, he admits to writing with international readers in mind.[65] He abstains from puns, colloquialisms and alliteration, and selects universal themes that will appeal to future readers as well as present ones. At the same time, he is conscious of the trap of writing in a way in which differences are smoothed over and commodified.

O'Brien's censures are almost benign in comparison with the damnation pronounced on Ishiguro's fourth novel, *The Unconsoled*. Kate Kellaway questioned anxiously: 'What has gone wrong? ... It's almost as if the elegant butler in *The Remains of the Day* ... has suddenly thrown his sleek, constraining waistcoat away, stripped off and gone on a dangerous, unruly bender.'[66] This could serve as an apt description of what some of the reviewers were doing, as they threw off their constraining waistcoats and attacked *The Unconsoled*. Ned Rorem compared the novel to Chinese water torture,[67] whilst Robert Kiely invoked the fanciful image of Ishiguro as a Mozart in a trance at his piano, pounding the same chords again and again without end.[68] James Wood thought the novel was 'ponderous, empty, and generally unaffecting' and unabashedly declared that it 'invents its own category of badness'[69] – a judgement which, it might be countered, invents its own category of scathingness. A repeated charge in this invective was that the book was boring. Ned Rorem stated that 'nothing is more boring than another person's dream. When that person is himself a bore, the result is fatal.'[70] Michael Wood, more tolerant of the novel's 'determined equanimity of tone',[71] still wondered if the reader would notice whether or not they had fallen asleep whilst reading. Tom Wilhelmus was more favourable, comparing this 'monument to boredom'[72] to a play by Eugène Ionesco, although even he couldn't resist a snipe when he proposed *The Unrelenting* as an alternative title for the novel.

What had gone wrong, to echo Kellaway? Until this point, Ishiguro had enjoyed very positive feedback from his peers and the press. Why did the novel inspire such apparent loathing? Salman Rushdie shrewdly identified two possible factors.[73] The first is bound up with the length of the book, and the limited time available to reviewers to digest its densities. It is not a novel amenable to speed-reading. Given the pressures on the media to be perpetually topical, one wonders how a Marcel Proust would fare in a climate of instant sound-bite judgements. Ishiguro has asserted that 'Journalism is about working yourself up into a lather over things you felt nothing about', whilst the task of the novelist is 'very slowly to try to discover what it is you really think about things.'[74] Another possibility Rushdie raises as to why *The Unconsoled* was given such short shrift is that it frustrated expectations: 'Ishiguro has done something remarkable. He has said, "I am going to be someone else now."'[75] Reviewers were disappointed because they wanted a *Son of Remains of the Day* or a *Remains of the Day: The Sequel,* and it wasn't forthcoming. This comes back to the subtle snares of stereotyping again, and the demand for safe, brand-distinctive product. *The Unconsoled* is *sui generis*, and resistant to easy pigeonholing. There is a third reason to add to Rushdie's two suggestions as to why the book was panned: the reviewers simply misunderstood what Ishiguro was trying to do. For some time, he had been dismayed by the literal-minded readings of his work. *The Remains of the Day* was interpreted as if it was a historical novel 'about the fall of the British Empire or something like that',[76] whilst its author suggested that it should be read more metaphorically. *The Unconsoled* is a premeditated attempt to 'move out of a straight, naturalistic, realistic landscape and emphasize the mythic or the metaphorical aspects of my work.'[77] By displacing the setting beyond any recognisable geographical co-ordinates and breaking the laws of narrative, the novel becomes a riddle in which both Ryder and reader reach out for meaning. The words of artist Albert Ryder would make a suitable epigraph for the book: 'Have you ever seen an inch worm crawl up a leaf or twig, and then clinging to the very end, revolve in the air, feeling for something, to reach something? That's like me. I am trying to find something out there beyond the place on which I have a footing.'[78]

Most commentators were not prepared to leap into open space to grasp the significance of *The Unconsoled*, and felt safer on their familiar leaves and twigs. The novel did, however, have its supporters, and they came from unexpected quarters. Anita Brookner – author of quiet, romantic tragicomedies such as *Hotel du Lac* (1984) – is hardly the type of writer one would expect to be wooed by the verbal virtuosities of metafiction. Yet she defended *The Unconsoled* in 'A Superb Achievement' and claimed it had been misread. Like Rushdie, she blamed the 'short attention span of readers and critics in the electronic age'[79] for many of the misapprehensions, and the overdone comparisons with Kafka. She applauded the way in which Ishiguro rendered hermetic processes in such 'limpid unstressed language',[80] and was sorry that the book wasn't received with more dignity – a sentiment, no doubt, with which Stevens would agree.

The Archbishop of Canterbury, of all people, volunteered

such a dignified reading. In a lecture titled 'The Mission of the Christian Church in the Post-Modern World', the Archbishop used the novel to illustrate the nature of postmodernism. He proclaimed that *The Unconsoled* 'offers a powerful depiction of recent cultural change – and particularly of the increasing sense of fragmentation and loss of community experienced in many parts of the world today'.[81] He isolated three factors as characteristic of postmodernism, each of which is interrogated in Ishiguro's novel: the collapse of global ideology, the relativising of values and the loss of hope. The town into which Ryder arrives has abandoned its communal purpose, and desperately struggles to believe that music can fill its vacuum. They have had many disappointments in the recent past, with the failure of Christoff (note the religious significance of the name) and Brodsky to revive their fortunes. Consequently the citizens burden Ryder with their individual requests, no longer acting for the good of the town as a whole. They live without hope, and with few expectations.

Ishiguro, because of his own displaced background, is especially well equipped to appreciate the relativity of values: 'I've always been aware that a society's mores can be quite artificial constructs that don't carry over necessarily to a different culture, because that was actually my experience and at a very personal, crucial level.'[82] His hybrid upbringing probably also accounts for why his novels are often located in transitional moments of history, when one set of values is replaced by another. Individuals caught in the middle of such a juncture (Japan after the Second World War, Britain in the 1950s) cannot help realising the impermanence of moral truths. In times of flux, societies are threatened with chaos until a new equilibrium can be reached, and a search begins for someone to re-establish order: a saviour. This is the role in which Ryder is cast by the citizens of *The Unconsoled*. As the Archbishop proposes in his lecture, Ryder is seen as someone who can revive the fortunes of the city in a Christ-like way. And yet he is only a musician, albeit in a displaced world where music is the touchstone of civic health. Thus he is asked to adjudicate upon disputes both massive and minute in a society where music has replaced religion and every other ideology as the measure of significance.

A novel defended by the strange bedfellows of Anita Brookner and the Archbishop of Canterbury, and attacked by just about everyone else, deserves closer scrutiny. If it is a failure, as Amit Chaudhuri thinks it is, then 'that itself is a brave and old-world thing to be in a time when the idea of artistic success and failure no longer really applies … it is a failure, and failure usually implies the presence of artistic vision and talent.'[83] One thing that it apparently failed to do was amuse: the funny thing about *The Unconsoled* is that most reviewers did not find the thing funny. Yet Ishiguro wrote it 'as a kind of dark comedy',[84] and there are passages which rank alongside the best of Samuel Beckett and Evelyn Waugh for their zany despair and wry satire.

Such radical misconstruals are unavoidable. When the critical lantern shines, some aspects of the work are illuminated, others cast into shadow; some themes are overinterpreted, others overlooked. Is it better, therefore, for the text to remain in darkness? Barthes, in his book on Japan, exalts the poetic form of the *haiku* (a seventeen-syllabled poem) because it refuses to 'moisten everything with meaning',[85] to use the delicious phrase of the translation. Its language is flat, without symbolic lamination: the only way to explicate it is to repeat it. But novels are not *haiku*. Their terrain is saturated with meanings and they invite multiple interpretations. Nor are novels like the canvases which Mori-san places in the middle of a room for others to 'debate and ponder' (*AFW*, 139), whilst the painter stays silent and aloof. An author speaks through the literary work, even if his or her voice is lost in the cacophony of other voices.[86]

My own critical lantern has tried to shed some light on the works of Kazuo Ishiguro. It has shone its beam on to the Japaneseness and post-atomic silences of *A Pale View of Hills*; the treatment of shame and guilt in *An Artist of the Floating World* and its self-conscious, cinematic structure; the dissection of dignity in *The Remains of the Day*, and Stevens's inauthenticity; the dreams and displacements of *The Unconsoled*; and, in the

Postscript, it will shine on the childhood abandonments in *When We Were Orphans*. But where is the author in all this? He is not at home in the texts. Or he is hiding in the shadows cast by the words on the page.

If we attend to the authorial voice outside the work, it might seem possible to finally place this displaced person. Yet this is also to strive to retrieve the irretrievable, to revolve in the air, feeling for something beyond our footing. After all, that voice is also another text, another darkness, no more to be privileged than any other. Nevertheless, let's listen to that voice with keen hearing:

> What I'm interested in is not the actual fact that my characters have done things they later regret ... I'm interested in how they come to terms with it. On the one hand there is a need for honesty, on the other hand a need to deceive themselves – to preserve a sense of dignity, some sort of self-respect. What I want to suggest is that some sort of dignity and self-respect does come from that sort of honesty.[87]

Dignity, then, is what Ishiguro's novels are 'about' – according to Ishiguro. Yet I have argued the opposite, and proposed that they are equally about displacement, which is the removal of dignity. Michael Wood disagrees with both of us, and states that Ishiguro's 'deepest subject' is storytelling: 'the comedy and the pathos of the stories we tell ourselves to keep other stories away.'[88] None of these is correct; all of them are. Or perhaps dignity and displacement and storytelling are just different ways of saying that the books address what Ishiguro calls the 'scariest arena in life, which is the emotional arena.'[89] Emotion: a simple noun – with tentacles. Yet in Ishiguro's fictions, the heart is where the home is.

Postscript on
When We Were Orphans

'LITERATURE', writes Allon White, 'without displacement is unthinkable, but literature written for readers alerted to this fact is inevitably self-obscuring.'[1] Ishiguro's novel *The Unconsoled* was an example of literary displacement *par excellence*, and its self-obscurities perplexed readers and critics alike. This presented Ishiguro with a challenge. Given the negative reactions to Ryder and his singular universe, how should the next project be shaped? Continuing to experiment might risk losing a portion of his fan-base, whilst a return to the more 'homely' vein of the earlier novels could be construed as capitulation.

When We Were Orphans is an elegant solution to the dilemma. It marries the outward realism of *An Artist of the Floating World* or *The Remains of the Day* with the perpendicular dreamscapes of *The Unconsoled*. The first half of the novel presents a convincing portrait of detective Christopher Banks as he rises in the society of 1930s London. In the second half, Banks travels to Shanghai to solve the case of his parents' mysterious disappearance there eighteen years earlier. The obsessions of his boyhood return to dominate his mature behaviour. As Ishiguro comments, 'The child's logic has been carried into the adult world.'[2]

The presence of a detective as the central protagonist should not surprise us. All of Ishiguro's previous narrators are detectives of a kind, investigating their past lives with Holmes-like meticulousness. Banks begins as a variant of Etsuko, Ono and Stevens, a mariner of memory, trawling for clues in his consciousness to help explain who he is. He ends up, however, more like Ryder, a fragmented subject driven by forces he can scarcely identify let alone control.

The movement from fully rounded character to fractured self is relayed through seven sections. Part One, 'London, 24th July 1930', introduces Banks at the onset of his sleuthing career. He meets Sarah Hemmings, an ambitious *femme fatale* who ingratiates herself with the up-and-coming detective to gain entrance to a prestigious banquet at Claridge's. There she charms Sir Cecil Medhurst, a notable statesman (whom she later marries). Banks is beguiled by Sarah, but like Stevens will not allow desire to come before duty.

In Part Two, 'London, 15th May 1931', Banks dwells upon his Shanghai past. His father worked for Butterfield and Swire, a company profiting from the opium trade in the Far East. His beautiful mother, Diana, campaigned against the invidiousness of her husband's employers. When both parents disappeared from the family home in suspicious circumstances, one after the other, Christopher was forced to travel to England to be looked after by his aunt in Shropshire.

By Part Three, 'London, 12th April 1937', Banks is celebrated in metropolitan circles, but is restless to face up to his responsibilities concerning his parents, a matter increasingly connected by him with the maelstrom of current world affairs. When he bumps into Sarah at a wedding of a mutual acquaintance, and is told that she is leaving for Shanghai with Sir Cecil, he decides to do the same – even though this means leaving behind his adopted child, Jennifer, in the care of her nanny Miss Givens. Misgivings indeed.

In Part Four, 'Cathay Hotel, Shanghai, 20th September 1937', Banks is welcomed back to his childhood haunt by the British consulate, Mr MacDonald, and Mr Grayson of the Shanghai Municipal Council. They harbour considerable expectations about how the detective's arrival might improve the fortunes of the International Settlement, now that the Japanese are attacking their Chinese foes. It is around this point that the atmosphere of the book changes. Banks confuses his mission to rescue his parents with single-handedly averting the impending global catastrophe.

In Part Five, 'Cathay Hotel, Shanghai, 29th September 1937', Banks's situation is swathed in the nightmare shadows associated with Ryder in the previous novel. Banks, like the musician, seems to find remnants of his past obtruding into the present wherever he turns. He is telephoned by an old school-friend, Anthony Morgan, who takes the detective on an unarranged visit to the house of the Lin family. There he is cleft by the startling realisation that 'the entire rear half of the room in which I was standing was in fact what used to be the entrance hall of our old house' (*WWWO*, 185–86). The past is peeping into the present like an under-painting beneath a weathered oil canvas.

Events in Part Six, 'Cathay Hotel, Shanghai, 20th October 1937', deviate further from the norms of realism. Following a tip from the retired Inspector Kung, Banks relinquishes the Inter-national Settlement – a haven of security in the military chaos surrounding it – to track down a house where he believes his parents are still being held by unknown captors. He fails to fulfil a plan to flee from Shanghai with Sarah, who wishes to escape from the increasing debts caused by Sir Cecil's gambling addiction. Instead, guided by local policeman Lieutenant Chou, he picks his way through the rubble of the warren, the devastated tenements where much of the fighting between the Japanese and the Chinese is concentrated. Chou will only go so far with Banks, and the detective is left to pursue his task in the most dangerous of conditions beyond the front line. He rescues a wounded Japanese soldier from the hostile intentions of some Chinese citizens who are eager to revenge the loss of friends and kin. It is Akira, his childhood friend. This is the sort of coinci-dence that can only happen in dreams or in Dickens. With the help of Akira's directions, Banks finally reaches the house where he hopes to find his parents. But all he discovers are the mutilated bodies of a Chinese family caught in the bombing. The only survivor is a young girl who, still in shock, is anxious about the injuries sustained by her pet dog. It is a grisly scene, mercifully ended when Banks is captured by Japanese soldiers, and transported back to the International Settlement. His case remains unsolved until Uncle Philip, a family friend from his early years – whom Banks has long suspected in assisting his mother's disappearance – summons him. Philip reveals all in a surprising *dénouement*.

Part Seven, 'London, 14th November 1958', leaps ahead some twenty years. Banks, back in England, recalls a recent trip to Hong Kong where he was at last reunited with his mother. Domiciled in Rosedale Manor, an institution for the mentally ill governed by nuns, she is incapable of recognising her son. Banks returns to London to ponder the future of Jennifer, who is yet to settle down and marry. He also muses over a single letter he received from Sarah in 1947 in which she declares her current happiness and expresses no regrets about what might have been between them. Banks doubts that she has found what she wanted, any more than he has, and concludes that 'for those like us, our fate is to face the world as orphans, chasing through long years the shadows of vanished parents' (*WWWO*, 313).

When We Were Orphans invites comparisons with J. G. Ballard's *Empire of the Sun* (1984). Ballard, himself born in Shanghai in 1930, gained a wide audience with his semi-autobiographical account of the internment of young James Graham and his family in a Japanese camp following the collapse of the International Settlement. What became apparent with the publication of this work is that the distorted environments of Ballard's earlier 'elemental' novels – such as *The Drowned World* (1962), *The Drought* (1964) and *The Crystal World* (1965) – were displacements of his own wartime experiences. He admitted in an interview that, in a sense, he had always been attempting to return to the Shanghai landscape from which he was so abruptly excluded.[3] Something similar seems to be true of Ishiguro, who left Nagasaki at the age of five, but who has frequently revisited the Japan of his imagination in his fictions.

Like Ballard's book, Ishiguro's novel is a persuasive evocation of childhood, particularly in its depiction of the relationship between the young Christopher Banks and his Japanese friend,

Akira. Following the disappearance of Mr Banks, the boys acted out 'detective' fantasies centred on the fantasy of his rediscovery. These games were the genesis of Christopher's subsequent career and psychological fixations. A touching parallel between two scenes in the book demonstrates his bond with Akira. As kids, they invaded the privacy of Ling Tien, a feared servant rumoured to hoard all manner of monstrosities amongst his personal belongings. They pluck up the courage to intrude into his room when he is away for a few days, and enter this forbidden zone linked arm-in-arm. Many years later, when as an adult Banks chances upon his wounded friend in the warren, Akira directs him to the house where the detective hopes to find his lost parents. As before, they enter the threshold whilst clinging on to each other.

Ishiguro's novel is partly about how 'our childhood becomes like a foreign land once we have grown' (*WWWO*, 277). But it is also equally about how childhood can persist through to maturity, when it colours the search for somewhere to belong and be included. *En route* to England after his parents' disappearance, the young Banks reacted angrily to the suggestion that he was 'going home': 'As I saw it, I was bound for a strange land where I did not know a soul, while the city steadily receding before me contained all I knew' (*WWWO*, 28). Yet by the end of the book, Banks is older and wiser and reconciled to his exile: 'This city ... has come to be my home' (*WWWO*, 313).

Adam Zachary Newton claims that 'literary texts play host to various kinds of homelessness, even and perhaps especially that most *heimlich* of discursive forms, first-person narrative, where 'home' fits into the quiet chamber of the narrating "I"'.[4] *When We Were Orphans* is a homefelt exploration of the quiet chamber of the self.

Notes

Chapter 1

1 Robert Frost, 'The Death of the Hired Man', in *The Complete Poems of Robert Frost* (London, Jonathan Cape, 1951), 58.

2 Peter L. Berger, Brigitte Berger and Hansfried Kellner, *The Homeless Mind: Modernization and Consciousness* (Harmondsworth, Penguin, 1974), 165.

3 Kazuo Ishiguro, *The Gourmet*, Granta, 43 (1993), 125.

4 See Janet Hawley, 'Grousebeating with Royals', *Sydney Morning Herald*, 5 March 1988, 72.

5 Kenzaburo Oe and Kazuo Ishiguro, 'Wave Patterns: A Dialogue', *Grand Street*, 10:2 (1991), 82–83.

6 See Graham Swift, 'Kazuo Ishiguro', *Bomb* (Autumn 1989), 22. When asked by his fellow novelist whether or not he feels himself to be 'particularly English', Ishiguro fudges the reply by stating that people are often a 'funny homogeneous mixture', and that it is difficult to give a definitive answer.

7 Kate Kellaway, 'The Butler on a Bender', *Observer Review*, 16 April 1995, 7.

8 Pico Iyer, 'The Nowhere Man', *Prospect* (February 1997), 30.

9 Iyer, 'Nowhere', 32.

10 Kazuo Ishiguro, letter to Salman Rushdie, in Steve MacDonogh (ed.), *The Rushdie Letters: Freedom to Speak, Freedom to Write* (London, Brandon, 1993), 80.

11 Jatinda Verma, letter to Salman Rushdie, in MacDonogh, *Rushdie Letters*, 49.

12 Abdul R. JanMohamed, 'Worldliness-without-World, Homelessness-as-Home', in Michael Sprinkler (ed.), *Edward Said: A*

Critical Reader (Oxford, Blackwell, 1992), 101.

13 Pico Iyer, 'A New Kind of Travel Writer', *Harper's Magazine* (February 1996), 30. This is from an edited transcript of a discussion between Ishiguro and Iyer, part of the Lannan Foundation's 'reading and conversation' series at the Center Green Theatre, West Hollywood, CA, US, 19 October 1995.

14 Joseph Coates, 'Deceptive Calm', *Chicago Tribune*, Books, 1 October 1989, 5.

15 Kana Oyabu, 'Cross-Cultural Fiction: The Novels of Timothy Mo and Kazuo Ishiguro' (Ph.D. thesis, University of Exeter, England, 1995), 233.

16 David Sexton, 'Interview: David Sexton Meets Kazuo Ishiguro', *Literary Review* (January 1987), 19.

17 Pico Iyer, 'Waiting upon History', *Partisan Review*, 58:3 (1991), 586.

18 See *AFW*, 15–16, 32–34, 81–82; and Eleanor Wachtel, 'Kazuo Ishiguro', *More Writers and Company* (Toronto, Knopf, 1996), 20.

19 Blake Morrison, 'It's a Long Way from Nagasaki', *Observer*, 29 October 1989, 35.

20 Morrison, 'Long Way', 35.

21 Susan Chira, 'A Case of Cultural Misperception', *New York Times*, 28 October 1989, 13. For further comments by Ishiguro on why he wanted to try something new, see Maya Jaggi, 'Dreams of Freedom', *Guardian*, 29 April 1995, 28.

22 Morrison, 'Long Way', 35.

23 Anthony Thwaite, 'In Service', *London Review of Books*, 18 May 1989, 17.

24 Oe and Ishiguro, 'Wave Patterns', 77.

25 Robert Clark, introduction to Christopher Bigsby, 'Interview with Kasuo [sic] Ishiguro', *European English Messenger*, zero issue (1990), 26.

26 Tony Tanner, *Jane Austen* (London, Macmillan, 1986), 1.

27 Iyer, 'Waiting', 588.

28 Terrence Rafferty, 'The Lesson of the Master', *New Yorker*, 15 January 1990, 104.

29 Patrick Parrinder, 'Manly Scowls', *London Review of Books*, 6 February 1986, 16.

30   See David Gurewich, 'Upstairs, Downstairs', *New Criterion*, 8:4 (1989), 77.

31   Caroline Patey, 'When Ishiguro Visits the West Country: An Essay on *The Remains of the Day*', *Acme*, 44:2 (1991), 135–55.

32   Allan Vorda, 'Stuck on the Margins: An Interview with Kazuo Ishiguro', in Allan Vorda (ed.), *Face to Face: Interviews with Contemporary Novelists* (Houston, TX, Rice University Press, 1993), 15. Originally published as Allan Vorda and Kim Herzinger, 'An Interview with Kazuo Ishiguro', *Mississippi Review*, 20 (1991), 131–54.

33   Gregory Mason, 'Inspiring Images: The Influence of the Japanese Cinema on the Writings of Kazuo Ishiguro', *East West Film Journal*, 3:2 (1989), 50.

34   Tom Wilhelmus, 'Between Cultures', *Hudson Review*, 49:2 (1996), 322.

35   Iyer, 'Nowhere', 32.

36   See Bill Ashcroft, Gareth Griffiths and Helen Tiffin (eds), *The Post-Colonial Studies Reader* (London & New York, Routledge, 1995) for critical extracts by JanMohamed (18–23), Spivak (24–28), Bhabha (29–35, 176–77) and Said (87–91).

37   Vorda, 'Stuck', 12. Emphasis in original.

38   Pico Iyer, 'The Empire Writes Back', *Time*, 8 February 1993, 54.

39   Susie O'Brien, 'Serving a New World Order: Postcolonial Politics in Kazuo Ishiguro's *The Remains of the Day*', *Modern Fiction Studies*, 42:4 (1996), 797.

40   Bruce King, 'The New Internationalism: Shiva Naipaul, Salman Rushdie, Buchi Emecheta, Timothy Mo and Kazuo Ishiguro', in James Acheson (ed.), *The British and Irish Novel Since 1960* (New York, St. Martin's Press, 1991), 209.

41   King, 'New', 210.

42   See Oyabu, 'Cross-Cultural', 259 and Steven Connor, 'Outside In', in *The English Novel in History: 1950–1995* (London, Routledge, 1996), 104.

43   Edward Said, 'Jane Austen and the Empire', in *Culture and Imperialism* (London, Chatto & Windus, 1993), 95–116.

44   Iyer, 'Waiting', 586.

45   George Steiner, *Extraterritorial: Papers on Literature and the Language Revolution* (Harmondsworth, Penguin, [1971] 1975), 21.

46 Salman Rushdie, 'The Empire Writes Back With a Vengeance',
    Times, 3 July 1982, 8. The remark is made with reference to the
    Indian writer G. V. Desani.

47 Ihab Hassan, 'An Extravagant Reticence', *The World and I*, 5:2
    (1990), 369.

48 Connor, 'Outside', 108.

49 Edward Said, *Orientalism: Western Conceptions of the Orient*
    (New York, Vintage, 1978), 1.

50 Bigsby, 'Interview', 27.

51 Jaggi, 'Dreams', 28.

52 See 'Displacement', *Oxford English Dictionary*, 2nd ed., vol. 4,
    prepared by J. A. Simpson and E. S. C. Weiner (Oxford, Clarendon
    Press, 1989), 656–57. Subsequent definitions in this paragraph are
    from the same source.

53 Mark Krupnick (ed.), introduction to *Displacement: Derrida and
    After* (Bloomington, IN, Indiana University Press, 1983), 3–4.

54 Samuel Beckett, *All That Fall*, in *The Complete Dramatic Works*
    (London, Faber & Faber, 1986), 175.

Chapter 2

1 Ruth Benedict, *The Chrysanthemum and the Sword: Patterns of
   Japanese Culture* (London, Routledge & Kegan Paul, [1946]
   1967). Although this seminal anthropological study has dated
   somewhat, many of its observations still hold true. Notoriously,
   Benedict never actually visited Japan before writing the book.

2 Benedict, *Chrysanthemum*, 2.

3 See Nancy R. Rosenberger (ed.), introduction to *Japanese Sense of
   Self* (Cambridge, Cambridge University Press, 1992), 2–3.

4 Vorda, 'Stuck', 4.

5 Kazuo Ishiguro, introduction to Yasunari Kawabata, *Snow Country*
   and *Thousand Cranes*, trans. Edward G. Seidensticker (Harmondsworth, Penguin, 1986), 1.

6 Vorda, 'Stuck', 26.

7 Anthony Thwaite, 'Ghosts in the Mirror', *Observer*, 14 February
   1982, 33.

8 Geoff Dyer, 'On Their Mettle', *New Statesman*, 4 April 1986, 25.

9   Gabriele Annan, 'On the High Wire', *New York Review of Books*, 7 December 1989, 3.

10   Thwaite, 'Ghosts', 33.

11   Mason, 'Inspiring', 47.

12   Chira, 'Misperception', 13.

13   Jonathan Spence, 'Two Worlds Japan Has Lost Since the Meiji', *New Society*, 13 May 1982, 267.

14   It did not satisfy this demand immediately. The first performance at Milan in February 1904 was booed off by a hostile crowd. Puccini recast the opera into three acts, and it was this version that was more successful at Brescia in May of the same year.

15   Bigsby, 'Interview', 28.

16   Gurewich, 'Upstairs', 80.

17   See Gurewich, 'Upstairs', 80.

18   See John Rothfork, 'Zen Comedy in Postcolonial Literature: Kazuo Ishiguro's *The Remains of the Day*', *Mosaic*, 29:1 (1996), 79–102.

19   Iyer, 'Waiting', 587.

20   See Clive Sinclair, 'The Land of the Rising Son', *Sunday Times Magazine*, 11 January 1987, 36. Sinclair also conducted an interview at the Institute of Contemporary Arts, released as 'Kazuo Ishiguro in Conversation', *The Roland Collection*, video, 34 minutes, 1987. Topics discussed include growing up in the shade of the atomic bomb; the moral crisis of post-war Japan; the codes of modern Japanese fiction; the function of research and critical encouragement in the writing process; and the difficulties of using English to portray Japanese worlds.

21   Nicholas Clee (ed.), 'The Butler in Us All', *Bookseller*, 14 April 1989, 1328.

22   Roland Barthes, *Empire of Signs*, trans. Richard Howard (London, Jonathan Cape, [1970] 1983), 3.

23   Barthes, *Empire*, 3.

24   Rocío G. Davis, 'Imaginary Homelands Revisited in the Novels of Kazuo Ishiguro', *Miscelanea*, 15 (1994), 149.

25   Gary Corseri, 'Ishiguro, Kazuo', in Hal May (ed.), *Contemporary Authors: New Revision Series*, 49 (Detroit, MI, Gale Research, 1999), 195.

26   Kazuo Ishiguro, 'A Family Supper', in Malcolm Bradbury (ed.), *The Penguin Collection of Modern Short Stories* (Harmondsworth, Penguin, 1987), 434–42.

27   Ishiguro, 'Family', 439.

28   Ishiguro, 'Family', 440.

29   See F. Hadland David, *Myths and Legends of Japan* (London, G. G. Harrap, 1913), 50–51, 127–29 and 177–80.

30   There is an echo of this ritual in *The Gourmet*, when Manley Kingston lays out food on the floor of a church vestry to entice the ghost of a man murdered there in 1884.

31   See Gustav Freytag, *The Technique of the Drama: An Exposition of Dramatic Composition and Art*, trans. Elias J. MacEwan (Chicago, Griggs, [1863] 1895).

32   It is a tableau repeated later in Chapter 10 (*PVH*, 166–68) when Sachiko drowns Mariko's kittens in the river, using the wooden box the little girl won at the *kujibiki* stall. On this second occasion, Etsuko watches Mariko watching her mother.

33   See Brian W. Shaffer, *Understanding Kazuo Ishiguro* (Columbia, SC, University of South Carolina Press, 1998), 27–31.

34   Annan, 'High Wire', 3. Annan even conjectures that Etsuko may take her own life after Niki's visit, though there is no textual evidence for this.

35   Paul Bailey, 'Private Desolations', *Times Literary Supplement*, 19 February 1982, 179.

36   See James Campbell, 'Kitchen Window', *New Statesman*, 19 February 1982, 25.

37   See Oyabu, 'Cross-Cultural', 198–202.

38   Kazuo Ishiguro, 'A Strange and Sometimes Sadness', in *Introduction 7: Stories by New Writers* (London, Faber & Faber, 1981), 13–27.

39   Kinoshita is an early sketch of the character Ogata in *A Pale View of Hills*.

40   Ishiguro, 'Sadness', 23.

41   Sexton, 'Interview', 17.

42   Michael Wood, 'Sleepless Nights', *New York Review of Books*, 21 December 1995, 18.

43   Wood, 'Sleepless', 18.

44   Wachtel, 'Kazuo', 20.

45   See John Whittier Treat, *Writing Ground Zero: Japanese Literature and the Atomic Bomb* (Chicago, University of Chicago Press, 1995).

46   Treat, *Ground Zero*, 21.

47   Treat, *Ground Zero*, 308.

48   Paul Boyer, *By the Bomb's Early Light: American Thought and Culture at the Dawn of the Atomic Age* (New York, Pantheon Books, 1985), 183.

49   Treat, *Ground Zero*, 27.

50   Joy Kogawa, *Obasan* (Harmondsworth, Penguin, [1982] 1983), 60.

51   Lawrence Langer, *The Holocaust and the Literary Imagination* (New Haven, CT, Yale University Press, 1975), 37.

52   Pierre Macherey, *A Theory of Literary Production in Literature in the Modern World*, trans. Geoffrey Wall (London, Routledge, 1978), 84.

53   Macherey, *Theory*, 87.

54   Bigsby, 'Interview', 28.

55   Kazuo Ishiguro, 'I Became Profoundly Thankful for Having Been Born in Nagasaki', *Guardian*, 8 August 1983, 9.

56   Ishiguro, 'I Became', 9.

57   See Sigmund Freud, 'The Uncanny' [1919], in *The Standard Edition of the Complete Psychological Works of Sigmund Freud*, vol. 17, trans. James Strachey (London, Hogarth Press, 1953), 217–56.

Chapter 3

1   Arthur Golden, *Memoirs of a Geisha* (London, Chatto & Windus, 1997).

2   I was made aware of Yasusada by the following: Brian McHale, 'Essentially Criminal Acts: Hoax Poetry, Mock-Hoaxes, and the Fabrication of Identity', lecture at Eighth Tampere Conference on North American Studies, University of Tampere, Finland, 24 April 1999.

3   Araki Yasusada, 'Doubled Flowering: From the Notebooks of Araki Yasusada', trans. Tosa Motokiyu, Okura Kyojin and Ojiu Norinaga, supplement, *American Poetry Review*, 25:4 (1996), 23–26.

4   Araki Yasusada, 'Mad Daughter and Big Bang: December 25, 1945', *First Intensity*, 5 (1996), 10.

5   See Takie Sugiyama Lebra, 'Self in Japanese Culture', in Rosenberger (ed.), *Japanese Sense*, 105–20.

6   Thwaite, 'Ghosts', 33.

7   Kazuo Ishiguro, 'The Summer after the War', *Granta*, 7 (1983), 121–37.

8   See Ishiguro, 'Summer', 133.

9   Ishiguro, 'Summer', 128.

10 At different stages of the drafting process, Ishiguro tried out several possible narrators: Ichiro, Nariko and even a character who did not appear in the final version of the book.

11 Shaffer, *Understanding*, 48.

12 Malcolm Bradbury, 'The Floating World', in *No, Not Bloomsbury* (London, André Deutsch, 1987), 365.

13 Bradbury, 'Floating', 364.

14 Peter J. Mallett, 'The Revelation of Character in Kazuo Ishiguro's *The Remains of the Day* and *An Artist of the Floating World*', *Shoin Literary Review*, 29 (1996), 19.

15 Anne Chisholm, 'Lost Worlds of Pleasure', *Times Literary Supplement*, 14 February 1986, 162. See *AFW*, 167–69 for a description of Ono's painting.

16 Again, this could be glossed as an allusion to the affected Japaneseness of Ishiguro's novel. It is enough for his purposes that his fiction 'looks' Japanese. Whether or not it is Japanese in substance is besides the point.

17 Margaret Scanlan, 'Mistaken Identities: First-Person Narration in Kazuo Ishiguro', *Journal of Narrative and Life History*, 3:2 & 3 (1993), 145.

18 This correspondence between the fictional and historical Matsuda has not, to the best of my knowledge, been spotted by critics or acknowledged by Ishiguro in his interviews.

19 A good model for this would be *Mishima: A Life in Four Chapters*, dir. Paul Schrader, prod. George Lucas and Francis Ford Coppola (Warner Brothers, 1985). This biopic features Ken Ogata as the Japanese writer, and parses his life into four discrete units: 1: 'Beauty', 2: 'Art', 3: 'Action', and 4: 'Harmony of Pen and Sword'. Incidentally, Ishiguro was unhappy with the film's use of Japanese stereotypes – see Sexton, 'Interview', 18.

20 Hollywood films usually have twenty-three or twenty-four sequences, but the number in Ishiguro's novel corresponds to the norm for European cinema, which tends to have between eleven and eighteen.

21   Gregory Mason, 'An Interview with Kazuo Ishiguro', *Contemporary Literature*, 30:3 (1989), 341.

22   Mason, 'Inspiring', 39.

23   Fumio Yoshioka, 'Beyond the Division of East and West: Kazuo Ishiguro's *A Pale View of Hills*', *Studies in English Literature* (1988), 75.

24   See Kathe Geist, 'Narrative Strategies in Ozu's Late Films', in Arthur Nolletti, Jr. and David Desser (eds), *Reframing Japanese Cinema: Authorship, Genre, History* (Bloomington & Indianapolis, IN, Indiana University Press, 1992), 92–111.

25   Geist, 'Narrative', 93.

26   Christopher Tookey, 'Sydenham, mon amour', *Books and Bookmen* (March, 1986), 34.

27   Mason, 'Inspiring', 44.

28   Noël Burch, *To the Distant Observer: Form and Meaning in the Japanese Cinema* (London, Scolar Press, 1979), 161. Burch's book is the definitive account of how Japanese cinema critiques Hollywood realist narrative cinema. The discontinuous, anti-linear style of directors such as Ozu is clearly a useful parallel to Ishiguro's fictional strategies.

29   Amit Chaudhuri, 'Unlike Kafka', *London Review of Books*, 8 June 1995, 30.

30   The nominations were as follows: Best Picture – Ismail Merchant, Mike Nichols, John Calley; Best Actor – Anthony Hopkins; Best Actress – Emma Thompson; Best Director – James Ivory; Best Original Score – Richard Robbins; Best Adapted Screenplay – Ruth Prawer Jhabvala; Best Art Direction/Set Decoration – Luciana Arrighi, Ian Whittaker; and Best Costume Design – Jenny Beavan, John Bright.

31   John Ash, 'Stick It Up Howard's End', *Gentleman's Quarterly* (August 1994), 43.

Chapter 4

1   Jessica Berry and Andrew Alderson, 'Japanese Mourn a Lost Britain of Tea, Butlers and Stiff Upper Lips', *Sunday Times*, 16 November 1997, 3.

2   Jeffrey Richards, *Films and British National Identity: From Dickens to Dad's Army* (Manchester and New York, Manchester University Press, 1997), 169.

3   Vorda, 'Stuck', 14. Emphasis in original.

4   Patey, 'West Country', 135.

5   Iyer, 'Waiting', 586.

6   Connor, 'Outside', 107.

7   See George Watson, 'The Silence of the Servants', *Sewanee Review*, 103:3 (1995), 480–86, for a larger overview of servants in literature from the comedies of Plautus through to Cervantes, Shakespeare and Dickens.

8   Hassan, 'World', 374.

9   Rafferty, 'Lesson', 103.

10 Norman Page, 'Speech, Culture and History in the Novels of Kazuo Ishiguro', in Mimi Chan and Roy Harris (eds), *Asian Voices in English* (Hong Kong, Hong Kong University Press, 1991), 164.

11 William Hutchings, 'English: Fiction', *World Literature Today*, 64:3 (1990), 464.

12 Thwaite, 'In Service', 17.

13 See bibliography for broadcast details. The initial 'J' in the title suggests Prufrockian echoes.

14 Kazuo Ishiguro, *A Profile of Arthur J. Mason*, unpublished manuscript, 18.

15 Ishiguro, *Profile*, 25.

16 Ishiguro, *Profile*, 10.

17 Clee (ed.), 'Butler in Us All', 1327.

18 R. A. W. Rudd, 'Storm over Port', *Times*, 7 November 1989, 17. See also General Sir John Hackett, 'A Letter to the Editor', *Daily Telegraph*, 16 December 1989, for some similar misguided objections.

19 Philip Howard, 'A Comedy of Authors', *Times*, supplement, 21 September 1993, vi.

20 See Francis King, 'A Stately Procession of One', *Spectator*, 27 May 1989, 31.

21 Annan, 'High Wire', 4.

22 Wachtel, 'Kazuo', 19.

23 Oe and Ishiguro, 'Wave Patterns', 83.

24 Wachtel, 'Kazuo', 26.

25 Rafferty, 'Lesson', 102.

26   Coates, 'Deceptive', 5.

27   Connor, 'Outside', 104.

28   Barthes, *Empire*, 108.

29   See Connor, 'Outside', 105–06.

30   The phrase applies to Mr George Ketteridge, a fellow butler, but Stevens could well have made it about himself.

31   See 'Dignity', *Oxford English Dictionary*, vol. 4, 814–15.

32   It is therefore deeply ironic that when Stevens's father comes to work at Darlington Hall, he is on the decline and is made to suffer various indignities. Before the 1923 conference, for instance, he is reduced to 'pushing a trolley loaded with cleaning utensils, mops, brushes … teapots, cups and saucers, so that it at times resembled a street-hawker's barrow' (*RD*, 78).

33   Edward de Bono, *The Happiness Purpose* (Harmondsworth, Penguin, 1977), 126. Emphasis in original.

34   See Jean-Paul Sartre, *Being and Nothingness: An Essay on Phenomenological Ontology*, trans. Hazel E. Barnes (London, Methuen, [1943] 1958), 49–50.

35   *White Lies* – with its connotations of ethnicity and trivial deceit – would make a splendid alternative title for the novel.

36   It is significant that this episode is bracketed by talk about a fake seventeenth-century stone arch leading into the dining room. Stevens likes to position himself under this arch when he is on duty, and the exchange with the Wakefields occupies what is almost the dead centre of the book.

37   Salman Rushdie, 'What the Butler Didn't See', *Observer*, 21 May 1989, 53.

38   Galen Strawson, 'Tragically Disciplined and Dignified', *Times Literary Supplement*, 19 May 1989, 535.

39   Mark Kamine, 'A Servant of Self-Deceit', *New Leader*, 13 November 1989, 21.

40   The theatrical connotations of the term are obvious.

41   Pamela Horn,*The Rise and Fall of the Victorian Servant* (Stroud, Alan Sutton, 1990), 167.

42   M. Griffiths, 'Great English Houses/New Homes in England?: Memory and Identity in Kazuo Ishiguro's *The Remains of the Day* and V. S. Naipaul's *The Enigma of Arrival*', *Span*, 36 (1993), 494.

43   Chie Nakane, *Japanese Society* (Harmondsworth, Penguin, 1973), 61.

44   The award of a knighthood is still today one of the greatest
       honours an Englishman can receive. Ishiguro himself received the
       Order of the British Empire in 1995 for services to literature
       (despite the fact that his fiction punctures the very notion of
       Empire). It is interesting to note in this context that in 1999 a
       portrait of Kazuo Ishiguro by Peter Edwards replaced one of Pitt
       the Younger by George Romney in the entertaining room of
       Number 10 Downing Street, the home of British Prime Minister
       Tony Blair. See David Lister, 'Revealed: The "Trendy" Art Chosen
       for Facelift at No 10', *Independent*, 18 September 1999, 1.

45   Ernest Barker, 'Some Constants of the English Character' [1947],
       in Judy Giles and Tim Middleton (eds), *Writing Englishness 1900–
       1950: An Introductory Sourcebook on National Identity* (London,
       Routledge, 1995), 59.

46   Lord Redesdale admired Hitler; Lord Londonderry was a friend of
       Goering; and five peers – Lord Stamp, Lord Clive, Lord Hollenden,
       Lord Brocket and Lord McGowan – attended the 1938 Nuremberg
       rally. Furthermore, the Duke of Wellington was a member of an
       anti-semitic secret society, and MI5 investigated the Duke of
       Westminster at the outbreak of the Second World War because of
       his pro-German sympathies.

47   See Rosenberger, introduction, *Japanese Sense*, 4.

48   See Nakane, *Japanese Society*, 24–40.

49   Hermione Lee, 'Quiet Desolation', *New Republic*, 22 January
       1990, 38.

50   David Lodge, 'The Unreliable Narrator', in *The Art of Fiction*
       (New York, Viking, 1992), 155.

51   Homi K. Bhabha, 'Of Mimicry and Man: The Ambivalence of
       Colonial Discourse', *October*, 28 (1984), 125–33.

52   Strawson, 'Tragically', 535.

53   Griffiths, 'Great English', 492. Incidentally, 'dignity' is also an
       oratorical term for the correct use of tropes and figures towards
       which Stevens strives.

54   Page, 'Speech', 165.

55   Annan, 'High Wire', 4.

56   Iyer, 'Waiting', 588.

57   Vorda, 'Stuck', 34.

58   Ishiguro told an interviewer that he spent weeks deciding whether
       or not to include this line. He decided to do so, in case he himself

was accused of the same sterility as his character. See Clee (ed.), 'Butler in Us All', 1328.

59   Derrick Mercer (ed.), *Chronicle of the 20th Century* (London, Longman, 1988), 786.

60   Rushdie, 'What', 53. See also John Sutherland, 'Why Hasn't Mr Stevens Heard of the Suez Crisis?', in *Where Was Rebecca Shot?: Puzzles, Curiosities and Conundrums in Modern Fiction* (London, Wiedenfeld & Nicolson, 1998), 185–89.

61   Coates, 'Deceptive', 5.

62   Tony Augarde (ed.), *The Oxford Dictionary of Modern Quotations* (Oxford, Oxford University Press, 1991), 229.

Chapter 5

1   See Oyabu, 'Cross-Cultural', 189.

2   Nigel Hunt, 'Two Close Looks at Faraway', *Brick*, 31 (1987), 38.

3   See Karine Zbinden, 'Self-Representation in Kazuo Ishiguro's Novels' (MA dissertation, University of Lausanne, Switzerland, 1996), 35.

4   See Sigmund Freud, 'The Dream-Work' [1916–17], in *Introductory Lectures on Psychoanalysis*, lecture 11, trans. James Strachey (Harmondsworth, Penguin, 1971), 204–18 for a fuller explanation of this process.

5   Freud, *Interpretation of Dreams* [1900], in *Standard Edition*, vol. 4, 308.

6   Pico Iyer, 'The Butler Didn't Do It, Again', *Times Literary Supplement*, 28 April 1995, 22.

7   Valentine Cunningham, 'A Pale View of Ills Without Remedy', *Guardian*, 7 May 1995, 15.

8   Wood, 'Sleepless', 17.

9   Linda Simon, 'Remains of the Novelist', *Commonweal*, 22 March 1996, 25.

10   Shaffer, *Understanding*, 115.

11   *A Christmas Carol* (1843) by Charles Dickens seems to be an important text for Ishiguro. In Chapter 7 of *A Pale View of Hills*, Sachiko tells Etsuko about her contact with the tale: 'I remember once ... my father brought a book back from America for me, an English version of *A Christmas Carol*. That became something of

an obsession of mine, Etsuko. I wanted to learn English well enough to read that book. Unfortunately, I never had the chance. When I married, my husband forbade me to continue learning. In fact, he made me throw the book away.' (*PVH*, 110) For a persuasive account of the ghost elements in Ishiguro's works, see Gabriel Brownstein, 'Kazuo Ishiguro', in Carol Howard and George Stade (eds), *British Writers Supplement IV* (New York, Scribner's, 1997), 301–17.

12   It is only much later, after Brodsky is involved in the 'hacksaw amputation' incident in Chapter 30, that Ryder and the reader find out about the extent of this earlier injury.

13   Tim Rayment, 'Niceness', *Sunday Times Magazine*, 8 February 1998, 48.

14   Iyer, 'Butler', 22.

15   Yoshioka, 'Beyond', 83.

16   For passages about Boris and 'Number Nine', see *U*, 40–42, 162, 206–16; for Ryder's musings about football matches, see *U*, 15, 24, 161–66 and 245–46; and for other soccer references, see *U*, 35 and 73.

17   Cynthia F. Wong, *Kazuo Ishiguro* (Tavistock, Northcote House, 2000), 76.

18   See Ishiguro, 'Summer', 121 for an earlier version of this assailant fantasy in the mind of Ichiro.

19   See the episode in Chapter 8 when Ryder ignores Boris's attempt to impress him by drawing a picture of Superman. Sophie upbraids the musician in the same terms as on the tram: 'You'll never feel towards him like a real father.' (*U*, 95)

20   Vorda, 'Stuck', 30–31.

21   Jaggi, 'Dreams', 28.

22   Paul Gray, 'Bad Dream: After *The Remains of the Day*, a Weird Non-Sequitur', *Time*, 2 October 1995, 82.

23   Ned Rorem, 'Fiction in Review', *Yale Review*, 84:2 (1996), 157.

24   Rorem, 'Fiction', 157.

25   Chaudhuri, 'Unlike', 30.

26   Chaudhuri, 'Unlike', 31.

27   Cunningham, 'Pale', 15.

28   Cunningham, 'Pale', 15.

29   Rorem, 'Fiction', 158.

30   Wood, 'Sleepless', 17. This feature is one of three 'rules' that Wood believes govern the world of *The Unconsoled*. The other two are that people appear in front of Ryder whenever he thinks about them, and that when they do they invariably inflict the musician with their monologues of misery.

31   Malcolm Bradbury, 'Breaking Loose', *W Magazine*, 1 (1995), 36–37.

32   Tamsin Todd, 'Down and Out in Central Europe', *Austin Chronicle*, 7 June 1996, 32.

33   Vorda, 'Stuck', 12.

34   Vorda, 'Stuck', 29. Emphasis in original.

35   Vorda, 'Stuck', 16.

Chapter 6

1   Macherey, *Theory*, 84.

2   See Oyabu, 'Cross-Cultural', 246–47.

3   Kazuo Ishiguro, 'Waiting for J', in *Introduction 7: Stories by New Writers* (London, Faber & Faber, 1981), 28–37.

4   Kazuo Ishiguro, 'Getting Poisoned', in *Introduction 7*, 38–51.

5   Sinclair, 'Land', 36.

6   These games include torturing the family cat by starving it, then tethering its collar to somewhere in the kitchen just out of reach of a bowl of food. The sadism culminates in a nasty scene where the cat is poisoned with weed-killer. It is a rehearsal for the narrator's later attempt to murder his potential step-sister, Carol. (As a matter of curiosity, the cat is called Naomi – the same name Ishiguro later gave to his daughter.)

7   Sexton, 'Interview', 16.

8   Shaffer, *Understanding*, 57.

9   Shaffer, *Understanding*, 90.

10   See Wong, *Ishiguro*, 18–19, 27–28. The terms 'homodiegetic' and 'extradiegetic' have been popularised by Shlomith Rimmon-Kenan, *Narrative Fiction: Contemporary Poetics* (London, Methuen, 1983).

11   Wong, *Ishiguro*, 51.

12   Wong, *Ishiguro*, 58.

13   Wong, *Ishiguro*, 69.

14 Wong, *Ishiguro*, 66. The phrase is borrowed from Zygmunt Bauman.

15 Jaggi, 'Dreams', 28.

16 See Clee (ed.), 'Butler in Us All', 1327.

17 Iyer, 'Butler', 22.

18 The pattern largely holds true in *When We Were Orphans*, too, as is discussed in the Postscript.

19 Ishiguro's initial ambitions were not literary but musical. See Rorem, 'Fiction', 155; Dylan Otto Krider, 'Rooted in a Small Place: An Interview with Kazuo Ishiguro', *Kenyon Review*, 20 (1998), 146–48; and Miyuki Hama, 'A Pale View', *Switch*, 8:6 (1991), 76–102. This last article, although written in Japanese, reproduces the lyrics (in English) of a pop song Ishiguro wrote in 1977 called 'Old Sixties Records'. It also lists his favourite musicians, who include Bob Dylan, Miles Davis and Bruce Springsteen.

20 Lee, 'Quiet', 36.

21 Lee, 'Quiet', 37.

22 Mason, 'Interview', 3.

23 Francis King, 'Shimmering', *Spectator*, 27 February 1982, 25.

24 Spence, 'Two Worlds', 267.

25 Yoshioka, 'Beyond', 72.

26 Cynthia F. Wong, 'The Shame of Memory: Blanchot's Self-Dispossession in Ishiguro's *A Pale View of Hills*', *Clio*, 24:2 (1995), 127–45.

27 Iyer, 'Waiting', 588.

28 Allan Massie, *The Novel Today: A Critical Guide to the British Novel 1970–1989* (London & New York, Longman, 1990), 64.

29 Penelope Lively, 'Backwards and Forwards', *Encounter*, 58:6 & 59:1 (1982), 90.

30 King, 'Shimmering', 25.

31 Ishiguro, introduction to *Snow Country*, 3.

32 King, 'New', 207.

33 Bradbury, 'Floating', 364.

34 Annan, 'High Wire', 4. Giorgio Morandi (1890–1964) was an Italian artist, but the serenity of his bottles and vases and narrow tonal palette have affinities with the Japanese tradition.

35 Charles Sarvan, 'Floating Signifiers and *An Artist of the Floating World*', *Journal of Commonwealth Literature*, 32:1 (1997), 97.

36 Bradbury, 'Floating', 365.

37 It was also shortlisted for the Booker Prize that year, alongside *The Old Devils* by Kingsley Amis (the winner), *The Handmaid's Tale* by Margaret Atwood, *Gabriel's Lament* by Paul Bailey, *What's Bred in the Bone* by Robertson Davies and *An Insular Possession* by Timothy Mo.

38 The other competitors were: *Cat's Eye* by Margaret Atwood, *The Book of Evidence* by John Banville, *Jigsaw* by Sybille Bedford, *A Disaffection* by James Kelman and *Restoration* by Rose Tremain.

39 Philip Howard, 'A Butler's Tale Wins Booker for Ishiguro', *Times*, 27 October 1989, 24.

40 See Clee (ed.), 'Butler in Us All', 1328.

41 Howard, 'Butler's Tale', 24.

42 Vorda, 'Stuck', 8.

43 Salman Rushdie, 'Imaginary Homelands', in *Imaginary Homelands: Essays and Criticism 1981–1991* (London, Granta Books, 1991), 10.

44 Rushdie, 'Imaginary', 12. Emphasis in original.

45 Rushdie, 'What', 53.

46 Vorda, 'Stuck', 9.

47 Rushdie, 'What', 53.

48 Coates, 'Deceptive', 5.

49 Strawson, 'Tragically', 535.

50 Lawrence Graver, 'What the Butler Saw', *New York Times Book Review*, 8 October 1989, 3.

51 Daniela Carpi, 'The Crisis of the Social Subject in the Contemporary English Novel', *European Journal of English Studies*, 1:2 (1997), 183.

52 Patey, 'West Country', 136.

53 Rocío G. Davis, '*The Remains of the Day*: Kazuo Ishiguro's Sonnet on His Blindness', *Cuadernos de Investigación Filológica*, 21–22 (1995–96), 57–67.

54 Kathleen Wall, '*The Remains of the Day* and Its Challenges to Theories of Unreliable Narration', *Journal of Narrative Technique*, 24:1 (1994), 18–42.

55 Rafferty, 'Lesson', 102.

56 Rafferty, 'Lesson', 104.

57   Gurewich, 'Upstairs, Downstairs', 79–80.

58   Susie [sic] Mackenzie, 'Into the Real World', *Guardian*, 15 May 1996, 12.

59   Wachtel, 'Kazuo', 291.

60   Wood, 'Sleepless', 18.

61   Martin Dodsworth, 'The Novel Since 1950', in Martin Dodsworth (ed.), *The Penguin History of Literature: Volume 7, The Twentieth Century* (Harmondsworth, Penguin, 1994), 344.

62   Annan, 'High Wire', 4.

63   Susie O'Brien, 'Serving a New World Order: Postcolonial Politics in Kazuo Ishiguro's *The Remains of the Day*', *Modern Fiction Studies*, 42:4 (1996), 787–806.

64   O'Brien, 'Serving', 797. Emphasis in original.

65   When asked by Pico Iyer if he deliberately wrote for an international audience, Ishiguro replied that when he writes he has an unconscious image of a bunch of Norwegians in his head. This stems from promotional tours, where he might be in Oslo for four days and faced by some tough questions on issues he hadn't foreseen. See Iyer, 'New Kind', 30.

66   See Kellaway, 'Bender', 6.

67   Rorem, 'Fiction', 159.

68   Robert Kiely, 'In an Unknown City to an Unknown Destination', *Boston Book Review*, 1 October 1995, 32.

69   James Wood, 'Ishiguro in the Underworld', *Guardian*, 5 May 1995, 5.

70   Rorem, 'Fiction', 159.

71   Wood, 'Sleepless', 18.

72   Wilhelmus, 'Between', 322.

73   Rushdie, quoted in Kellaway, 'Bender', 6.

74   Mackenzie, 'Into', 12.

75   Rushdie, quoted in Kellaway, 'Bender', 6.

76   Vorda, 'Stuck', 28.

77   Wachtel, 'Kazuo', 19.

78   See entry in Ian Chilvers (ed.), *The Concise Oxford Dictionary of Art and Artists* (Oxford and New York, Oxford University Press, 1990), 415. Albert Pinkham Ryder (1847–1917), an American tonalist painter, was influenced by Japanese prints and literature.

79   Anita Brookner, 'A Superb Achievement', *Spectator*, 24 June 1995, 40.

80   Brookner, 'Superb', 40.

81   The lecture, delivered by the Archbishop of Canterbury – George Carey – at the University of Notre Dame, IN, 24 July 1996, has not been officially published. However, a full transcript is available on the World Wide Web at the following address: http://www.nd.edu/~ktrembat/www-EDNIN/text/Mission.Post.Modern.html

82   Wachtel, 'Kazuo', 23.

83   Chaudhuri, 'Unlike', 31.

84   Rorem, 'Fiction', 157.

85   See Barthes, *Empire*, 70.

86   It is too early to see if that voice is heard in the reception accorded to *When We Were Orphans*, published when this study was in press.

87   Graver, 'Saw', 3.

88   Wood, 'Sleepless', 18.

89   Vorda, 'Stuck', 18.

Chapter 7

1   Allon White, *Uses of Obscurity: The Fiction of Early Modernism* (London, Routledge & Kegan Paul, 1981), 3.

2   Wong, *Ishiguro*, 81.

3   See Thomas Frick, 'J. G. Ballard', *Paris Review*, 94 (1984), 132–60.

4   Adam Zachary Newton, 'Telling Others: Secrecy and Recognition in Dickens, Barnes, and Ishiguro', in *Narrative Ethics* (Cambridge, MA, Harvard University Press, 1997), 243.

Select bibliography

Works by Kazuo Ishiguro

NOVELS

A Pale View of Hills (London, Faber & Faber, 1982; New York, G. P. Putnam's Sons, 1982).

An Artist of the Floating World (London, Faber & Faber, 1986; New York, G. P. Putnam's Sons, 1986).

The Remains of the Day (London, Faber & Faber, 1989; New York, Knopf, 1989).

The Unconsoled (London, Faber & Faber, 1995; New York, Knopf, 1995).

When We Were Orphans (London, Faber & Faber, 2000; New York, Knopf, 2000).

SHORT STORIES

'A Strange and Sometimes Sadness', in *Introduction 7: Stories by New Writers* (London, Faber & Faber, 1981), 13–27.

'Getting Poisoned', in *Introduction 7: Stories by New Writers* (London, Faber & Faber, 1981), 38–51.

'Waiting for J', in *Introduction 7: Stories by New Writers* (London, Faber & Faber, 1981), 28–37.

'A Family Supper', in T. J. Binding (ed.), *Firebird 2* (Harmondsworth, Penguin, 1983), 121–31; also in Malcolm Bradbury (ed.), *The Penguin Collection of Modern Short Stories* (Harmondsworth, Penguin, 1987), 434–42; and *Esquire*, (March 1990), 207–11.

'The Summer After the War', *Granta 7* (1983), 121–37.

SCREENPLAYS

A Profile of Arthur J. Mason, unpublished manuscript. Originally broadcast in the UK by Channel 4, 18 October 1984, dir. Michael Whyte, prod. Ann Skinner (Skreba/Spectre), with Bernard Hepton, Charles Gray and Cheri Lunghi.

The Gourmet, *Granta*, 43 (1993), 89–127. Originally broadcast in the UK by Channel 4, 8 May 1986, dir. Michael Whyte, prod. Ann Skinner (Skreba/Spectre), with Charles Gray and Mick Ford.

OTHER WRITINGS

'I Became Profoundly Thankful for Having Been Born in Nagasaki', *Guardian*, 8 August 1983, 9.

Introduction to Yasunari Kawabata, *Snow Country* and *Thousand Cranes*, trans. Edward G. Seidensticker (Harmondsworth, Penguin, [1971], 1986), 1–3.

Letter to Salman Rushdie, in Steve MacDonogh (ed.), *The Rushdie Letters: Freedom to Speak, Freedom to Write* (London, Brandon, 1993), 79–80.

Reviews

A PALE VIEW OF HILLS

Bailey, Paul, 'Private Desolations', *Times Literary Supplement*, 19 February 1982, 179.

Campbell, James, 'Kitchen Window', *New Statesman*, 19 February 1982, 25.

King, Francis, 'Shimmering', *Spectator*, 27 February 1982, 25.

Lively, Penelope, 'Backwards and Forwards', *Encounter*, 58:6 & 59:1 (1982), 86–91.

Milton, Edith, 'In a Japan Like Limbo', *New York Times Book Review*, 9 May 1982, 12–13.

Spence, Jonathan, 'Two Worlds Japan Has Lost Since the Meiji', *New Society*, 13 May 1982, 266–67.

Thwaite, Anthony, 'Ghosts in the Mirror', *Observer*, 14 February 1982, 33.

AN ARTIST OF THE FLOATING WORLD

Chisholm, Anne, 'Lost Worlds of Pleasure', *Times Literary Supplement*, 14 February 1986, 162.

Geoff Dyer, 'On Their Mettle', *New Statesman*, 4 April 1986, 25.

Hunt, Nigel, 'Two Close Looks at Faraway', *Brick*, 31 (1987), 36–38.

Morton, Kathryn, 'After the War was Lost', *New York Times Book Review*, 8 June 1986, 19.

Parrinder, Patrick, 'Manly Scowls', *London Review of Books*, 6 February 1986, 16.

Stuewe, Paul, 'Genuine Japanese … Slush-Pile Saviour … for God and Greed', *Quill and Quire*, 52:12 (1986), 31.

Wasi, Jehenara, 'Book Reviews', *Indian Horizons*, 36:1&2 (1987), 52–54.

THE REMAINS OF THE DAY

Annan, Gabriele, 'On the High Wire', *New York Review of Books*, 7 December 1989, 3–4.

Coates, Joseph, 'Deceptive Calm', *Chicago Tribune*, Books, 1 October 1989, 5.

Dyer, Geoff, 'What the Butler Did', *New Statesman and Society*, 26 May 1989, 34.

Graver, Lawrence, 'What the Butler Saw', *New York Times Book Review*, 8 October 1989, 3, 33.

Gray, Paul, 'Upstairs, Downstairs', *Time*, 30 October 1989, 55.

Gurewich, David, 'Upstairs, Downstairs', *New Criterion*, 8:4 (1989), 77–80.

Hutchings, William, 'English: Fiction', *World Literature Today*, 64:3 (1990), 463–64.

Iyer, Pico, 'Waiting Upon History', *Partisan Review*, 58:3 (1991), 585–89.

Kamine, Mark, 'A Servant of Self-Deceit', *New Leader*, 13 November 1989, 21–22.

King, Francis, 'A Stately Procession of One', *Spectator*, 27 May 1989, 31–32.

Rafferty, Terrence, 'The Lesson of the Master', *New Yorker*, 15 January 1990, 102–04.

Rubin, Merle, 'A Review of *The Remains of the Day*', *Christian Science Monitor*, 13 November 1989, 13.

Rushdie, Salman, 'What the Butler Didn't See', *Observer*, 21 May 1989, 53; reprinted as 'Kazuo Ishiguro', in Salman Rushdie, *Imaginary Homelands: Essays and Criticism 1981–1991* (London, Granta Books, 1991), 244–46.

Strawson, Galen, 'Tragically Disciplined and Dignified', *Times Literary Supplement*, 19 May 1989, 535.

Thwaite, Anthony, 'In Service', *London Review of Books*, 18 May 1989, 17–18.

THE UNCONSOLED

Allen, Brooke, 'Leaving Behind Daydreams for Nightmares', *Wall Street Journal*, 11 October 1995, A12.

Brookner, Anita, 'A Superb Achievement', *Spectator*, 24 June 1995, 40–41.

Chaudhuri, Amit, 'Unlike Kafka', *London Review of Books*, 8 June 1995, 30–31.

Cunningham, Valentine, 'A Pale View of Ills Without Remedy', *Guardian*, 7 May 1995, 15.

Cusk, Rachel, 'Journey to the End of the Day', *Times*, 11 May 1995, 38.

Eder, Richard, 'Meandering in a Dreamscape', *Los Angeles Times Book Review*, 8 October 1995, 3, 7.

Gray, Paul, 'Bad Dream: After *The Remains of the Day*, a Weird Non-Sequitur', *Time*, 2 October 1995, 81–82.

Hughes-Hallett, Lucy, 'Feeling No Pain', *Sunday Times*, Books, 14 May 1995, 7, 9.

Innes, Charlotte, 'Fiction Without Frontiers', *Los Angeles Times*, 5 November 1995, 11.

Innes, Charlotte, 'Dr Faustus Faces the Music', *Nation*, 6 November 1995, 546–48.

Iyer, Pico, 'The Butler Didn't Do It, Again', *Times Literary Supplement*, 28 April 1995, 22.

Kauffmann, Stanley, 'The Floating World', *New Republic*, 6 November 1995, 42–45.

Kaveney, Roz, 'Tossed and Turned', *New Statesman and Society*, 12 May 1995, 39.

Kiely, Robert, 'In an Unknown City to an Unknown Destination', *Boston Book Review*, 1 October 1995, 32.

Menand, Louis, 'Anxious in Dreamland', *New York Times Book Review*, 15 October 1995, 7.

Passaro, Vince, 'New Flash from an Old Isle', *Harper's Magazine* (October 1995), 71–75.

Rorem, Ned, 'Fiction in Review', *Yale Review*, 84:2 (1996), 154–59.

Rorty, Richard, 'Consolation Prize', *Village Voice Literary Supplement* (October 1995), 13.

Rubin, Merle, 'Probing the Plight of Lives "Trapped" in Others' Expectations', *Christian Science Monitor*, 4 October 1995, 14.

Shone, Tom, 'Chaos Theory', *Harper's Bazaar*, 1 October 1995, 132.

Simon, Linda, 'Remains of the Novelist', *Commonweal*, 22 March 1996, 25–26.

Steinberg, Sybil, 'A Book About Our World', *Publisher's Weekly*, 18 September 1995, 105–06.

Sweet, Nick, 'Kafka Set to Music', *Contemporary Review* (October 1995), 223–24.

Todd, Tamsin, 'Down and Out in Central Europe', *Austin Chronicle*, 7 June 1996, 32.

Wilhelmus, Tom, 'Between Cultures', *Hudson Review*, 49:2 (1996), 316–22.

Wood, James, 'Ishiguro in the Underworld', *Guardian*, 5 May 1995, 5.

Wood, Michael, 'Sleepless Nights', *New York Review of Books*, 21 December 1995, 17–18.

WHEN WE WERE ORPHANS

Barrow, Andrew, 'Clueless in Shanghai', *Spectator*, 25 March 2000, 44–45.

Carey, John, 'Few Novels Extend the Possibilities of Fiction. This One Does', *Sunday Times*, Culture, 2 April 2000, 45.

Francken, James 'Something Fishy', *London Review of Books*, 13 April 2000, 37.

Hensher, Philip, 'It's the Way He Tells It …', *Observer Review*, 19 March 2000, 11.

Jaggi, Maya, 'In Search of Lost Crimes', *Guardian*, 1 April 2000, 8.

Jones, Russell Celyn, 'Shanghai Search', *Times 2*, 6 April 2000, 15.

Leith, Sam, 'Shanghai Sherlock', *Daily Telegraph*, Arts and Books, 25 March 2000, 4.

McWilliam, Candia, 'Painful, Lovely, Limpid in Freezing Fog', *Financial Times*, Weekend, 8 April 2000, 4.

Oates, Joyce Carol, 'The Serpent's Heart', *Times Literary Supplement*, 31 March 2000, 21–22.

Sutcliffe, William, 'History Happens Elsewhere', *Independent on Sunday*, Sunday Review, 2 April 2000, 56–58.

Interviews and profiles

Bigsby, Christopher, 'An Interview with Kasuo [sic] Ishiguro', *European English Messenger*, zero issue (1990), 26–29.

Bradbury, Dominic, 'Making Up a Country of His Own', *Times 2*, 6 April 2000, 12–13

Bradbury, Malcolm, 'Breaking Loose', *W Magazine*, 1 (1995), 34–37.

Bryson, Bill, 'Between Two Worlds', *New York Times*, 29 April 1990, sec. 6, 38, 44, 80.

Chira, Susan, 'A Case of Cultural Misperception', *New York Times*, 28 October 1989, 13.

Clee, Nicholas (ed.),'The Butler in Us All', *Bookseller*, 14 April 1989, 1327–28.

Field, Michele, 'This Britisher is Japanese', *Sydney Morning Herald*, 12 March 1988, 74.

Hawley, Janet, 'Grousebeating with Royals', *Sydney Morning Herald*, 5 March 1988, 72.

Hensher, Philip, 'Books', *Harper's and Queen* (May 1995), 21.

Howard, Philip, 'A Butler's Tale Wins Booker for Ishiguro', *Times*, 27 October 1989, 24.

Howard, Philip, 'A Comedy of Authors', *Times*, supplement, 21 September 1993, vi.

Iyer, Pico, 'A New Kind of Travel Writer', *Harper's Magazine* (February 1996), 30, 32.

Jaggi, Maya, 'Dreams of Freedom', *Guardian*, 29 April 1995, 28.

Jaggi, Maya, 'Kazuo Ishiguro Talks to Maya Jaggi', *Wasafiri*, 22 (1995), 20–24.

de Jongh, Nicholas, 'Life After the Bomb', *Guardian*, 22 February, 1982, 11.

Kellaway, Kate, 'The Butler on a Bender', *Observer Review*, 16 April 1995, 6–7.

Krider, Dylan Otto, 'Rooted in a Small Space: An Interview with Kazuo Ishiguro', *Kenyon Review*, 20 (1998), 146–54.

Mackenzie, Suzie, 'Into the Real World', *Guardian*, 15 May 1996, 12.

Mackenzie, Susie [sic], 'Between Two Worlds', *Guardian*, Weekend, 25 March 2000, 10–11, 13–14, 17.

Mason, Gregory, 'An Interview with Kazuo Ishiguro', *Contemporary Literature*, 30:3 (1989), 335–47.

Morrison, Blake, 'It's a Long Way from Nagasaki', *Observer*, 29 October 1989, 35.

Oe, Kenzaburo, and Kazuo Ishiguro, 'The Novelist in Today's World: A Conversation', *Boundary 2*, 18 (1991), 109–22. Reprinted as 'Wave Patterns: A Dialogue' in *Grand Street* 10 (1991), 75–91; originally published in Japanese in *Kokusai Koryu*, 53 (1989), 100–08.

Ohno, Barbara, 'Who Is the Unconsoled?': A Profile of Novelist Kazuo Ishiguro', *Mars Hill Review*, 5 (1996), 137–42.

Sexton, David, 'Interview: David Sexton Meets Kazuo Ishiguro', *Literary Review* (January 1987), 16–19.

Sinclair, Clive, 'The Land of the Rising Son', *Sunday Times Magazine*, 11 January 1987, 36–37.

Sinclair, Clive, 'Kazuo Ishiguro in Conversation', *The Roland Collection*, video, 34 minutes, 1987.

Smith, Julia Llewellyn, 'A Novel Taste of Criticism: Kazuo Ishiguro', *Times*, 3 May 1995, 17.

Swift, Graham, 'Kazuo Ishiguro', *Bomb* (Autumn 1989), 22–23.

Tonkin, Boyd, 'Artist of His Floating World', *Independent*, Weekend Review, 1 April 2000, 9.

Tookey, Christopher, 'Sydenham, mon amour', *Books and Bookmen* (March 1986), 33–34.

Vorda, Allan, and Kim Herzinger, 'An Interview with Kazuo Ishiguro', *Mississippi Review*, 20 (1991), 131–54. Reprinted as 'Stuck on the Margins: An Interview with Kazuo Ishiguro' in Allan Vorda (ed.), *Face to Face: Interviews with Contemporary Novelists* (Houston, TX, Rice University Press, 1993), 1–36.

Wachtel, Eleanor, 'Kazuo Ishiguro', in *More Writers and Company* (Toronto, Alfred A. Knopf, 1996), 17–35.

Wilson, Jonathan, 'The Literary Life: A Very English Story', *New Yorker*, 6 March 1995, 96–106.

Criticism

BOOKS

Bradbury, Malcolm, 'The Floating World', in *No, Not Bloomsbury* (London, André Deutsch, 1987), 363–66.

Bradbury, Malcolm, *The Modern British Novel* (London, Secker & Warburg, 1993), 423–25.

Connor, Steven, 'Outside In', in *The English Novel in History: 1950– 1995* (London, Routledge, 1996), 83–127.

Dodsworth, Martin (ed.), *The Penguin History of Literature: Volume 7, The Twentieth Century* (Harmondsworth, Penguin, 1994), 344.

Doyle, Wadick, 'Being an Other to Oneself: First-Person Narration in Kazuo Ishiguro's *The Remains of the Day*', in *L'Alterité dans la litterature et la culture du monde anglophone* (Le Mans, University of Maine, 1993), 70–76.

Graham, Gordon, *Philosophy of the Arts: An Introduction to Aesthetics* (London & New York, Routledge, 1998), 121–27.

Hall, Laura, 'New Nations, New Selves: The Novels of Timothy Mo and Kazuo Ishiguro', in A. Robert Lee (ed.), *Other Britain, Other British: Contemporary Multicultural Fiction* (London, Pluto Press, 1995), 90–110.

Hitchens, Christopher, 'Kazuo Ishiguro', in *For the Sake of Argument: Essays and Minority Reports* (London, Verso, 1993), 320–22.

King, Bruce, 'The New Internationalism: Shiva Naipaul, Salman Rushdie, Buchi Emecheta, Timothy Mo and Kazuo Ishiguro', in James Acheson (ed.), *The British and Irish Novel Since 1960* (New York, St. Martin's Press, 1991), 192–211.

Lodge, David, 'The Unreliable Narrator', in *The Art of Fiction* (New York, Viking, 1992), 154–57.

Luyat, Anne, 'Myth and Metafiction: Is Peaceful Co-Existence Possible? Destruction of the Myth of the English Butler in Kazuo Ishiguro's *The Remains of the Day*', in Max Duperray (ed.), *Historicité et metafiction dans le roman contemporain des Iles Britanniques* (Aix-en-Provence, University of Provence, 1994), 183–96.

Massie, Allan, *The Novel Today: A Critical Guide to the British Novel 1970–1989* (London & New York, Longman, 1990), 64.

Newton, Adam Zachary, 'Telling Others: Secrecy and Recognition in Dickens, Barnes, and Ishiguro', in *Narrative Ethics* (Cambridge, MA, Harvard University Press, 1997), 241–85.

Page, Norman, 'Speech, Culture and History in the Novels of Kazuo Ishiguro', in Mimi Chan and Roy Harris (eds), *Asian Voices in English* (Hong Kong, Hong Kong University Press, 1991), 161–68.

Peters, Sarah, *York Notes Advanced: The Remains of the Day* (London, York Press, 2000).

Petry, Mike, *Narratives of Memory and Identity: the Novels of Kazuo Ishiguro* (Frankfurt, Peter Lang, 1999).

Salecl, Renata, 'I Can't Love You Unless I Give You Up', in Renata Salecl and Slavoj Zazek (eds), *Gaze and Voice as Love Objects* (Durham, SC, Duke University Press, 1996), 179–207.

Shaffer, Brian W., *Understanding Kazuo Ishiguro* (Columbia, SC, University of South Carolina Press, 1998).

Stevenson, Randall, *A Reader's Guide to the Twentieth-Century Novel in Britain* (Lexington, KY, University Press of Kentucky, 1993), 130–36.

Sutherland, John, 'Why Hasn't Mr Stevens Heard of the Suez Crisis?', in *Where Was Rebecca Shot?: Puzzles, Curiosities and Conundrums in Modern Fiction* (London, Wiedenfeld & Nicolson, 1998), 185–89.

Wong, Cynthia F., *Kazuo Ishiguro* (Tavistock, Northcote House, 2000).

Wood, Michael, 'The Discourse of Others', in *Children of Silence: Studies in Contemporary Fiction* (London, Pimilico, 1995), 171–81.

ARTICLES AND ESSAYS

Arai, Megumi, 'Ishiguro's Floating Worlds: Observations on His Visions of Japan and England', *General Education Review*, 22 (1990), 29–34.

Ash, John, 'Stick It Up Howard's End', *Gentleman's Quarterly* (August 1994), 43.

Cardullo, Bert, 'The Servant', *Hudson Review*, 47:4 (1995), 616–22.

Carpi, Daniela, 'The Crisis of the Social Subject in the Contemporary English Novel', *European Journal of English Studies*, 1:2 (1997), 165–83.

Davis, Rocío G., 'Imaginary Homelands Revisited in the Novels of Kazuo Ishiguro', *Miscelanea*, 15 (1994), 139–54.

Davis, Rocío G., '*The Remains of the Day*: Kazuo Ishiguro's Sonnet on his Blindness', *Cuadernos de Investigación Filológica*, 21–22 (1995–96), 57–67.

Garland, Alex, 'On the Shelf: *An Artist of the Floating World*', *Sunday Times*, Books, 10 May 1998, 9.

Griffiths, M., 'Great English Houses/New Homes in England?: Memory and Identity in Kazuo Ishiguro's *The Remains of the Day* and V. S. Naipaul's *The Enigma of Arrival*', *Span*, 36 (1993), 488–503.

Guth, Deborah, 'Submerged Narratives in Kazuo Ishiguro's *The Remains of the Day*', *Forum for Modern Language Studies*, 35:2 (1999), 126–37.

Hama, Miyumi, 'A Pale View', *Switch* (1991), 8:6, 76–102.

Hassan, Ihab, 'An Extravagant Reticence', *The World and I*, 5:2 (1990), 369–74.

Janik, Del Ivan, 'No End of History: Evidence from the Contemporary English Novel', *Twentieth-Century Literature*, 22 June 1995, 160–89.

Lee, Hermione, 'Quiet Desolation', *New Republic*, 22 January 1990, 36–39.

Mallett, Peter J., 'The Revelation of Character in Kazuo Ishiguro's *The Remains of the Day* and *An Artist of the Floating World*', *Shoin Literary Review*, 29 (1996), 1–20.

Mason, Gregory, 'Inspiring Images: The Influence of the Japanese Cinema on the Writings of Kazuo Ishiguro', *East West Film Journal*, 3:2 (1989), 39–52.

O'Brien, Susie, 'Serving a New World Order: Postcolonial Politics in Kazuo Ishiguro's *The Remains of the Day*', *Modern Fiction Studies* 42:4 (1996), 787–806.

Patey, Caroline, 'When Ishiguro Visits the West Country: An Essay on *The Remains of the Day*', *Acme*, 44:2 (1991), 135–55.

Rothfork, John, 'Zen Comedy in Postcolonial Literature: Kazuo Ishiguro's *The Remains of the Day*', *Mosaic*, 29:1 (1996), 79–102.

Sarvan, Charles, 'Floating Signifiers and *An Artist of the Floating World*', *Journal of Commonwealth Literature*, 32:1 (1997), 93–101.

Scanlan, Margaret, 'Mistaken Identities: First-Person Narration in Kazuo Ishiguro', *Journal of Narrative and Life History*, 3:2 & 3 (1993), 145.

Slay, Jr., Jack, 'Ishiguro's *The Remains of the Day*', *Explicator*, 55:3, 180–82.

Tamaya, Meera, 'Ishiguro's *The Remains of the Day*: The Empire Strikes Back', *Modern Language Studies*, 22:2 (1992), 45–56.

Wain, Peter, 'The Historical-Political Aspect of the Novels of Kazuo Ishiguro', *Language and Culture*, 23 (1992), 177–205.

Wall, Kathleen, '*The Remains of the Day* and Its Challenges to Theories of Unreliable Narration', *Journal of Narrative Technique* 24:1 (1994), 18–42.

Watson, George, 'The Silence of the Servants', *Sewanee Review*, 103:3 (1995), 480–86.

Wong, Cynthia F., 'The Shame of Memory: Blanchot's Self-Dispossession in Ishiguro's *A Pale View of Hills*', *Clio*, 24:2 (1995), 127–45.

Yoshioka, Fumio (1988), 'Beyond the Division of East and West: Kazuo Ishiguro's *A Pale View of Hills*', *Studies in English Literature* (1988), 71–86.

DISSERTATIONS

Nagaoka, Tomoko, 'Playing with Margins in the Works of Kazuo Ishiguro' (MA dissertation, International Christian University of Tokyo, Japan, 1999).

Oyabu, Kana, 'Cross-Cultural Fiction: The Novels of Timothy Mo and Kazuo Ishiguro' (Ph.D. thesis, University of Exeter, England, 1995).

Zbinden, Karine, 'Self-Representation in Kazuo Ishiguro's Novels' (MA dissertation, University of Lausanne, Switzerland, 1996).

REFERENCE

Brownstein, Gabriel, 'Kazuo Ishiguro', in Carol Howard and George Stade (eds), *British Writers Supplement IV* (New York, Scribner's, 1997), 301–17.

Corseri, Gary, 'Ishiguro, Kazuo', in Hal May (ed.), *Contemporary Authors: New Revision Series*, 49 (Detroit, MI, Gale Research, 1999), 194–97.

Forceville, Charles, 'Kazuo Ishiguro', in Johannes Willem Bertens (ed.), *Post-War Literatures in English: A Lexicon of Contemporary Authors*, 17 (Groningen, Wolters-Noordhoff, 1992), 1–12.

Mesher, D., 'Kazuo Ishiguro', in Merrit Moseley (ed.), *Dictionary of Literary Biography: British Novelists Since 1960, Second Series*, 194 (Asheville, NC, Gale Research, 1998), 145–53.

Moritz, Charles (ed.), 'Kazuo Ishiguro', in *Current Biography*, 51:9 (1990), 30–33.

Pear, Nancy, 'Ishiguro, Kazuo', in Hal May (ed.), *Contemporary Authors*, 120 (Detroit, MI, Gale Research, 1987), 184–85.

Taylor, Anna-Marie, 'Kazuo Ishiguro', in Susan Windisch Brown (ed.), *Contemporary Novelists*, 6th ed. (London, St. James Press, 1996), 518–19.

General

Ashcroft, Bill, Gareth Griffiths and Helen Tiffin (eds), *The Post-Colonial Studies Reader* (London & New York, Routledge, 1995).

Augarde, Tony (ed.), *The Oxford Dictionary of Modern Quotations* (Oxford, Oxford University Press, 1991).

Barker, Ernest, 'Some Constants of the English Character' [1947], in Judy Giles and Tim Middleton (eds), *Writing Englishness 1900–1950: An Introductory Sourcebook on National Identity* (London, Routledge, 1995), 55–63.

Barthes, Roland, *Empire of Signs*, trans. Richard Howard (London, Jonathan Cape, [1970] 1983).

Beckett, Samuel, 'All That Fall', in *The Complete Dramatic Works* (London, Faber & Faber, 1986), 169–99.

Benedict, Ruth, *The Chrysanthemum and the Sword: Patterns of Japanese Culture* (London, Routledge & Kegan Paul, [1946] 1967).

Berger, Peter L., Brigitte Berger and Hansfried Kellner, *The Homeless Mind: Modernization and Consciousness* (Harmondsworth, Penguin, 1974).

Berry, Jessica and Andrew Alderson, 'Japanese Mourn a Lost Britain of Tea, Butlers and Stiff Upper Lips', *Sunday Times*, 16 November 1997, 3.

Bhabha, Homi K., 'Of Mimicry and Man: The Ambivalence of Colonial Discourse', *October*, 28 (1984), 125–33.

de Bono, Edward, *The Happiness Purpose* (Harmondsworth, Penguin, 1977).

Boyer, Paul, *By the Bomb's Early Light: American Thought and Culture at the Dawn of the Atomic Age* (New York, Pantheon Books, 1985).

Burch, Noël, *To the Distant Observer: Form and Meaning in the Japanese Cinema* (London, Scolar Press, 1979).

Carey, George, 'The Mission of the Church in a Post-Modern World', lecture at University of Notre Dame, IN, 24 July 1996.

Chilvers, Ian (ed.), *The Concise Oxford Dictionary of Art and Artists* (Oxford & New York, Oxford University Press, 1990), 415.

David, F. Hadland, *Myths and Legends of Japan* (London, G. G. Harrap, 1913).

Freud, Sigmund, *Interpretation of Dreams* [1900], in *The Standard Edition of the Complete Psychological Works of Sigmund Freud*, vols 4 & 5, trans. James Strachey (London, Hogarth Press, 1953).

Freud, Sigmund, 'The Uncanny' [1919], in *The Standard Edition of the Complete Psychological Works of Sigmund Freud*, vol. 17, trans. James Strachey (London, Hogarth Press, 1953), 217–56.

Freud, Sigmund, 'The Dream-Work' [1916–17], in *Introductory Lectures on Psychoanalysis*, lecture 11, trans. James Strachey (Harmondsworth, Penguin, 1963), 204–18.

Freytag, Gustav, *The Technique of the Drama: An Exposition of Dramatic Composition and Art*, trans. Elias J. MacEwan (Chicago, Griggs, [1863],1895).

Frick, Thomas, 'J. G. Ballard', *Paris Review*, 94 (1984), 132–60.

Frost, Robert, 'The Death of the Hired Man', in *The Complete Poems of Robert Frost* (London, Jonathan Cape, 1951), 54–60.

Geist, Kathe, 'Narrative Strategies in Ozu's Late Films', in Arthur Nolletti, Jr. and David Desser (eds), *Reframing Japanese Cinema: Authorship, Genre, History* (Bloomington & Indianapolis, IN, Indiana University Press, 1992), 92–111.

Golden, Arthur, *Memoirs of a Geisha* (London, Chatto & Windus, 1997).

Horn, Pamela, *The Rise and Fall of the Victorian Servant* (Stroud, Alan Sutton, 1990).

Iyer, Pico, 'The Empire Writes Back', *Time*, 8 February 1993, 54.

Iyer, Pico, 'The Nowhere Man', *Prospect* (February 1997), 30–33.

JanMohamed, Abdul R., 'Worldliness-without-World, Homelessness-as-Home', in Michael Sprinkler (ed.), *Edward Said: A Critical Reader* (Oxford, Blackwell, 1992), 96–119.

Kogawa, Joy, *Obasan* (Harmondsworth, Penguin, [1982] 1983).

Krupnick, Mark (ed.), *Displacement: Derrida and After* (Bloomington, IN, Indiana University Press, 1983).

Langer, Lawrence, *The Holocaust and the Literary Imagination* (New Haven, CT, Yale University Press, 1975).

Lebra, Takie Sugiyama, 'Self in Japanese Culture', in Nancy R. Rosenberger (ed.), *Japanese Sense of Self* (Cambridge, Cambridge University Press, 1992), 105–20.

Lister, David, 'Revealed: The "Trendy" Art Chosen for Facelift at No 10', *Independent*, 18 September 1999, 1.

MacDonogh, Steve, (ed.), *The Rushdie Letters: Freedom to Speak, Freedom to Write* (London, Brandon, 1993).

McHale, Brian, 'Essentially Criminal Acts: Hoax Poetry, Mock-Hoaxes, and the Fabrication of Identity', lecture at Eighth Tampere Conference on North American Studies, University of Tampere, Finland, 24 April 1999.

Macherey, Pierre, *A Theory of Literary Production in Literature in the Modern World*, trans. Geoffrey Wall (London, Routledge, 1978).

Mercer, Derrick (ed.), *Chronicle of the 20th Century* (London, Longman, 1988).

Nakane, Chie, *Japanese Society* (Harmondsworth, Penguin, 1973).

Rayment, Tim, 'Niceness', *Sunday Times Magazine*, 8 February 1998, 44–45, 47–48.

Richards, Jeffrey, *Films and British National Identity: From Dickens to Dad's Army* (Manchester & New York, Manchester University Press, 1997).

Rimmoth-Kenan, Shlomith, *Narrative Fiction: Contemporary Poetics* (London, Methuen, 1983).

Rosenberger, Nancy R., (ed.), Introduction to *Japanese Sense of Self* (Cambridge, Cambridge University Press, 1992), 1–18.

Rushdie, Salman, 'The Empire Writes Back With a Vengeance', *Times*, 3 July 1982, 8.

Rushdie, Salman, 'Imaginary Homelands', in *Imaginary Homelands: Essays and Criticism 1981–1991* (London, Granta Books, 1991), 9–21.

Said, Edward, *Orientalism: Western Conceptions of the Orient* (New York, Vintage, 1978).

Said, Edward, 'Jane Austen and the Empire', in *Culture and Imperialism* (London, Chatto & Windus, 1993), 95–116.

Sartre, Jean-Paul, *Being and Nothingness: An Essay on Phenomenological Ontology*, trans. Hazel E. Barnes (London, Methuen, [1943] 1958).

Steiner, George, *Extraterritorial: Papers on Literature and the Language Revolution* (Harmondsworth, Penguin, [1971] 1975).

Tanner, Tony, *Jane Austen* (London, Macmillan, 1986).

Treat, John Whittier, *Writing Ground Zero: Japanese Literature and the Atomic Bomb* (Chicago, University of Chicago Press, 1995).

White, Allon, *Uses of Obscurity* (London, Routledge & Kegan Paul, 1981).

Yasusada, Araki, 'Doubled Flowering: From the Notebooks of Araki Yasusada', trans. Tosa Motokiyu, Okura Kyojin and Ojiu Norinaga, supplement, *American Poetry Review*, 25:4 (1996), 23–26.

Yasusada, Araki, 'Mad Daughter and Big Bang: December 25, 1945', *First Intensity*, 5 (1996), 10.

Index

Note: 'n' after a page reference indicates the number of a note on that page.